Community-Based Psych
with Young People

CW00822767

In the last 50 years, emotional and behavioural problems among young people have increased dramatically, yet only a minority are receiving treatment. Many young people who would benefit from psychotherapy are reluctant to be treated in traditional clinical settings, and it is doubtful whether these settings are the most effective way to deal with these patients.

Community-Based Psychotherapy with Young People offers a fresh perspective on working with difficult groups of patients. It addresses the difficulties in engaging with and treating young people with mental health problems, describing approaches and techniques for working with them and taking into account the developmental, psychiatric, psychological and biological issues of those in need of help. Part I covers the likely problems and difficulties encountered in such work, addressing issues such as engaging young men who are depressed and hard to reach. Part II describes services for high priority groups of young people, including those who are disabled or from ethnic minority backgrounds. Part III describes how the outcome of the work is evaluated, and considers the impact present developments in child and adolescent mental health may have on community-based organisations.

This book will appeal to professionals working in more traditional settings who want to explore different ways of working with young patients, including psychotherapists, counsellors, clinical psychologists, social workers and mental health service planners.

Geoffrey Baruch is Director of the Brandon Centre for Counselling and Psychotherapy for Young People, and is a qualified psychoanalyst. He also works as a part-time senior lecturer at Sub-department of Clinical Health Psychology, University College London.

Community-Based Psychotherapy with Young People

Evidence and innovation in practice

Geoffrey Baruch

First published 2001
by Brunner-Routledge
27 Church Road, Hove, East Sussex BN3 2FA

Simultaneously published in the USA and Canada
by Taylor & Francis Inc
325 Chestnut Street, Suite 800, Philadelphia, PA 19106

Brunner-Routledge is an imprint of the Taylor & Francis Group

Typeset in Times by Regent Typesetting, London
Printed and bound in Great Britain by Biddles Ltd, Guildford and
King's Lynn
Cover design by Richard Massing

British Library Cataloguing in Publication Data
A catalogue record for this book is available from the British
Library

Library of Congress Cataloging-in-Publication Data
Community-based psychotherapy with young people : evidence
and innovation in practice / [edited by] Geoffrey Baruch.
     p. ; cm.
  Includes bibliographical references and index.
  ISBN 0-415-21510-2--ISBN 0-415-21511-0 (pbk.)
    1. Adolescent psychotherapy. 2. Child psychotherapy. 3. Youth--Counseling of. 4.
Children--Counseling of. 5. Community mental health services. I. Baruch, Geoff.
  [DNLM: 1. Psychotherapy--Adolescence. 2. Community Mental Health
Services--Adolescence. WS 463 C734 2001]
RJ503 .C645 2001
616.89'14'0835--dc21
                                                            00-054708
  ISBN 0-415-21510-2 (hbk)
  ISBN 0-415-21511-0 (pbk)

Contents

Contributors

Mellany Ambrose, MBBChir, BA, worked at the Brandon Centre as a doctor delivering contraceptive services. She is a member of the Royal College of General Practitioners and a Diplomate of the Faculty of Family Planning. She has worked in general practice, family planning and sexual health. As well as her qualification in medicine she has a degree in psychology and a foundation certificate in counselling.

Olivia Amiel, MSc, is a senior psychotherapist at the Brandon Centre where she has worked since 1987. She is a member of the Guild of Psychotherapists. She has a background in social work and higher education and has a special interest in working with troubled students from the performing arts.

Rajinder K. Bains, MSc, is a clinical psychologist who provided on-site psychotherapy to pupils presenting with behavioural problems at local mainstream and special schools as well as being a psychotherapist at the Brandon Centre where she worked mainly with young people from ethnic minority backgrounds. Currently she works for Camden and Islington Community Health Services NHS Trust in London.

Geoffrey Baruch, PhD, is Director of the Brandon Centre and part-time senior lecturer in the Sub-department of Clinical Health Psychology, University College London. He is a member of the British Psycho-Analytical Society and is qualified to treat adults, adolescents and children.

Suzanne Blundell, MACP, is a child and adolescent psychotherapist who trained at the Tavistock Clinic, London. She is responsible for delivering bereavement services for young people aged 12 to 18 years at the Brandon Centre. She is also principal child psychotherapist at Alder Hay Children's Hospital in Liverpool where she works in the inpatient psychiatric unit. She is a tutor teaching on the MSc course in psychoanalytic psychotherapy in Liverpool, in conjunction with the Tavistock and Portman NHS Trust and the University of East London.

Caroline Essenhigh, LLB, BA, is a child and adolescent psychotherapist who trained at the Anna Freud Centre where she continues to work and teach. Over a period of 3 years, until she left the Brandon Centre, she was responsible for delivering an on-site psychotherapy service to pupils attending a special school for children who present with emotional and behavioural problems.

Pasco Fearon, PhD, is a lecturer in the Sub-department of Clinical Health Psychology at University College London and teaches on the Doctorate in Clinical Psychology at UCL. His research work is focused primarily on attachment processes in infancy, childhood and adulthood.

George Mak-Pearce, MA, is a psychotherapist at the Brandon Centre who also works on the Centre's conduct disorder project. He has worked as a team leader at the Arbours Crisis Centre and as a student counsellor at Kingston University. He runs a private practice in Norwich, Norfolk.

Zora Radonic, MA, MACP, is a child and adolescent psychotherapist who works as a psychoanalytical psychotherapist at the Brandon Centre and as a child psychotherapist at Woodbury Down Child and Family Consultation Service in east London. She is also a visiting teacher at the Tavistock and Portman NHS Trust.

James Rose, PhD, is a senior psychotherapist at the Brandon Centre where he has worked since 1987. He is also a member of the British Psycho-Analytical Society and works as a psychoanalyst in private practice.

David Trevatt, M Psych Psych, is a child and adolescent psychotherapist who, as part of his work for the Brandon Centre, is responsible for delivering on-site psychotherapy to pupils attending a special school for children who have severe physical disabilities. He also provides psychotherapy for refugee pupils at a local mainstream school. He is responsible for the Parent Consultation Service at the Open Door Young Person's Consultation Service. He is also professional manager of the Adolescent Counselling Service in Redbridge and Waltham Forest.

Charles Wells, C Psychol MSc, is a chartered counselling psychologist at the Brandon Centre. He is responsible for administering the interventions for a randomised controlled trial, which is testing treatments for reducing re-offending among persistent young offenders.

Figures

Foreword by Peter Wilson
Young Minds

Adolescents have been, and continue to be, much on our adult minds. Their predicament, ever more perplexing in a confusing world, is not unfamiliar to any of us. However detached some of us may try to be, or impassioned others cannot help but be, none of us can be indifferent to them. Their immersion in growing up, changing all the time with so little surely resolved, is an experience that touches our memories and indeed our current lives. It is that absorbing process of transition, that uncertain pathway from childhood to adulthood with all of its possibilities and unpredictabilities, which captures our imagination and challenges us all.

For the most part, for much of the time, most adolescents manage this transition well enough, and in many respects we know how to prepare them for it – through setting the right foundations of trust and security in infancy and childhood, and through the back-up and stimulation of supportive loving families and caring well-resourced schools. But there always persists a significant proportion, 10 to 20 per cent according to how severe the problems may be, who do not do so well, who trail, trip and flounder often quite desperately. These are teenagers in poor mental health – not enjoying or learning from their relationships or opportunities, feeling overwhelmed by what has or is happening to them, too afraid, mistrustful and angry to go forward and make the most of their development. They, unlike the majority, need help – additional, professional help, over and above what their parents, friends and schools can provide. They need a special place to go to.

Despite all our understanding, despite all of the alarms that are raised in our daily media about 'the youth of today', and despite the ever increasing number of weighty reports that intone the need for improved services for young people – there are in fact remarkably few places for troubled adolescents to go to. There are of course examples of good practice (accessible and effective) in some statutory and youth counselling services, but overall the national provision is patchy, variable in quality and all too often vulnerable in terms of funding and long-term stability. Caught between the traditional professional and managerial domains of 'child' and 'adult', adolescent services in their own right forever seem to get bypassed. And yet we know that in the very developmental process of adolescence there arises a crucial second chance to learn from past experience and find new ways of living. We know too that if the more vulnerable teenagers are simply left to themselves, not helped or treated by people with skill and experience, they are likely to enter adult life with major handicaps in their capacity to work and to love. The provision of a service designed specifically for adolescents based conveniently within its community, accountable to and responsive to the needs of that community, is of the greatest importance – not only in the interests of relieving the distress of troubled young people, but also in improving the quality of life of the whole community.

The Brandon Centre is just such a service – and this book in many ways is a celebration of its work and of what it has achieved in the 30 years of its existence. I have a particularly deep affection for the Brandon Centre, not least because I was its Director for almost 8 years. I succeeded its founder, Dr Faith Spicer, in 1984, building on her pioneering work and developing a more broadly based psychotherapy service. Dr Geoffrey Baruch took over in 1992 and has taken the Centre further, establishing it as a highly regarded multi-disciplinary specialist service for adolescents within the broad framework of local child and adolescent mental health service provision. The Centre provides a wide range of services (including brief and long-term psychotherapy, family planning, bereavement counselling); it surveys and seeks to meet the differing needs of young people in its community, including those who are anti-social and the more difficult to reach; it provides consultation in schools; and, last but not least, it carries out research and evaluation of its services.

With such rich experience there is a great deal of value to be read in the various chapters of this book. The Centre contains in fact a quite unique mixture of skills and approaches – and this is very much reflected in the diversity of language and perspective expressed in the book. There is here much to learn about the nature of adolescence, of the various kinds of disturbance that can occur within it and of the effects of trauma and neglect on the mental health of the young; so too about ways of helping young people and evaluating how these are practised. These are two interesting lines of enquiry and the book stands out as admirable in its endeavour to address them. The first has to do with the application of psychoanalytic therapy to meet the needs of teenagers; the second to do with the building of a research culture in a community-based clinic setting.

Psychoanalysis has resided at the core of much of the psychotherapy that has been practised at the Brandon Centre over the years. Most of the Centre's psychotherapists have been trained in one way or another to approach clients (or patients) with a certain discipline and posture that is sensitive to both conscious and unconscious expressions of anxiety, defence and transference. This has enabled them to pay respect to the sensibilities of the young people who have come to the Centre, to listen properly to their stories, to allow them space and time for reflection, to understand their distress and give appropriate support. This has been felt by many young people to be very helpful in enabling them to change. There has however for some time been a serious question about how well this approach has suited all young people who have come to the Centre, particularly those who are aggressive, antisocial and apparently unmotivated. Many of these people have not responded positively and the Centre, through its examination of the participation of young people in its service, now knows more clearly than before that those who drop out of therapy are younger and have greater behavioural problems than those who continue with therapy. Faced with this fact and with a growing concern that many of these younger teenagers may well be in the greatest need, the Centre has looked critically at what needs to be done on the part of psychotherapists to engage and maintain therapeutic contact with these young people. It has also studied what can be achieved in brief psychotherapy work and in particular with young delinquents.

Much of the strength of this book derives from the force of this scrutiny, focusing as it must on the application of established psychoanalytic technique, taking into account the particular fears of the adolescents who come for help, their cultural and ethnic differences, their levels of cognitive development and the severity of their past traumatic experiences. Whilst clearly the psychotherapists at the Centre retain their allegiance to their learnt traditional skills – and appropriately apply them in relation to many of the adolescents, particularly the older ones, who attend the Centre – they also show a readiness in the chapters of this book to take a different, more active stance, focusing more on strengthening cognitive skills, cultivating emotional literacy and generally taking more 'responsibility for the direction of the sessions'. No doubt this has constituted a challenge for them, but the over-riding sense from reading their chapters is that it has also become an enlivening and imaginative opportunity. George Mak-Pearce's chapter, for example, on how he engages troubled adolescents in six sessions through what he calls the 'future transference' – i.e. through focusing on how they might anticipate the relationship with the therapist – is an interesting illustration of the kind of creative thinking that has been engendered.

A similar quality of innovation is to be seen in those chapters of the book that focus on research and evaluation. During the last 7 years or so, the Centre has taken seriously – and more so than most – its responsibility to evaluate its services and to conduct research into areas of critical concern in its practice. It has carried out systematic studies investigating the use made of the Centre by young people, and the mental health outcomes of the work that it engages with. On top of this, it has set up a random controlled study of psychotherapeutic effectiveness with young people who are probably the most difficult to treat – those diagnosed as having a conduct disorder. All of this work is clearly described in this book and gives an encouraging indication of the value of the psychotherapy that is undertaken at the Centre. What is perhaps most striking is the well-considered and determined way in which this research activity is being pursued at the Centre. As in many psychotherapy centres, there have been understandable reservations about the introduction and 'intrusion' of research methodology. However, at the Brandon Centre, through the strong conviction and leadership of its Director, the involvement of senior management and all staff in the running and administration of the research, as well as the involvement of the research expertise of a local university department, this area of resistance has been, and is being, overcome. The result is a centre that is moving beyond the subjective observations and impressions of its practitioners – valuable though these may be – and which is creating a climate in which more objective findings can also be made and learned from. An added bonus – and a surprise to some – has been that the young people themselves have responded positively to the spirit of research interest in them – not at all put off, and indeed in some cases stimulated by, the invitation to fill in forms!

In many respects the Brandon Centre is at the forefront in its realm of scientific enquiry and in its readiness to look at clinical problems that many would prefer to avoid. In its provision of a community-based psychotherapy service for young people, particularly for those at greatest risk, it is carrying out a highly commendable task. Its achievement is all the more remarkable given the modesty of its basic resources. Having read through the breadth of work described in this book, I can well imagine that many who don't know the Centre might think it to be a large, well-endowed institution, rooted within the mainstream of service and research activity. In fact it practices in a relatively small building, operating on its own as a medium-sized charity in the uncertain waters of the voluntary sector, without the advantage of a large infrastructure. That the Brandon Centre has established its own distinctive identity and produced such a relevant and contemporary book is testimony to its sheer courage and energy and indeed to the innovative spirit of the voluntary sector in which it has grown.

Foreword by Peter Fonagy

You are holding a hallmark volume in your hands. The collection of essays in this book marks a new departure in the application of psychoanalytic ideas. Psychoanalysis's second century must be different from the first if Freud's understanding of psychological disorder is to survive. The theory has fared exceptionally well given the rapid pace of scientific advances in fields adjacent to analysis (Fonagy, in press). The therapeutic work of psychodynamic therapists and psychoanalysts has fared less well in an environment where short-term interventions are prized by a health care system shaped as much by accountancy as clinical knowledge, as much by misinformation taken from inappropriate and flawed experimental evaluations of outcome as by genuine scientific knowledge (Fonagy, Target, Cottrell, Phillips and Kurtz, 2000). If they are not to be buried under wave after wave of reorganisations of the public and private mental health delivery systems in which they work, psychoanalytic psychotherapists need urgently to rethink the clinical service they offer. To survive, and survive they must, they need to be intelligent, imaginative, inspired but also remain integrated with their traditional knowledge base. To achieve the remarkable leap into the second century, many books like this will be needed; books, which in a highly practical and enlightening way reconfigure the psychoanalytic approach to a clinical problem and provide a set of profoundly helpful insights for improving the care offered in a specific specialty.

Of the many challenges of child psychiatry, suicidality, disordered or delinquent behaviour in adolescents present the most awesome difficulties. It is not that the psychological problems of adolescence are inherently more difficult to solve than those of other developmental periods, but rather that the developmental concerns of this age with individuation combine with the vulnerable psychological structures characteristic of individuals with severe conduct problems to make these individuals extremely hard to reach, and treatment processes extremely hard to maintain. Working with this group one frequently has the feeling that much could be achieved, yet persuading these young people of the value of what we have to offer appears to be a Herculean task. In the past, these challenges often triggered hospital admissions with the implicit hope, all too frequently unrealised, that a supportive inpatient setting would facilitate therapeutic engagement. In most

Western countries, hospitalisation is an increasingly scarce resource. Specialist adolescent units are rapidly disappearing. Community treatment is the only realistic option.

There are relatively few models for offering specialist psychological help to adolescents and young adults. In the United States multisystemic therapy is increasingly frequently offered. This is an intensive community-based method incorporating a range of therapeutic approaches delivered to the family by a single therapist (Borduin, 1999). However, it requires extensive training and supervision, and is currently unavailable outside the United States. In the UK, the Brent (Walk-in) Consultation Centre has had an enduring influence on the shape of psychodynamic psychotherapeutic services to this age group (Laufer and Laufer, 1989). The Brandon Centre model, I believe, is an alternative approach with immense potential to inspire the development of psychological services for this age group. The Brandon Centre approach has the potential to become a dominant frame of reference for addressing psychological problems of adolescents and young adults.

Under Geoffrey Baruch's inspired leadership, the Centre is in the process of evolving a unique set of therapeutic strategies for the wide-ranging and complex problems of this difficult group of young people. As you read this collection of chapters, you will not only be gripped by the vivid clinical descriptions of lives in developmental turmoil but you will also be increasingly impressed by the coherence of an approach to these young people that has as its hallmarks a deep commitment to a pragmatic psychodynamic approach and a deep respect for the individuality of the adolescents who presented to the Centre either directly or through one of its outreach programmes. The services cater for a variety of needs. The special force of the programme described lies in its rapid responsiveness to the needs of the young person. The service clearly fills a gap in statutory service provision, the prototypical role for a voluntary organisation.

Technical innovation is a central feature of the Brandon Centre approach. If psychodynamic ideas are going to continue to impact on adolescent psychosocial treatments, it is clear that they have to be adapted to the rapidly changing cultural and social contexts in which our young people live. Techniques that were effective two decades ago simply will not do for a generation whose childhood years were dominated by the Internet and MTV. They may face problems of reconciling the conflicting demands for separateness and relatedness as generations upon generations of adolescents before them, but the same struggle may now manifest in the context of disintegrating family structures, the realistic potential of ethnic alienation, the rapid disappearance of social institutions embodying a value system that incorporates interpersonal respect, etc. Changing culture is forcing us to update the therapeutic techniques of yesteryear. The need is most acute with adolescents, who always represent the vanguard of cultural change. The Brandon Centre is at the forefront of generating a radically new model for the application of psychoanalytic ideas. This book contains many of its key messages.

Just one unique marker of the change signalled by this book is the commitment to empirical evaluation. The Brandon Centre has led the child psychotherapy field in providing information on the impact of its service upon the client group it serves. A series of publications by Baruch and colleagues have not only established the value of the interventions offered by the Centre's programmes, but also evolved a method for the routine scrutinising of clinical effectiveness which could help the majority of services that provide help for this age group. That the work emanates from a psychodynamic rather than behavioural or cognitive behavioural organisation speaks volumes about the quality of leadership of the Centre and the sensitivity to current social concerns of its board of management.

This is a model book: a model of how to deliver an effective psychotherapy service, a model of how to use psychoanalytic insights and yet retain respect for the community, a model of how to bring the psychoanalytic approach up to date and make it relevant to current mental health problems without significant distortion of this tradition, and a model of how to present this in a readable, informative and entertaining way. I congratulate the editor and the authors.

References

Borduin, C. M. (1999). 'Multisystemic treatment of criminality and violence in adolescents'. *Journal of the American Academy for Child and Adolescent Psychiatry* 38: 242–9.

Fonagy, P. (in press). 'The place of psychodynamic theory in developmental psychopathology'. *Development and Psychopathology*.

Fonagy, P., Target, M., Cottrell, D., Phillips, J. and Kurtz, Z. (2000). *A Review of the Outcomes of All Treatments of Psychiatric Disorder in Childhood* (MCH 17-33). London: National Health Service Executive.

Laufer, M. and Laufer, M. E. (1989). *Breakdown and Psychoanalytic Treatment in Adolescence*. New Haven: Yale University Press.

Preface

This volume brings together the work of a number of clinicians who have accumulated valuable experience in practising psychotherapy and in providing a birth control service to young people in a community-based setting, the Brandon Centre (formerly the London Youth Advisory Centre). There has been a growing recognition that young people need access to mental health and contraceptive services that are tailored to meet their needs. They should not be constrained to fit in with mental health services for children nor should they be forced into using adult mental health and contraceptive services. For many years, these views were voiced by young people and practitioners working with them but were largely ignored by successive governments. However, the rising rate of teenage pregnancy, of at-risk behaviour such as deliberate self-harm, eating disorder, drug and alcohol abuse, conduct disorder, their adverse impact on the mental health of young people, the consequent damage to their lives and the severe consequences for the community have finally persuaded government to take notice and respond.

The Brandon Centre has existed for over 30 years and is now seen as a model of service delivery for young people. In 1998 the Centre was short-listed for an award for excellence in community health work in the SmithKline Beecham Community Health Awards in partnership with the King's Fund. In 1999 the work of the Centre with young offenders and with adolescents who present with severe behavioural difficulties was cited as a model of good practice in a report, *Children Health and Crime*, by the National Association for the Care and Resettlement of Offenders (NACRO). The Centre's work supporting troubled young people at risk of school exclusion was cited by the Department of Health in 1999 as a service model and an example of good practice in the *National Service Frameworks for Mental Health*. In 2000 the Centre's psychotherapy service was described as a model of service delivery in *Sidelined: Young Adults' Access to Services* carried out by the New Policy Institute and supported by Calouste Gulbenkian Foundation and The Children's Society.

The contributors are enormously grateful for the support and guidance we have received from Richard Astor, Richard Taffler, John Cape, Felicity Crowther, Dolores Curry, Anna Higgitt, Jane Roberts and Olivia Tatton Brown, who are current members of the Centre's Council of Management, in preparing this volume. We want to thank Sarah Charlton, the Centre's Administrator, for her invaluable contribution and Alison Webster who is our Information Officer. It is no coincidence that the recognition the Centre has received in recent years coincides with the impetus Sarah has given to our efforts since she arrived in 1997. We also want to thank a number of people who have been enormously helpful and influential in the Brandon Centre's development including Brandon Cadbury, Professor Peter Fonagy, Sandra Ramsden, Dr Mary Target, Peter Wilson, Andrew Gerber, Dr Veronique Moens, Dr Julie Nye, Nicky Cloutman, Dr David Citron, Ginnie Lawlor, David Robins and Olivia Harvard Watts. The Centre's services would not be possible without continuing financial support from central and local government, from the local health authority, from a wide range of charitable trusts, from generous individual donations and from the corporate sector, for which we are very grateful. However, we want most of all to thank the young people who use our services, whose problems and vivacity make our work so challenging and compelling.

Geoffrey Baruch PhD
1 September 2000

Introduction

Geoffrey Baruch

BACKGROUND

This book focuses on the engagement and maintenance of troubled young people in psychotherapy at the Brandon Centre (formerly the London Youth Advisory Centre). The Centre is a charitable organisation that has existed for over 30 years. It was started as a contraceptive service for young women aged 12 to 25 years. The founder, Dr Faith Spicer, recognised that young women needed to have access to a service that allowed them time to talk through emotional issues that accompanied requests for contraception. Shortly after the founding of the contraceptive service an information service and a psychotherapy service were initiated for young women and young men due to the scale of the emotional needs of young people in the local community. These services were made accessible by allowing self-referral and confidentiality, by providing comfortable, welcoming and 'non-institutional premises' in the heart of the local community and by receptionists being friendly without being intrusive. The contraceptive service quickly gained a reputation for working effectively with young women from dysfunctional backgrounds that put them at risk of unwanted pregnancy and sexually transmitted diseases. The Centre also acquired a reputation for imaginatively applying psychotherapeutic principles in devising innovatory services for young people, especially high priority groups of young people, and in combining service delivery with audit and research, including the rigorous evaluation of mental health outcome. The objective of the book is to describe this approach to helping troubled young people.

ADOLESCENT DEVELOPMENT, PSYCHOSOCIAL DISORDERS IN YOUNG PEOPLE

The developmental changes that take place between the ages of 12 to 25 years are profound (Leffert and Petersen, 1995; Freud, 1969; Blos, 1967; Graham and Rutter, 1985; Bleiberg, 1988; Kazdin, 1993a; Laufer and Laufer, 1984; Edgcumbe, 1993; Wilson, 1991; Bloch, 1995). From early adolescence there are marked biological changes in height, weight and reproductive system development. There are psychological changes in cognitive development from concrete operational thinking to formal abstract thinking (Inhelder and Piaget, 1958). There are also major intrapsychic changes that involve an intensification of Oedipal and pre-Oedipal conflicts (Freud, 1969; Blos, 1967) which if overcome successfully lead to a disengagement from the internalised 'Oedipal parents' and the external parents. There is a move towards external partnerships independent of the family, initially with friends of the same sex and then around 15 years of age with the opposite sex leading to the first sexual relationship. In young adulthood these moves may lead to marriage and parenthood. Along with the acquisition of psychological and social autonomy, the relationship of the young person to the wider community changes, for instance in being allowed to drive, to vote, to drink alcohol legally, and to leave school either for further study or for starting work.

During adolescence many psychosocial disorders increase and peak in frequency: offending behaviour, suicide and suicidal and self-harming behaviours, depression, eating disorders and the abuse of alcohol and drugs other than for medical conditions (Smith and Rutter, 1995). There are differences in the rate of particular disorders for boys and girls. The crime rate, substance abuse and suicide are higher among boys than among girls whereas the rate of eating disorders, depression and suicidal behaviour in adolescence is higher among girls than boys. Although not well understood, these differences are perhaps connected with salient characteristics of boys and girls. Boys tend to be impulsive and aggressive, characteristics that feature strongly in offending behaviour and suicide, whereas girls are more introspective and concerned with their feelings and these characteristics are associated with depression and suicidal behaviour (Smith and Rutter, 1995).

The mental health of young people is enormously vulnerable because of many, diverse challenges they face in adolescence and also because of a propensity to engage in at-risk behaviour. Some young people are also exposed to harmful circumstances which affect their mental health (Kazdin, 1993a). Examples of at-risk behaviours are drug and alcohol abuse, running away from home, sexual promiscuity, teenage pregnancy and dropping out of school. Harmful circumstances may include family discord, unemployment, a parent (particularly the mother) suffering from psychiatric disorder, homelessness, physical and sexual abuse, divorce and parental separation and lone parenting of children born to unmarried mothers (Kurtz, 1992). There is also a greater risk of psychosocial disorder in young offenders (Gunn, Maden and Swinton, 1991) and in young people who have a learning difficulty especially in connection with literacy (Rutter, 1989) or a learning disability (Bone and Meltzer, 1989). Singly, or more usually in combination, these at-risk behaviours and adverse circumstances increase the vulnerability of young people to psychosocial disorders. Graham (1986) estimated the overall prevalence of mental health problems in the adolescent population at 20 per cent with 7 to 10 per cent having moderate to severe problems.

A commonly held view is that as young people grow up they grow out of their problems. However, there is strong evidence to show that if left untreated psychosocial disorders in young people persist into adulthood with harmful consequences for their lives (Achenbach, Howell, McConaughy and Stanger, 1998; Stanger, MacDonald, McConaughy and Achenbach, 1996; Achenbach, Howell, McConaughy and Stanger, 1995; Ferdinand, Verhulst and Wiznitzer, 1995). Despite improvements in living standards and physical health over the last 50 years many psychosocial disorders in young people have become significantly more prevalent including offending behaviour, substance abuse, depressive disorders, and suicide and suicidal behaviours (Smith and Rutter, 1995).

Historically National Health Service provision for young people suffering from psychosocial disorders, with some notable exceptions such as the Adolescent Department of the Tavistock Clinic in London (Anderson and Dartington, 1998), has either been in conjunction with children's mental health services or in the context of adult mental health services. However, a few distinguished community-based psychotherapy centres in the voluntary sector and counselling services for students and other troubled young people have recognised their special needs and have led the way in making mental health services available for troubled adolescents and young people who do not require inpatient treatment. In the last decade, the case for providing services for young people which are independent of services for children and adults has been recognised (Parry-Jones, 1995). The reasons cited include the increasing value society attaches to adolescence and youth, the recent increase in status of adolescent medicine and the need to invest in prevention and mental health provision due to the link between psychosocial disorder in adolescence and adulthood. The influential Health Advisory Service report on child and adolescent mental health services recommends that mental health services for young people aged 16 to 25 years are specifically commissioned and provided (Health Advisory Service, 1995). Currently the Department of Health is instructing health authorities to implement the recommendations of this report.

THE FOCUS OF THE BOOK

The focus of the book is the engagement and maintenance of troubled young people in psychotherapy. The meaning of 'psychotherapy' requires some explanation since the range of treatment techniques considered to be psychotherapy is vast – there are over 230 documented psychotherapies for children and adolescents (Kazdin, 1999). The model used at the Centre is psychoanalytic. Basically this involves a psychotherapist meeting with the young person on a weekly basis for 50 minutes and engaging in a process, through listening to and commenting on what the young person says, of helping the young person to gain insight into their problems. It is to be hoped that this understanding leads to a modification of maladaptive behaviour and states of mind and to an increased capacity to meet the challenges of the adolescent process. This model has been adapted to meet the needs of young people who seek help at the Centre.

A number of factors have influenced the delivery of psychotherapy. First the young people who seek help from the Brandon Centre usually have more than one problem for which they are seeking help. This is usually referred to as co-morbidity and means that there are two or more separate problems, which may be interconnected, for instance conduct disorder, substance abuse and depression. A therapeutic technique appropriate for one problem may be inappropriate for the other problems. According to therapists' ratings of 508 young people assessed between 1993 and 1999 the median diagnosis (that is the representative number) is three according to the ICD-10 diagnostic system (World Health Organisation, 1990). Using a checklist of problem areas describing the young person's current situation we found that the median number of problems presented by young people is five. The principal diagnoses are anxiety-related disorders, mood disorder, conduct disorder almost exclusively among young people aged 12 to 16 years and personality disorder. Three of the most frequent problems presented are family problems, relationship and sexual problems, and social isolation. The same client population also has a high score on conditions that make them at risk of psychosocial disorders. On a scale used to rate the severity of psychosocial and environmental stressors experienced by the young person, the Severity of Psycho-social Stressors Scale for Children and Adolescents (American Psychiatric Association, 1994), the median stressor on a scale of 1–6 is 4. That is severe events or circumstances such as divorce of parents, unwanted pregnancy, arrest, harsh or rejecting parents, chronic life-threatening illness in a parent or multiple foster home placements. Over 41 per cent score 4 and a further 24 per cent score 5, an extreme event such as sexual or physical abuse or death of a parent. According to the Global Assessment of Functioning Scale (GAF) (American Psychiatric Association, 1994) the population of young people assessed are moderately to severely impaired psychologically, socially and occupationally, for example they may have few friends, have suicidal ideation and truant from school. The mean score is 51.8. These measures of Brandon Centre clients indicate a high risk of psychosocial disorder and a low level of psychosocial functioning. These characteristics usually suggest that the prospects of engagement in and improvement from psychotherapy are poor (Luborsky, Diguer, Luborsky, McLellan, Woody and Alexander, 1993).

A second influence on the delivery of psychotherapy is the influence of age and development. We have already noted that between the ages of 12 and 25 years young people pass through 'a variety of stages, or levels in which experience with the environment and affective, cognitive, and behavioural repertoires are evolving and mingling in a dynamic way' (Kazdin, 1993a, p. 282). The changes in development markedly affect treatment. Clearly a young person aged 22 years is cognitively better prepared to use interpretative interventions than an adolescent aged 13 or 14 years. The experience of the Brandon Centre suggests that some adaptation in psychotherapeutic technique may be necessary in order to take account of cognitive maturity and other aspects of development which change with age

A third influence concerns the impetus for seeking treatment. Younger adolescents usually do not refer themselves for psychotherapy. Many who are referred do not see themselves as having problems. Parents, teachers, social workers and other adults in positions of responsibility usually refer them because the young person is a cause of problems to them and others, this is particularly true of adolescents who present with conduct disorder. These referrers may also recognise the difficulties and stresses affecting the young person which underlie their antisocial behaviour. The absence of recognition on the part of the young person of their problems affects their motivation for seeking psychotherapy and for engaging in the therapeutic process. Like all models of psychotherapy, psychoanalytic psychotherapy relies on the individual making a therapeutic alliance with the psychotherapist that partly may involve some recognition by the client of their difficulties and a willingness to collaborate with the therapist. This is hardly likely to happen if the young person is unaware that they have a problem. Indeed their feeling that they are being made to comply may increase their resistance to therapy. Obviously these young people cannot be left untreated because their behaviour does not conform to an ideal of appropriate participation. The problem of the engagement in psychotherapy of young people who are not motivated to seek treatment is not peculiar to psychoanalytic psychotherapy. Studies of cognitive behavioural treatment of conduct-disordered adolescents also report high levels of premature termination (see Kazdin, 1990; Kazdin, Holland and Crowley, 1997).

In summary, a combination of the young person's presenting problems, their age and stage of development and their motivation for treatment all affect whether they engage in and are retained in psychotherapy. A study at the Brandon Centre comparing the difference between young people who terminated treatment prematurely and those who continued in treatment confirmed the importance of these factors. Young people who dropped out of therapy were younger (mean = 17.51 years, SD = 3.29) and had greater behavioural problems compared to young people who continued in therapy. They were older (20.2 years, SD = 3.22), had fewer behavioural problems and were likely to be self-referred which is an indicator of self-recognition of problems and self-motivation for therapy (Baruch, Gerber and Fearon, 1998). Interestingly 'continuers' were likely to be treated by psychotherapists who used supportive techniques. When the pattern of engagement of young people aged under 20 years was examined, ethnic minority status and being treated by a supportive therapist predicted continuing in treatment and a diagnosis of conduct disorder predicted premature termination. The findings from this study and the Centre's evaluation of mental health outcome raise the issue of the modification of psychotherapeutic technique and service delivery in order to improve the engagement of young people in psychotherapy.

A fourth influence on the practice and delivery of psychotherapy at the Centre is ethnic minority status. Approximately 25 per cent of young people who come to the Centre for psychotherapy are from an ethnic minority background. As yet psychotherapy interventions for young people rarely consider the effect of factors such as ethnic background and racial and cultural differences. Young people coming from such backgrounds may vary in their at-risk behaviours, family circumstances, psychosocial problems, their pattern of seeking help and how they use treatment. Moreover some ethnic minority backgrounds may be strongly associated with adverse social conditions which put young people at greater risk of psychosocial disorders. For instance, in the last few years, in the area of London where the Centre is situated there has been a great influx of refugees from many different countries (Camden and Islington Health Authority, 1997). It is not uncommon for refugee children and adolescents to be separated from their parents in traumatic circumstances. Clearly these children and adolescents, because of the nature of the separation, are at great risk of developing psychosocial disorders. Complications may also arise for some young people who are caught in a conflict of identification between the mores of Western culture and the mores of their background – they too may be at an increased risk of psychosocial disorder. The therapeutic process is further complicated by the likelihood that therapists treating these young people do not share their background and also by the diverse backgrounds from which young people come, all with their own separate cultural identities (Kazdin, 1993b; Tharp, 1991).

As well as this group of young people, there are other high priority groups such as young people with severe physical disabilities, the homeless young, bereaved young people and young offenders, who may require modifications in therapeutic technique and changes in service delivery. Developing interventions that are sensitive to the special circumstances of all these groups of young people is an enormous challenge. This book describes how the challenge of developing appropriate and acceptable therapeutic interventions for young people has been met by the Brandon Centre by diversifying the models of treatment offered and by introducing innovative and experimental methods of care.

AUDIT AND EVALUATION

Since the 1980s audit has become a fundamental requirement in clinical practice. Although clinical audit in psychotherapy services has been somewhat ambivalently received by psychotherapists, by the late 1990s even these services have begun to implement the principles of audit (Davenhill and Patrick, 1998). According to Parry (1998) 'the purpose of clinical audit is to improve services to patients by a formal process of setting standards, gathering data to find out how the service is performing in relation to them and changing practice as a result' (p. 15). The model adopted by the Brandon Centre in 1993 is very similar to a model of outcome study recently described by Weiss (1998) as the routine monitoring of effectiveness. Weiss argues that responsible application of psychotherapy in a clinic requires that the therapy be evaluated in the setting where the treatment is being implemented and with the therapists who are administering the intervention where the objective is to treat clients effectively. In other words 'The objective of routine monitoring studies is ... to determine, for a particular clinic or practice group, the parameters of the treatment's effectiveness' (Weiss, 1998, p. 943).

The Brandon Centre audit of mental health outcome follows the recommendations of Fonagy and Higgitt (1989) for the auditing of psychotherapy services. This involves the use of reliable and valid methods of measuring the functioning of young people and using different sources of information on the young person's functioning, including information from the young person, their therapist and a significant other in their life such as a parent or partner. The audit of mental health outcome also involves assessments that are taken at the beginning of treatment, during treatment, at the end of treatment and at repeated follow-ups after treatment has terminated. Part III describes this approach in more detail.

To date the Brandon Centre audit has yielded three areas of study which have led to publications. First there has been the evaluation of mental health outcome, that is treatment effectiveness in Weiss's terms (Baruch, 1995; Baruch, Fearon and Gerber, 1998). A second area of study, which we referred to earlier, has been an examination of the participation of young people in treatment, that is their attendance and the factors which affect this participation (Baruch, Gerber and Fearon, 1998). Finally, we have investigated the correspondence between the assessment made by young people and their significant others of the young person's internalising (emotional) problems, externalising (disruptive or behavioural) problems and total problems (Baruch, Fearon and Gerber, 1999). This investigation was prompted by the frequent discrepancy between the young person's view of themselves and the view of their significant other and hence the urgent need to understand the nature of this discrepancy in order to arrive at a valid assessment of the young person's problems.

The audit of the Centre's psychotherapy service has had a profound impact on service development and psychotherapeutic technique. The investigation of mental health outcome and premature termination have shown that on the whole young people who are over 19 years old tend to continue in long-term treatment, present mainly with internalising problems which show a significant response to psychoanalytic psychotherapy. On the other hand young people aged under 18 years who present with conduct disorder terminate treatment prematurely and are much less likely to benefit significantly from psychotherapy. These findings have led to an extensive reconsideration of the treatment of conduct disorder in young people. We have initiated a number of psychotherapy projects at schools that have problems with pupils who present with severe disruptive behaviour sufficiently serious for them to be excluded from school. We have also initiated a randomised controlled trial to test the effectiveness of a manualised cognitive behavioural treatment against supportive counselling. The population being treated are persistent young offenders aged between 14 and 16 years. We describe these projects and some preliminary findings in Part II. At this point we want to highlight the way audit is integrated with service delivery and how practice changes as a result of the evaluation of treatment.

Behind the theories and the statistics is the human predicament of the young people who seek help from the Centre. In the rest of the book we hope to give the reader a sense of their struggles and how we try to help them.

OUTLINE OF THE BOOK

Part I includes contributions that consider theoretical and practical aspects of engaging and maintaining young people in treatment. Chapter 1, by George Mak-Pearce, describes the role of a short-term intervention designed to assist the engagement of young people in therapy. The young person receives up to six sessions, which allow the therapist and young person to address the client's presenting problems and assess the need for continuing treatment at the Centre. Pearce explores the advantages and disadvantages of the intervention. In Chapter 2, Olivia Amiel describes work with young people who have had a psychotic breakdown. In the three case examples Amiel discusses, despite the evident fragility of the young people, useful therapeutic work is possible by harnessing their drive to continue their development. For this to happen the setting has to be carefully established as part of developing and maintaining a working alliance. Amiel shows how therapy contributed to the three young people, whose functioning had come to a standstill as a result of a psychotic illness, being able to re-establish their lives. Chapter 3 by James Rose focuses on engaging young men who are depressed and apathetic and therefore difficult to reach. As well as describing some technical issues that arise in working with this group Rose considers theoretical issues in seeking to understand their internal and external functioning. In Chapter 4, Geoffrey Baruch discusses problems faced by psychoanalytic psychotherapists in engaging hard-to-reach young people in psychotherapy who present with severe developmental disturbance. He argues that the difficulties in engaging these young people in treatment are due to a poorly developed capacity to reflect on their own and others' mental states. The technical implications for the therapeutic approach are described and case material is presented which illustrates this approach.

Part II describes services for high priority groups of young people. In the psychotherapy literature there is a dearth of publications on the impact of race and culture on therapeutic practice with young people. Based on her experience of psychotherapy at the Brandon Centre with young people from ethnic minority backgrounds Rajinder Bains, in Chapter 5, proposes a model for such work which highlights the modifications in therapeutic technique when working with young black people. The doctors who run the contraceptive service at the Brandon Centre attend both to the contraceptive needs of young women and practice a counselling approach that offers the time to listen to young people in order to help them understand relevant personal issues. In Chapter 6, Mellany Ambrose vividly uses case material to illustrate how a young woman's request for contraception is frequently an expression of unrecognised emotional conflict and need as well as a straightforward request for protection. She shows the careful work that the doctor does in helping the young person address their inner difficulties. David Trevatt has worked for a number of years at a school for severely disabled young people. In Chapter 7 he describes this project. Of particular interest is the adaptation in therapeutic technique necessitated by pupils' learning difficulties. In some cases they are so severe that the young person can only communicate with the assistance of sophisticated technological support. Suzanne Blundell runs a bereavement service at the Centre for young people aged between 12 and 18 years. The work of this project is described in Chapter 8. Generally, young bereaved people who are referred for treatment present with multiple problems as well as having to cope with a bereavement. For instance many are from lone parent or divorced backgrounds which makes coping with bereavement a complex task when the parent who has passed away has not been part of the family for several years. A major issue for most bereaved young people is coping with the developmental tasks of adolescence in the context of losing a parent. In Chapter 9 Caroline Essenhigh presents her work at a local school for boys who present with severe emotional and behavioural disorders who are unlikely to return to mainstream education. Many of the boys have had a disappointing experience of therapy in the past. Essenhigh shows how, despite the enormous demands of the setting and the severe and complex problems presented by the boys, in-depth therapeutic work of a high quality is possible. The conduct disorder project represents a significant departure for the Brandon Centre. In Chapter 10, Charles Wells describes this research project that is designed as a randomised controlled trial. The trial is evaluating a manualised intervention based on best practice that has been adapted by us for convicted young offenders and conduct-disordered youth. The intervention is compared with supportive counselling. Both treatments are targeted at young people who are persistent and serious offenders or who have been permanently excluded from mainstream school due to severe disruptive behaviour. The project has been designed to be close to 'real life' conditions so that others can replicate a model of effective intervention.

Part III is devoted to the Centre's programme for evaluating mental health outcome. The Brandon Centre introduced a programme evaluating mental health outcome in 1993 and has continued this programme on an ongoing basis since then. In Chapter 11 Baruch and Fearon describe the reasons for introducing the programme. They also consider a number of options for evaluating mental health outcome including the approach adopted by the Centre. They discuss the implementation of the programme and finally report on various outcomes. In Chapter 12, Zora Radonic elucidates the significance of the programme from a clinical perspective. She considers the effect of evaluation methodology on her work as a psychotherapist and the impact on the therapeutic process. She draws on clinical material in showing the unexpected ways in which young people can use the outcome questionnaires in establishing contact with their therapist. Chapter 13 considers the impact that present developments in child and adolescent mental health may have on community-based mental health centres like the Brandon Centre. Baruch argues that findings from research, in particular, will profoundly influence practice and challenge practitioners and organisations dedicated to a single therapeutic technique. The Brandon Centre will need to be flexible and adaptable so that it can incorporate new findings, as they arise, into service provision while retaining its distinctive character.

THE USE OF CASE MATERIAL

Traditionally psychotherapists have used case material from their work with patients as the basis for advancing ideas about unconscious mental functioning and about the clinical process. The importance and meaning of patient confidentiality is taught during the course of clinical training – it is the essence of responsible practice. However, in recent years standards regarding confidentiality have become much more stringent, so much so that there are considerable anxieties among psychotherapists about using case material in publications. Signed consent is now regarded as the *sine qua non* when publishing case material about a particular client even when personal details are disguised.

In preparing this book we adopted two approaches regarding the inclusion of case material. We obtained signed consent from the client or we used fictitious descriptions of cases. Case descriptions are based on the author's clinical experience at the Centre but do not constitute reports of a particular case. The process of ensuring that the authors kept to this guideline was both painstaking and at times painful. As editor, I had the unenviable task of asking authors to resubmit their manuscript, in some cases on several occasions, until I was satisfied with their use of case material. I am acutely conscious of confidentiality being the bedrock on which our services are founded. Any breach of our clients' trust could have disastrous implications for the way the community perceives us. I am satisfied that we have not betrayed their trust.

References

Achenbach, T. A., Howell, C. T., McConaughy, S. H. and Stanger, C. (1995). 'Six-year predictors of problems in a national sample: III. Transitions to young adult syndromes'. *Journal of the American Academy of Child and Adolescent Psychiatry* 34: 658–69.

—— (1998). 'Six-year predictors of problems in a national sample: IV. Young adult signs of disturbance'. *Journal of the American Academy of Child and Adolescent Psychiatry* 37: 718–27.

American Psychiatric Association (1994). *Diagnostic and Statistical Manual of Mental Disorders*, 4th edn, Washington DC: American Psychiatric Association.

Anderson, R. and Dartington, A. (1998) *Facing it Out: Clinical Perspectives on Adolescent Disturbance*. London: Duckworth.

Baruch, G. (1995). 'Evaluating the outcome of a community-based psychoanalytic psychotherapy service for young people between 12 and 25 years old: Work in progress'. *Psychoanalytic Psychotherapy* 9: 243–67.

—— Gerber, A. and Fearon, P. (1998). 'Adolescents who drop out of psychotherapy at a community-based psychotherapy centre: a preliminary investigation of the characteristics of early-drop-outs, late drop-outs and those who continue treatment'. *British Journal of Medical Psychology* 71: 233–45.

—— Fearon, P. and Gerber, A. (1998). 'Evaluating the outcome of a community-based psychoanalytic psychotherapy service for young people: one year repeated follow-up'. In Davenhill, R. and Patrick, M. (eds), *Rethinking Clinical Audit*. London: Routledge.

—— (1999). 'Emotional and behavioural problems in adolescents/young adults receiving treatment at a community-based psychotherapy centre for young people: a preliminary study of the correspondence among adolescent/young adult and significant other reports'. *British Journal of Medical Psychology* 72: 251–65.

Bleiberg, E. (1988). 'Adolescence, sense of self, and narcissistic vulnerability'. *Bulletin of the Menninger Clinic* 52: 211–28.

Bloch, H. S. (1995). *Adolescent Development, Psychopathology and Treatment*. Madison, CT: International Universities Press.

Blos, P. (1967). 'The second individuation process of adolescence'. *Psychoanalytic Study of the Child* 22: 162–86.

Bone, M. and Meltzer, H. (1989). *The Prevalence of Disability Among Children*. OPCS Surveys of Disability in Great Britain, Report 3. London: HMSO.

Camden and Islington Health Authority (1997). *Camden and Islington Public Health Report 1997*.

Davenhill, R. and Patrick, M. (eds). 1998. *Rethinking Clinical Audit: The Case of Psychotherapy Services in the NHS*. London: Routledge.

Edgcumbe, R. (1993). 'Developmental disturbances in adolescence and their implications for transference technique'. *Bulletin of the Anna Freud Centre* 16: 107–20.

Ferdinand, R. F., Verhulst, F. C., and Wiznitzer, M. (1995). 'Continuity and change of self-reported behaviors from adolescence into young adulthood'. *Journal of the American Academy of Child and Adolescent Psychiatry* 34(5): 680–90.

Fonagy, A. and Higgitt, A. (1989). 'Evaluating the performance of departments of psychotherapy'. *Psychoanalytic Psychotherapy* 4: 121–53.

Freud, A. (1969). 'Adolescence'. In *The Writings of Anna Freud: Vol. 5. Research at the Hampstead Child Therapy Clinic and Other Papers*, 136–66. New York: International Universities Press. (Original work published 1958.)

Graham, P. and Rutter, M. (1985). 'Adolescent disorders'. In Rutter, M. and Hersov, L. (eds), *Child and Adolescent Psychiatry: Modern Approaches*. London: Blackwell Scientific Publications.

Graham, P. J. (1986). 'Behavioural and intellectual development in childhood epidemiology'. *British Medical Bulletin* 42: 155–62.

Gunn, J., Maden, A. and Swinton, M. (1991). 'Treatment needs of prisoners with psychiatric disorders'. *British Medical Journal* 303: 338–41.

Health Advisory Service (1995). *Child and Adolescent Mental Health Services: Together We Stand*. London: HMSO.

Inhelder, B. and Piaget, J. (1958). *The Growth of Logical Thinking From Childhood to Adolescence*. New York: Norton.

Kazdin, A. E. (1990). 'Premature termination from treatment among children referred for antisocial behaviour'. *Journal of Child Psychology and Psychiatry* 31: 415–25.

——(1993a). Treatment of Conduct Disorder. *Development and Psychopathology* 5: 277–310.

——(1993b). 'Adolescent mental health: prevention and treatment programs'. *American Psychologist* 48: 127–41.

——(1999). Commentary on: 'Weiss, B. C., Catron, C. and Harris, V. (1999). "The effectiveness of traditional child psychotherapy". *Journal of Consulting and Clinical Psychology* 67: 82–94'. In *Evidence-Based Medicine* 2: 86.

——Holland, L. and Crowley, M. (1997). 'Family experience of barriers to treatment and premature termination from child therapy'. *Journal of Consulting and Clinical Psychology* 65: 453–63.

Kurtz, Z. (1992). *With Health in Mind: Mental Health Care for Children and Young People.* London: Action for Sick Children.

Laufer, M. and Laufer, M.E. (1984). *Adolescence and Developmental Breakdown: A Psychoanalytic View.* London: Yale University Press.

Leffert, N. and Petersen, A.C. (1995). 'Patterns of development during adolescence'. In Rutter, M. and Smith, J. (eds), *Psychosocial Disorders in Young People: Time Trends and Their Causes*, 67–103. Chichester: John Wiley & Sons.

Luborsky, L., Diguer, L., Luborsky, E., McLellan, A. T., Woody, G. and Alexander, L. (1993). 'Psychological Health-Sickness (PHS) as a predictor of outcomes in dynamic and other psychotherapies'. *Journal of Clinical and Consulting Psychology* 61: 542–49.

Parry, G. (1998). 'Psychotherapy services, healthcare policy and clinical audit'. In Davenhill, R. and Patrick, M. (eds), *Rethinking Clinical Audit*. London: Routledge.

Parry-Jones, A. Ll. (1995). 'The future of adolescent psychiatry'. *British Journal of Psychiatry* 166: 299–305

Rutter, M. (1989). 'Isle of Wight revisited: twenty-five years of child psychiatric epidemiology'. *Journal of the American Academy of Child and Adolescent Psychiatry* 28: 633–53.

Smith, D. J. and Rutter, M. (1995). *Psychosocial Disorders in Young People: Time Trends and Their Causes.* Chichester: John Wiley & Sons.

Stanger, C., McConaughy, S. H. and Achenbach, T. A. (1995). 'Three-year course of behavioral/emotional problems in a national sample of 4– to 16– year-olds: II. Predictors of syndromes'. *Journal of the American Academy of Child and Adolescent Psychiatry* 31(5): 941–50.

—— MacDonald, V. V., McConaughy, S. H. and Achenbach, T. A. (1996). 'Predictors of cross-informant syndromes among children and youth referred for Mental Health Services'. *Journal of Abnormal Child Psychology* 24(5): 597–614.

Tharp, R. G. (1991). 'Cultural diversity and treatment of children'. *Journal of Consulting and Clinical Psychology* 59: 799–812.

Weiss, B. (1998). 'Annotation: Routine monitoring of the effectiveness of child psychotherapy'. *Journal of Child Psychology and Psychiatry* 39: 943–50.

Wilson, P. (1991). 'Psychotherapy with adolescents'. In Holmes, J. (ed.), *Textbook of Psychotherapy with Adolescents*, 443–67. London: Churchill.

World Health Organization (1990). ICD-10, 1990. Draft of Chapter V, 'Mental and Behavioural Disorders (Including Disorders of Psychological Development)', Geneva: World Health Organization.

Part I

Theoretical and practical aspects of engaging young people in treatment

Chapter 1

Engaging troubled adolescents in six-session psychodynamic therapy

George Mak-Pearce

THE PROBLEM OF ENGAGEMENT OF ADOLESCENTS

This chapter considers the question of how to engage psychodynamically in a time-limited intervention with young people aged 12 to 25 years. The question of engagement came to the fore following a review of attendance for psychotherapy at the Brandon Centre. This review is described in more detail in the Introduction to this book. One problem, no doubt familiar to other psychotherapy services for young people, was that demand for psychotherapy exceeded the resources that we could provide. As a result many young people's requests for help did not get a rapid response. Another key area highlighted by the review was the high drop-out rate early on in the therapy.

High levels of attrition during the engagement phase of therapy is wasteful and damaging not just because the session times are lost (whilst there are many waiting who could use the therapy) but because one suspects that those who drop out are often those in greatest need of help. Moreover, experience has shown that those with pernicious problems in adolescence do not simply 'get better' later on in life. Healing does not occur simply through a process of maturation. As discussed in the Introduction recent studies have shown that disorders in adolescence, if untreated, continue into adulthood with similar or increased severity. Problems do not ameliorate without treatment and consequently the high attrition rate is, in effect, a 'storing-up' of problems for the future.

These considerations led the Brandon Centre to introduce a rapid response project with the aim of improving both take-up and engagement of young people. Any young person approaching the Centre who has not had previous experience of counselling or therapy, or who seems at risk of harming either themselves or others, is placed on a six-session waiting list. The waiting time for the first session is then usually up to 4 weeks. The young person is offered once-weekly meetings for 6 weeks. After the six sessions are completed they have the option of being put on the waiting list for long-term, once-weekly therapy. Therapy can then continue either with the same or a different therapist. The length of the wait between the six sessions and the longer-term work is usually about 8 weeks. This structure has proved effective in reducing waiting times but to reduce early drop out requires effective engagement of the young person in therapy and to this matter I now turn.

ENGAGEMENT AND FEAR OF THE FUTURE

Messer and Warren (1995) describe starting work with adolescents thus:

> Adolescents can be especially difficult to engage in psychotherapy. They are often counterdependent and oppositional, struggling to develop autonomy and independence from parents. They also may be anxious about losing control, being controlled, or experiencing shame and inadequacy. The idea of revealing one's concerns to an adult is filled with the unconscious dread of infantile regression and loss of a new-found and tenuously held sense of self. (p. 305)

In addressing the issue of engaging young adolescents psychodynamically within a time-limited framework I want to draw attention to what, I believe, is a critical feature of this phase of life. This is the intensity of the young person's anxieties about how they will perform in the future. Adolescence is essentially a period of abrupt and dramatic changes to both psyche and soma. These changes are cognitive, emotional, social, physical and sexual. There are intense anxieties about future performance, in particular how to establish a degree of social status, a favourable ranking with peers and how to establish a sexual relationship. The young person has to negotiate new responsibilities and manage a burgeoning physical, sexual and intellectual potency. It is a time for dreaming of the future; equally it is a time of nightmarish anticipations.

Starting therapy can provoke unrealistic dreams and nightmares! A young person may approach therapy with trepidation or false bravado. It is not difficult to picture the 16-year-old who might start by saying that he didn't want to talk about his feelings but what he could do with is sorting out a set of wheels and a place to live! What do we do with those situations where there is an apparent chasm between the client and the therapist in their understanding of what psychotherapy may provide? How does one move towards a therapeutic relationship? Many of the obstacles to engagement that one may suppose – for example that therapy will dig up the past, create shame, inadequacy, or dependency, cause infantile regression or loss of sense of self – are all fears that can apply at any age. What is the pertinent characteristic of adolescence that explains the high drop-out rate? I have chosen to approach this question by focusing upon the intensity of the adolescent's fear of the future. To look into this fear I shall start with issues to do with attachment and rank.

ATTACHMENT AND RANK

Early attachment experiences, as Bowlby (1982) argued, are deeply pervasive in our capacity to establish and maintain future relationships. So where mother–child bonding has been significantly disrupted the individual is prone to form what Bowlby called 'anxious attachments'. Such individuals may feel lacking in confidence, insecure, shy or hostile. In more extreme circumstances they may become phobic, anxiety-ridden, depressed, or conduct-disordered. I am sure most psychodynamic therapists are sensitive to and listen out for indications of early attachment difficulties. In particular, attachment issues tend to get played out in the transference and thus can strongly influence the young person's anticipation of the future of the therapy and how it will end.

Issues of rank are to do with how one perceives one's social standing, one's sense of self-esteem, status and entitlement. Stevens and Price (1996), who develop an evolutionary perspective, have recently emphasised the significance of rank in mental health. They argue that being able to accurately sense and respond to one's rank and status with peers and with the wider society is a good indicator of mental health. Whilst such skills are important at any stage of life, to my mind they are acutely so for the adolescent. This is so because the young person, on the cusp of adulthood, can be in the confusing position of sensing life holds great potential whilst at the same time sensing that their actual social status is at an all-time low. One 16-year-old girl who had recently left care put it succinctly in her first session when she said of herself 'I could be Whitney Houston, not a total zilch!'

I am sure it is not contentious to emphasise that adolescence is generally a time of low social status. Equally it is generally a time of (unrealistically) high individual expectations. This clash can generate great turmoil. One has lost the 'charm value' of being a child but the compensating values of adult social competence and emotional tolerance are frequently not exercisable with any confidence. Even for those young people who are safely within the social norms for their age, leaving school or leaving university and starting employment they are generally 'at the bottom of the pile'.

A more devastating downward shift in social status but upward shift in expectations can pertain for those from more deprived backgrounds. Those who are socially excluded, have little education or employment prospects and may already have a criminal record stand a high risk of finding themselves destitute. Statutory provisions for those reaching age 16 abruptly change and homelessness for this age group is high. Unemployment, poverty, the risk of being mugged, attacked or raped is at its peak. Yet even so expectations increase. The young person leaving school or care is expected to budget, shop, cook and find work. The need to belong to a group or gang can become urgent; particularly where such a group has its own mores through which one can quickly gain status and acceptance. Many 'bold' and illegal acts are performed to win the kudos and admiration of peers.

How issues of rank manifest themselves in the therapy will be fashioned in a complex way by the client's attachment history, their age and other individual traits. Yet one truth that inevitably prevails is that the therapist out-ranks the client. The younger the client the more this is so. I state this rather obvious point because there may be many pressures upon the therapist that tend to inhibit awareness of ranking differences. Some that I have been conscious of within myself are a reluctance to be seen as an authority figure, a longing to be young again or over-identification with the adolescent phase of life, and, of course, projective identification with the client's own sense of worthlessness and low status.

For the young person entering therapy, especially when it is for the first time, the ranking difference can exacerbate those factors that make therapy and the therapist seem threatening. This in turn can evoke the more primitive responses to a sense of being under threat; namely to fight back, behave submissively or flee. Whilst fighting back or being submissive can be worked with, the latter option leaves the therapist with an empty chair. In any event issues to do with rank can quickly evoke the deeper and darker elements of earlier attachment experiences and a concomitant dread of the future.

FEAR OF THE FUTURE IN TIME-LIMITED THERAPY

It may be supposed that the six-session structure would give relief to certain anxieties about engagement with the therapist. The fear of being trapped, becoming dependent or too regressed, would be abated by a time-limited setting. This has not been my experience. If anything it seems to me that the emphasis upon a time limit tends to evoke such feelings, can provoke performance anxiety in the client and, equally damaging, performance anxiety in the therapist. Am I, the therapist, able to provide enough? Are the sessions too intensive or perhaps not focused enough? Is there time for some working through of transference issues? There are myriad questions and it is easy to enter a short intervention with a sense of pressure, ambition or at least a full 'agenda'.

Clients sensitive to such pressures can easily (mis)understand them in terms of their own performance. Thus they may feel they ought to quickly 'get rid' of problem X or 'stop feeling' Y or 'solve' conflict Z. In reality the therapist may be attempting to elicit, explore and 'stay with' problem X, feeling Y or conflict Z. This divergence can lead to all kinds of problems for engagement.

In time-limited therapy anxiety about performance and outcome – both the client's and the therapist's – can be present from the outset. It may just take the form of a vague but pernicious fear of the future. The task, it seems to me, is to be able to convert this vague fear into a more specific, articulated fear of engagement. And this is most directly tackled through talking about the fantasies of the future relationship. Of course exploring future fantasy is only one of many possible ways to approach such fears, but it is one that it is hoped will engage the person quickly and therapeutically.

It is particularly important in time-limited work that future fantasies of success and failure are made explicit and treated with openness and humour. In the process of doing so there is scope for playfulness and togetherness. When spoken about, future fantasy can portray both hope and despair but be free of the humiliation and pain connected with events that have actually happened. The work can be more 'plastic'; future fantasies can be treated with a freedom and exploration not so readily permitted in talk of the past. Likewise the transference that 'will be' is open to being talked about if the therapist is prepared to introduce the subject in an easy manner. Let me expand on this.

FUTURE TRANSFERENCE

The future transference is a term I use for the current feelings about how the relationship with the therapist will be at some point in the future. To my mind it is the key to engagement, for in actuality the therapist and client do have to share a future time together in order to work, they do have to negotiate issues of attachment and rank, and do have to end and separate. What kind of figure will the therapist be? How potent, how useless, how intimate, how loved, how hated will the therapist be? What is the perceived value of the therapist as a potential introject?

It has been almost universal in my experience that the younger the person the less notion they have that it is desirable, permitted, or indeed relevant to explore their feelings about the therapist. It is of necessity a sensitive and delicate task on the part of the therapist to present in a meaningful way that exploring such feelings is a useful part of the work. I have found this especially important but difficult for those under the age of about 16.

A 13-year-old boy I saw, who seemed intelligent but bossy, was keen to quickly set out a problem he had. The hope was that I would have practical advice that would help him. He launched into a very detailed and elaborate account of how his best friend had rejected him. The story went on for some time and I found I was losing track. I also found myself waiting for him to move on to what I would consider more 'important' things such as his family relationships. I made some comment about the best friend and with a look of disappointment he told me I had got it all wrong. I hadn't understood the situation at all. He went over it again in even greater detail.

My first reaction was to feel irritation and a need to reassert myself. I wanted to point out to him that I knew from the referral note that there were other more serious things going on in his life and within his family. But how should we decide what was spoken about in the session? He wanted to speak about his friend but I thought he was avoiding speaking about the family trauma. I discussed with him my concerns about the seriousness of the issues that had been mentioned in the referral note and then posed it as a question 'how should we decide what to focus on?' He replied that I should decide because I was the therapist.

Part of my reluctance to focus on the friend issue was that his expressed hope was that coming to therapy would result in winning his friend back. I felt I was seen as some kind of 'tool' that could be used to fix reality, a reality that was broken down, not working in the way he wanted. I was bound to fail. I decided to shift the focus towards his view of the future. I asked him how he imagined he would feel about me if at the end of the six sessions his friend was still rejecting him. He said, genuinely, that he would be very disappointed. He then added that at least we would have tried. The use of the word 'we' was the first indication of him seeing us as working together or at least being able to share a sense of failure together. So I agreed to stick with this issue.

We spent much of the six sessions talking through how he felt about this friend and what he could try to do to change things. He came up with the idea that while he had lost a friend, equally upsetting, he had lost status in his peer group. He was lower in the pecking order; he had been displaced in the gang and fallen out of favour. He came up with what I thought were some rather creative strategies to win his friend round. But, by the end of the six sessions he had not repaired the friendship – at least not in the way he had intended.

Yet there was a modest shift in the way that he felt about the loss of the friendship. Instead of only representing confirmation of his worthlessness he saw that the loss resulted from him expressing unpopular views. These unpopular views, however, were views that he believed in and that expressed his individuality. Following from this he was able to reassess the apparent loss of status within the gang and see that perhaps his growth and development represented a threat to a rather immature gang mentality. Internally the loss of the friendship became the price of progression towards a more autonomous future.

In this case exploring aspects of fantasies about the future helped develop a positive engagement in the here and now. In the next section I look at what could be called the negative future transference and try to separate out two forms this can commonly take.

SOME ILLUSTRATIONS OF NEGATIVE FUTURE TRANSFERENCE

Fated transference

Peter is a man in his early twenties who came looking for help because he was failing at university. Peter told me that throughout his life he had fought to gain independence. He had struggled to get to university, which represented freedom and future advancement. But now he was at university he had become deeply unsure of his worth. He felt his family expected him to fail and anticipated a humiliating 'I told you so' response from his mother.

His manner towards me was tired and passive. Yet he was quite specific about what he wanted: I should help him structure his time and give him the will power to get on with his studies. I should save him from a humiliating failure. On the surface this expectation can be seen as simply naive but otherwise reasonable. On a deeper level I felt he wanted to merge with me. I felt he wanted his failure and humiliation to become my failure and humiliation. Perhaps to triumph, perhaps so as not to feel so alone, perhaps to observe how I deal with and contain the pain, perhaps so he could say to me 'I told you so'.

There are many things that could be said about the above expectations and how they fit into the question of how to engage with Peter in therapy. Here I wish to draw attention to the predominant sense of being with Peter, namely a very depressed sense that whatever happened in therapy was fated – fated to humiliation and failure. Peter presented as a passive recipient of a future scripted by others. This maybe echoes an early attachment relationship that felt engulfing and controlling. It also seems to goes hand in hand with low self-esteem and a poor perception of potential social rank.

In thinking about this kind of initial presentation I have found very useful the notion of fate that has been carefully and elegantly distinguished from the notion of destiny by Bollas in his book *Forces of Destiny* (1991). In essence, where we do not feel that we are the authors of our future lives, where we feel that the script is already written and that things are done either to us or for us, we feel fated. Fated as, for example, Oedipus was fated to do the things he did. A sense of destiny, on the other hand, implies a feeling of freedom and potency in the future, a sense of authorship of the story of one's life, a sense that Bollas links with the Winnicottian notion of true self:

> A person who is fated, who is fundamentally interred in an internal world of self and object representations that endlessly repeat the same scenarios, has very little sense of a future that is at all different from the internal environment they carry around with them. The sense of fate is a feeling of despair to influence the course of one's life. A sense of destiny, however, is a different state, when the person feels he is moving in a personality progression that gives him a sense of steering his course. (p. 41)

Peter wanted recognition, independence and acceptance. He wanted his peers to rate him as worthwhile. However, he seemed fated to form merging relationships to provide security at the cost of autonomy and status. In his mind, accepting help from me equated with passively following my script. Naturally he resented being in this position and therein lay the threat to engagement in therapy.

It was through a detailed and explicit discussion of the implications of this stance to our relationship that he began to shift. Gradually the fantasies about what lay ahead broadened and diversified. By having a focus upon the future relationship somehow we were able to 'step over' the fears of being engulfed in the present. Peter developed a fledgling sense of having options for the future and he finished the six sessions having made several small but constructive decisions about his life. He returned to university and perhaps as importantly he left the door open to return to therapy should he wish to.

Utopian transference

While the fated transference indicates a very passive and depressed stance towards the future, the utopian transference indicates a more manic and aggressive attempt to be in control of one's destiny. The client battles to achieve unrealistic expectations sometimes at great personal cost. The therapist may be approached in an attempt to co-opt help in this endeavour. In so far as the therapist is seen as assisting in this goal the therapist is idealised.

The style in which a therapist is idealised probably says a great deal about the client's early attachment history. However, whatever the style in which it is done, the therapist who is idealised will almost inevitably at some later point be perceived as a threat to the client's stability and status. The initial idealisation can be a flimsy attempt to fend off this anticipated threat; as such it is a difficult barrier to genuine engagement.

In the normal course of things adolescents are prone to idealisation and often harbour unrealistic expectations. What can be difficult is to assess where this takes on an acute form. In my thinking about this I am indebted to Angela Molnos (1995) and her insights concerning utopian fantasies. She points out that most utopias contain a *tabula rasa* fantasy – that is to say that before the new order of utopian living can be instituted it is necessary to wipe clean the slate. What that invariably means is a wholesale destruction of the old order. There must be a coup, a bloody revolution or a period of anarchy before the new ideal state can be instituted.

In political utopias it is often implied that there should be no guilt about the destruction and violence – the end justifies the means. The narcissistic and omnipotent political fantasy of creating a perfect society must not be questioned. Usually the ideal future does not involve tolerating uncertainty, frustration or criticism! As politicians know it is important to be seen to occupy the moral high ground and adolescents, like Hitler's Youth, are easy fodder for manipulation through this domain of future fantasy. High expectations combined with low social ranking make young people particularly vulnerable to such manipulations.

A woman I saw in her mid-twenties seemed ambitious and set herself very high standards. She approached her therapy with a nervous, excited awe. In the first two sessions she was obsessed about a difficult work situation that could lead to either promotion or shame. The third session she did not attend. After writing to her she returned for the remaining sessions.

The feeling in the first two sessions was somewhat along the lines of 'together we can change the world'. However, at the end of the second session things changed when she thought I agreed with various criticisms others apparently made of her. As I said, she missed the third session and then returned on the fourth. She spent the first part of this session angry and mocking. She told me how useless therapy was. From being the 'guru therapist' breaking new ground I became a total stick-in-the-mud – and fit for elimination.

I tried to free associate with her to images of change and ending and asked her how she imagined leaving therapy. She seemed to quite enjoy describing how she would make a dramatic exit and I would be left behind dumped, therapy a complete debacle. If anything the pleasure in describing this seemed to engage her somewhat. It was not until the final session that we managed to pull things together a bit. Her idealisation of me in the initial period seemed a way of keeping me on her side. However, there was also an unconscious pressure to fall out with me. This was her opportunity to replay something that seemed to happen with her mother who was alternately controlling and rejecting. This unconscious longing to recreate and work through an early attachment drama in therapy was closely balanced with the fear of the humiliation entailed. However we did complete the six sessions due in part to the fact that we had a way of talking about the anticipated triumph followed by humiliation. Through talking about the transference in the future tense we were able to somewhat 'humanise' a rather cruel and paranoid view of the therapeutic relationship.

SOME EPISTEMOLOGICAL CONSIDERATIONS

Popper (1968) has emphasised that what gives a theory scientific status is that it can, at least in principle, be falsified. That is to say the theory will make predictions which can through empirical investigation be shown to be false. Falsification has a potency that verification lacks. A theory can be verified many times without necessarily meaning a great deal, but one falsification can be sufficient for its rejection. The approach towards truth through a process of falsification Popper calls verisimilitude.

It occurs to me that many of the young clients I see are engaged in a difficult process of what could be called 'emotional verisimilitude'. That is to say they come to the therapy with a dysfunctional 'paradigm' (a cluster of theories, conscious and unconscious, concerning amongst other things their potential for attachment and rank). The paradigm is believed verified by repeated past experiences. The compulsion to repeat (and the unconscious need to express) leads the client to establish a relationship with the therapist that pushes for further verification of the paradigm. Consequently the future transference becomes the domain of potential falsification.

In working with future fantasy one is, in effect, preparing the stage for falsification of the dysfunctional paradigm. To this end interpreting the transference is not so much aimed at the historic roots of distorted self-representations but rather towards clarifying the inherent implications and consequences of the paradigm. It is then for the therapist to draw upon the real relationship and highlight the discrepancies between the anticipated and actual state of affairs.

CONCLUSION

It is generally true that people in the age group 12 to 25 years do not like to tolerate frustration, pain or uncertainty for any length of time. As with adults but with more urgency this age group wants to be shot of bad feelings – not landed in them. In addition there is a common and (perhaps reasonable) expectation of feeling better after seeing a therapist. This expectation may be met or, equally likely, more bad feelings are discovered! The question of how the young adolescent understands this apparent 'failure' of treatment and tolerates attending therapy needs to be actively raised within the early stages of therapy.

To work with future fantasy is not to avoid working with thoughts, feelings and fantasies about the past. Both are important and usually one mirrors the other. To focus upon issues of rank and attachment embraces both domains. Our capacity to sustain social rank and intimate relations says so much about both what was and what will be in our lives.

My emphasis in this chapter has been to point out that for achieving engagement with adolescents an immediate exploration of future fantasy can be very containing. This is because it quickly opens the door to voicing critical and fearful feelings about the therapy and therapist. It is very easy and natural for the therapist to ask what the client is hoping to get from the therapy. One can ask how they imagine the therapy will end. These questions can lead straight to the anticipated relationship with the therapist – what I have called the future transference.

I have found that working with future fantasy can be done in a way that is free and more speculative than is sometimes the case with talk about past feelings. The latter, because they have a different ontological status, are usually felt to be much more revealing, much more private and personal, and much more blameworthy. I tend to think of future fantasy having the status of a dream. It is rich material for psychodynamic treatment. But, of course, it is a particular kind of dream. It is a dream that is created in the presence of another. It involves two people in its creation and as such it engages. It is a statement about their future relationship.

References

Bollas, C. (1991). *Forces of Destiny*. London: Free Association Books.
Bowlby, J. (1982). *Attachment and Loss*, vol. 1–3: *Attachment*. New York: New York Books.
Messer, S. B. and Warren, C. S. (1995). *Models of Brief Psychodynamic Therapy*. New York: The Guilford Press.
Molnos, A. (1995). *A Question of Time: Essentials of Brief Dynamic Psychotherapy*. London. Karnac Books.
Popper, K. (1968). *The Logic of Scientific Discovery*. London: Hutchinson.
Stevens, A. and Price, J. (1996). *Evolutionary Psychiatry*. London: Routledge.

Chapter 2

Why come, why come back

Developing and maintaining a long-term therapeutic alliance with young people who have had a psychotic breakdown

Olivia Amiel

INTRODUCTION AND BACKGROUND

This chapter focuses on the process of engaging young people who have experienced a psychotic breakdown before coming to the Brandon Centre. They had recently been hospitalised, or were being maintained in the community with the help of psychiatric or other medical input, that included medication. I hope to show that despite the severity of their symptoms it is possible to do useful therapeutic work in once-weekly psychotherapy.

Developing a therapeutic relationship can be difficult for all young people coming to the Centre but for this group it is particularly challenging. Unlike less troubled young people, their motivation for coming, their understanding of and adaptation to the setting cannot be taken for granted. They are often in a numbed, frightened state, full of terror, complexity and confusion. Their world has been narrowed by their fear, and taken over by their delusions, making it very hard to connect with reality. In the clinical work I shall describe, the biggest challenge, both for them and for me, was to find safe, accessible and consistent stepping-stones from their disintegrated, often paranoid state towards a position where they could have some sense of themselves as part of a world that was more meaningful and less threatening.

This involved very specific work aimed at getting them to come to their sessions and thereafter maintaining contact. Before illustrating this and the gradual development of the therapeutic process, I will describe the backgrounds of three young people who initially presented at the Centre with psychotic symptoms.

These young people had not sought help by referring themselves, although they were old enough to do so. They had stopped functioning altogether, and were of enormous concern to those who had referred them. They had dropped out of school, college or work; they had become socially isolated and they had begun behaving in bizarre, alarming and unpredictable ways.

Robyn (23) felt unable to return to college after her discharge from hospital. Although less deluded than she had been (she no longer, for example, believed she had a direct line to God), she was spending all day alone in her room, too terrified to talk to anyone in the flat she shared, playing discordant music at all hours, and planning how to die.

John (19) had been asked to leave college as he was no longer able to look after himself. He would forget to wash, eat or dress appropriately and had become increasingly paranoid. He was awake most of the night and slept at odd times during the day.

Ed (20) had stopped going to work and spent all day watching 'soaps' on TV. He felt he had become one of the characters and worried excessively about their/his life. He would not eat with his family and would only snack alone in his room.

Their isolation in some ways protected them but also effectively trapped them, not least by making it progressively more difficult to get help, particularly where that help involved relating to another person and sustaining that relationship. They had retreated from the stress and threats of everyday life and had blanked out the real world by cushioning themselves from the demands of others.

The difficulty in forming a relationship which would enable the development of a therapeutic alliance with these three young people was further compounded by the fact that, in common with many less disturbed people seeking help, they had all experienced severe difficulties in their early relationships with care givers. Fonagy and Target (1998) suggest that:

> In cases of abusive, hostile or simply totally vacuous relationships with the caregiver, the infant may deliberately turn away from the object; the contemplation of the object's mind is overwhelming as it harbours frankly hostile intentions towards the infant's self. This may lead to a widespread avoidance of mental states which further reduces the chance of identifying and establishing intimate links with an understanding object. (p. 27)

To a greater or lesser extent, this seemed to have been the case with all three, although their actual backgrounds differed markedly.

Robyn's mother had a serious breakdown soon after her birth and she was looked after by a number of different relatives. The family then moved to an isolated farmhouse in the country. When she was returned home, the main aim of her father was to keep her quiet in order to maintain a peaceful atmosphere for her mother. Often, this was achieved by placing Robyn on her own in front of a radio playing loud orchestral music. As a result, she was virtually always alone or ignored.

Throughout her early childhood, Robyn gained a good deal of attention as a result of her prodigious musical talent. But she was always on the edge of relationships, she would watch but not interact. By the time she reached early adolescence, she was no longer coping and had the first of a series of serious breakdowns, which were diagnosed as being characteristic of a manic-depressive illness and some of which necessitated hospitalisation. The shame and guilt of her family were enormous: once again she was made to be quiet and spent more and more time alone listening to music. She managed to get into music school but found the demands of the other students very threatening. By the time she reached the

Brandon Centre she was fearful that she was breaking down again and would lose the chance of attaining her one wish, to become a musician.

John's childhood could not have been more different. He was the much-loved and much the youngest child of parents who saw him as the solution to their increasing marital problems. He was effectively brought up as, and felt himself to be, an only child. His parents fought over him constantly and were intensely over-involved in every aspect of his life. He could not do anything without advice or counter-advice. Relating was a battlefield and was usually achieved by shouting. John did not know how to be with others, which resulted in a troubled childhood and a lonely school life: he found it extremely difficult to make or retain friends.

John was sent to a number of child psychotherapists, but he never remained in treatment for any length of time as his parents always found some reason why they were not good enough. By the time John came to the Brandon Centre, he had in any case defined his parents as the problem and thought that as soon as he got away from them he could learn to be himself. However, he quickly discovered at university that although he could not be with his parents, he could not be without them either.

John became increasingly paranoid about other students, feeling they were monitoring his every move: he shouted at them and abused them for this imagined persecution. He became obsessively concerned with getting unimportant parts of his written work to a state of perfection to the point where he never actually handed anything in. John lived in a state of external as well as internal chaos, neglecting his room and his personal care to the point of neither changing his clothes nor washing. He also became worryingly thin as he would often forget to eat. Complaints against and concern about him from students and staff led finally to John being asked to leave the university and seek hospital treatment. By the time he reached the Brandon Centre he feared he had gone mad.

Ed's father was black and had been born in South Africa: his mother was white and came from a small northern village. When he was 5 years old his father left and he had no further contact with him. Six years later his mother had a daughter by a white man who also left the family after a short while.

Ed was left as a black child in a white family with no contact with his father's family or friends. He felt different and isolated, identified as the 'bad one' like his father. He struggled to deal with his mixed parentage and the difficulties this posed for his identity. He felt on the edge, not part of any group. Always alone and separate, he had no friends and found it almost impossible to talk to others of his age.

Ed's childhood was spent with a succession of different childminders. As with Robyn he was made to feel that he had to behave and not make a fuss. He buried himself in his academic work and did exceptionally well in his small, strict but containing Catholic school.

Leaving school and going to college was very traumatic for Ed. He began to feel unable to cope and retreated into a world of fantasy centred around television, a world in which he became a white (and therefore acceptable) member of a family in an Australian soap. However, he also became afraid of his increasingly violent thoughts about harming his sister, and it was these that made him give in, albeit reluctantly, to his mother's and GP's insistence that he come to the Centre.

TREATMENT

A conducive therapeutic setting is seen as an important prerequisite for all psychotherapeutic work. This involves providing facilitative structures (physical surroundings, the setting out of procedures and ground rules) and processes (the style, orientation and perceived attitudes of the therapist) (Wilson, 1991, p. 451). With very acutely disturbed young people, creating a setting of any kind that feels safe for them is a critical first step and requires being much more active and re-active than is usual with less disturbed young people of their age. Key elements for the building of trust include clarity, containment, familiarity, consistency and flexibility.

I saw liaison with other professionals involved in the care of the three young people as essential, particularly where clarity was concerned. It was helpful for them to have other familiar professionals explaining and reinforcing our respect-ive roles, and supporting them in getting to and engaging with therapy. The exchange of background information and diagnostic perspectives, and the sharing of concerns were also helpful and supportive for me.

This worked particularly well in John's case. I worked closely with his Com-munity Psychiatric Nurse (CPN), who helped John plan his journey to the Centre and constantly reassured and encouraged him in attending. The CPN also provided a link to the psychiatrist who saw John intermittently and monitored his medica-tion. For Robyn this was more difficult as both her GP and her psychiatrist were extremely pessimistic about her prognosis and the use of psychotherapy. How-ever, clarification about her medication and assurance that she could be admitted to hospital if necessary was helpful in itself. Ed's GP encouraged his attendance as he wanted to keep him out of hospital. He found his silence impenetrable and therefore had difficulty in assessing his mental state.

Liaison with other professionals only occurred, of course, with the full know-ledge and consent of the young person. In general they were keen to know who I had spoken to and why, finding the interest shown in them comforting rather than threatening. Given that none of them had experienced relationships with their parents where communication had been open, consistent and/or inclusive, I was aware of the importance of demonstrating to them that such communication about and with them was possible. Without needing to explore this overtly by making interpretations that could perhaps not be tolerated in the early stages of therapy, my liaison work thus served a useful additional purpose in the transference at later stages.

The length of the sessions, the appointment times, why they were coming, etc. had to be restated on many occasions. Robyn, for example, had no conception of regularity and continuity: she had to be reminded at the end of each session that I would expect to see her the following week and I would go over briefly why it was necessary for her to come regularly to talk about why she was feeling so bad. When she seemed particularly perplexed, distracted or disengaged, I would additionally write her a note. It was several months before Robyn's attendance was automatic and understood.

Sessions were limited to one per week. This was positively beneficial in that it was not seen as being too threatening or intrusive. The regularity and structure of the sessions, and the familiarity of the setting became increasingly important in providing a sense of security and containment. Seemingly small things took on positive significance: the same receptionist letting them in; the same, small consulting room being there for them each week, and so on. These factors were perhaps particularly important to these three young people, given the level of their disturbance and its attendant distrust and fear.

Enabling the three young people to come to their sessions at the Centre in the first instance was only part of the therapeutic challenge; how to make therapy meaningful for them and worth repeated visits was a much greater challenge.

It was impossible during the early stages of treatment to work with any of them in an interpretive manner as one might with less disturbed young people. I experienced the difficulties Edgcumbe (1993) describes so clearly in working with patients who have psychotic symptoms:

> [the] processes of communication are hindered by the patients' inability to communicate with themselves within their own mind, that is to have an awareness and understanding of their own mental functioning, or to perceive the value of such communication and understanding. Such patients do not respond to interpretation of unconscious conflict because it is meaningless for them. (p. 109)

There began instead the slow and painstaking preliminary process described by Fonagy and Target (1998) as 'verbalising internal states, differentiating feelings, breaking down unmanageable, anxiety-provoking experiences into simpler, more manageable entities, helping the development of an "as if" attitude, where ideas can be thought of as ideas rather than reality' (p. 30). This appeared to be a necessary way forward, as all three young people's hold on reality and their ability to differentiate between themselves and others was too precarious.

I had to find a way of communicating that they found meaningful and that allowed them to want to engage, while at the same time respecting their defensive stance; a way of being able to reflect with them without being too threatening or intrusive. In coming to this view I can see how I was also reacting to my countertransference, in particular the powerful projections into me of their fragility, disturbance and confusion.

The early months with John were difficult to endure. He would arrive dishevelled and unwashed, in a very agitated state and would immediately attack me verbally, shouting uncontrollably. It was impossible to try and explore with him what these outbursts meant. John did not know how 'to be' with me in any other way.

Instead of interpreting his anger, I would insist he stopped shouting so that – paradoxically – I could hear what he was saying. I had to reassure him that the pictures in the room were not moving and that I was not making bizarre movements with my legs. Calm repetition, focusing on simple statements that clarified and defined what was going on in the room at that moment in time, seemed to be helpful. We would spend a good deal of time planning exactly how he would get home, what he would do if someone looked at him, etc. It was a slow learning process of reality testing and, more importantly, of how to be with another person.

In that long and often disheartening first year, there were some significant and poignant moments. John arrived at one session with a tatty carrier bag which split, pouring disconnected bits of his life on to the floor: old letters, combs, rotting food, medication. Together we taped up the bag and slowly put all the bits back into it. Much later in the therapy, he was able to see this moment as a metaphor for the process which he had undertaken and the reintegration he had been able to begin to achieve.

For Robyn also, coming to the Centre was at first threatening and anxiety provoking. She would sit rigid and tense throughout the early sessions, speaking in a quiet and polite manner on subjects which did not involve her personally. She could not bring herself into the room, but she brought her encased violin and placed it carefully on the floor between us, as a reminder of what she was no longer able to do, as a reproach and perhaps as a challenge. She was unable to practise or play with others. Having sought comfort through music in the past, she was now at a loss, feeling that part of herself had been removed, or perhaps encased. Her mood swings were becoming more marked and frightening and she was desperate not to be readmitted to hospital.

Paradoxically though, music became the only means of communication between us. Robyn talked about her violin, its tone, her long search to find the right instrument, her technical problems with her bowing arm, etc. She would bring sheet music into the room, setting it on the floor, trying to put it into some sort of order. She talked about music with a depth and complexity that I found difficult to understand as though she was testing my resolve to bear confusion.

Robyn could not tolerate a whole session and in those early sessions would either arrive late or leave early. It was difficult for her to be with another person in any degree of physical let alone emotional proximity. I was careful to respect her fragility: it was clear that if she felt pursued, threatened or even committed she would not be able to return.

When Robyn telephoned to cancel a session, I would attempt to speak to her myself. She usually cancelled when she was feeling bad, wanting it seemed to isolate herself with her music, as she had been made to do as a child. I would ask her what music she was listening to and from this get some idea as to how bad or out of control she was feeling. At particularly bad times, for example, she would listen to an anguished and violent Shostakovich symphony, whereas when she was feeling more sad and reflective, she might listen to a Schubert chamber work.

It was some months before Robyn could talk directly with me about her feelings. Gradually she put to one side the technical complexities of her musical world, as she felt safe enough to come back and bring into the open far greater complexities of her inner emotional world.

When Ed first came to the Centre, he could not make eye contact with anyone and could hardly bear even to give his name to the receptionist. In the room with me he was totally silent and when asked questions he was at best monosyllabic. He was obviously uncomfortable and anxious: I attempted to ameliorate this by filling some of the more painful silences with non-threatening observations. I started watching one or two 'soaps' myself, establishing a little common ground on which to base some remarks that did at least elicit a flicker of recognition and interest on Ed's face.

Perhaps this helped enable Ed to keep coming and he was eventually just about able to acknowledge that he was concerned about himself but found it difficult to share his thoughts. I knew he had become completely isolated, spending all his time watching television or playing on his computer, but he could not talk about what he did even on a superficial level, and was certainly unable to understand what it meant, why he did it, or what he was feeling about it. At this stage, it was impossible for Ed to engage in the difficult task of making sense psychologically of how the difference between him and his family in terms of colour mattered and affected him. This reticence was understandable, given that he had contrived over many years to deny being different by making himself invisible within his fantasy world. I had to find a way of relating to him before he could even look at me, let alone acknowledge or think about the 'difference' between us as a way of beginning to make sense of what was happening in his life. Difference was so terrifying and threatening to him, and the way he was dealing with it had become so dysfunctional, that I had to enable him to feel some connection with me before this could even begin to be looked at.

After several months of agonisingly slow and difficult sessions with Ed, he discovered a connection between us: we both used a particular palmtop computer. For the first time he became animated, as he was able to talk to me through a medium that was familiar and understandable for him. As music was for Robyn, so for Ed the computer was a safe 'transitional object' connecting us. He was able to talk to me about customising labelled fields in his database to catalogue the books he had read and the people he knew. By classifying, ordering and organising his world, albeit in a machine, Ed was making an attempt to fight the internal chaos and conflict that was overwhelming him. It gave him a certain sense of control and, in his relationship with me, also a means of connecting to another person.

Therapeutic work with these three young people, particularly in the early stages, was then rather different from that done with less disturbed young people in long-term treatment. I found myself more actively involved in setting up an environment which could enable a relationship to develop.

In the year that followed, John began to learn how 'to be' with other people. At first this was around the details of getting to the sessions: what, for example, to say to another passenger on the bus; what he felt when others were in the waiting room with him, etc. I was able to use what was going on in the room with me to begin to make sense for him of this process. It was an active feeding back to him of what he was doing, and the effect this might have on others. The CPN was very involved in reinforcing this work and liaising with both the psychiatrist and me, particularly when John's condition deteriorated and there was concern about whether he could be managed without a hospital admission.

Fortunately an admission was averted and John improved markedly as the year wore on. He began to be more reflective in the sessions. He was able to listen and no longer talked at me or over my words. He started to think about his childhood and the difficulties he had experienced in separating from his parents. Unavoidable breaks from our sessions were very important, and brought up a number of issues for him concerning separation and how to cope with it. He was able to make use of transference interpretations about separation and independence that reflected current difficulties he was having with his parents. He was eventually able to enrol at a local college, living at home initially, and continuing to attend his sessions with me. He began a relationship with a fellow student, which although fairly short-lived, gave a feeling of confidence and a belief that he could be 'normal' and have 'normal' things to be preoccupied about.

Robyn was also able to return to her studies. She gradually began to be able to tolerate being with other young people as long as there was no threat of real intimacy. Like John, she too was preoccupied by the details of relating: what to say to other members of her orchestral section; how to react when she felt certain things, etc. Robyn would rehearse in exhaustive detail what she would say or do in certain hypothetical situations that she feared, in particular how to react to tensions with her flatmates. She began to be more aware of her mood swings and more able to cope when she felt out of control. More significantly, she became able to come to her sessions even when she was feeling depressed or having suicidal thoughts. It was very important for her to know that I could tolerate her when she felt like this and that she could safely share with me details of her breakdowns, and the humiliation and shame she experienced from her parents which she then internalised.

Although this part of my work with Robyn increased as time went on, there was by no means a straightforward linear progression. Often Robyn would retreat back into her world of music and our sessions would have to follow suit. Although she became aware that this was happening, I accepted her need to step back and did not try to move her into other areas. She and I were both aware that, in her words, she 'would never be quite right'. However, she did appear to be more able to cope with day-to-day life and to make realistic plans for her future. She started taking her medication regularly and attending her psychiatric appointments.

Like Robyn, Ed would also retreat when more direct communication proved too threatening. The ease of communicating with and through his computer contrasted starkly with the difficulties he was experiencing in real life. At school, he had had an identity of sorts: unable to see himself as either one of the black or the white boys, he had become the quiet, intelligent one, spending most of his time in the library. This did not work so easily at college or at work, and the conflicts he experienced became increasingly difficult to cope with. As Gibbs (1987) has described, the task of developing and sustaining a separate and positive identity for adolescents of mixed parentage can be particularly complex and difficult. It would involve 'integrating dual racial identifications into a single identity that affirms the positive aspect of each heritage; acknowledges the reality of societal ambivalence and rejects the self-limitations of racial stereotypes or behaviours on the process of self-actualisation' (p. 275). This process was made impossible for Ed by the almost total negation on his mother's side (except in a pejorative sense) of both the black side of his family and of Ed himself.

At home, the quiet role was no longer working for him. He became increasingly explosive with his younger sister. This resulted in feelings of guilt and panic: from an early age, Ed had internalised the perception/accusation that he was just like his father, and if he was not good he would be sent away.

Our sessions moved forward very slowly over a period of 18 months. Familiarity, consistency and the connections we had established initially about our computers allowed for the gradual development of a trusting relationship. Ed began to realise that his bad thoughts could emerge in the room with me without him being sent away. As described above, it was difficult at first to acknowledge the difference between us. Gradually this did happen: his need to be quiet and to please diminished and his ability to express differences of opinion with me as well as his bad thoughts increased, albeit in a very tentative way at first. Thinking about his life and beginning to understand some of his responses to it became possible. Ed began to talk about his envy of his sister and his fury that the latter could get away with being demanding and difficult with their mother.

Slowly, Ed shifted from seeing his father, and himself, as all bad. He started to make enquiries about him and his life. Less worried about rocking the boat with his mother, he began to fill in some of the gaps in his history which in the past he had had to invent for himself. He also made contact with some of his black relatives and began from this slightly strengthened base to challenge his mother in a careful and thoughtful manner.

CONCLUSION

The cases I have described represent a group of young people commonly thought not to be amenable to once-weekly psychotherapy in the community. Their capacity for reflective thought is often absent or badly damaged, and their inability to initiate, tolerate or sustain relationships makes the establishment and maintenance of a therapeutic alliance very difficult.

The process may have been more prolonged than is usually the case in psychotherapy. The route taken was certainly more circuitous, requiring even more flexibility and adaptability than is usual with young people. Indeed, the process has seemed to me rather like a dance, initially between two strangers. One of them has no idea of the steps at first: the other may know the basic steps and is sometimes asked to lead. At other times, one may need to lead without being seen to do so and at still other times may need to be led. The tempo of the dance and the mood of the music it is danced to change frequently; many of the steps have to be repeated often, and some re-invented. The hoped for outcome is a shared under-standing of the direction of travel, a sharing of thoughts and feelings to provide a unity of purpose between the two participants, and a consolidation for the young person of those thoughts and feelings to the point where they can be sustained independently. For the young person, the experience of, the example provided by and the modest interpretations facilitated within the therapeutic relationship can enhance reflective capacity, enabling the development of an internal world which experiences others' behaviour towards them as being more comprehensible and meaningful, connected to them in a way which is not necessarily arbitrary and/or hostile.

After an average of 2 years of therapy, all three of the young people I have described demonstrated to a greater or lesser extent some of this reflective capacity. They were slowly and partially able to return to a path of more normal development, re-engaging with tasks and objectives that had been set for them or that they had set for themselves. Robyn completed her musical studies without readmission to hospital; John enrolled at a local university and eventually com-pleted a degree course; and Ed returned to college part time. Undoubtedly how-ever, they all remain vulnerable to further breakdowns. Ongoing availability of and support by mental health services is desirable and may well be necessary to try to pre-empt deterioration or hospitalisation. The transition from a young person's to an adult's service will in all likelihood be problematic in itself, not least because of the limited availability of ongoing psychotherapy for adults, especially those with a history of psychotic symptoms.

The achievements of these three young people were substantial but incomplete and may prove to be impermanent. Nonetheless, those achievements both reflect and will hopefully reinforce some of the work done by all of them during their therapeutic engagement with the Brandon Centre.

References

Edgcumbe, R. (1993). 'Developmental disturbances in adolescents and their implications for transference and technique'. *Bulletin of the Anna Freud Centre* 16: 109.

Fonagy, P. and Target, M. (1998). An interpersonal view of the infant. In Hurry, A. (ed.), *Psychoanalysis and Developmental Therapy*, 27.

Gibbs, J. T. (1987). 'Identity and marginality: issues in the treatment of biracial adoles-cents'. *American Journal of Orthopsychiatry* 57(2): 275.

Wilson P. (1991). 'Psychotherapy with Adolescents'. In Holmes, J. (1991). *Textbook of Psychotherapy in Psychiatric Practice*, 443–67. London: Churchill Livingstone.

Chapter 3

Absence and inertia in the transference

Some problems encountered when treating young men who have become developmentally stuck

James Rose

In this chapter I would like to describe and discuss problems I have encountered in engaging some young men in individual long-term psychotherapy at the Brandon Centre. They seemed to convey a message that appeared to say, 'You can't help me'. In addition, I have been frequently struck by how little progress they feel they have made in their lives. Young people of their age have often achieved much and experienced considerable inner psychic change, which has led to progress being made in their social and sexual relationships, in a field of study or in developing a choice of occupation. Because of this lack of progress, these young men seem to have become thoroughly demoralised and to be giving up struggling with life. This gives rise to the implicitly fatalistic sentiment of 'you can't help me'. And yet they come for help and therein lies a paradox because they clearly wish to be helped.

THE CLINICAL PROBLEM

It is comparatively common that a young person will come to a consultation de-scribing themselves as depressed; suffering from a lack of confidence and feeling devoid of ambition. Their psychic life can appear to be pervaded with emptiness to the point that it seems surprising to the psychotherapist that they have bothered to come to the consultation at all. Often there is evidence of disrupted family history, early bereavements and separations. Despite the apparently traumatic nature of these events, they are often dismissed as unimportant because they happened 'so long ago'. In short, while the psychotherapist can see many reasons for the young person's depressed state of mind, there is an apparent gulf between the young person's and the interviewer's understanding that seems unbridgeable and leaves the interviewer feeling hopeless and impotent. The apparent emptiness can seem like a deficit in functioning and it can appear that this young person is not suitable for psychotherapy because of their incapacity to symbolise or to reflect upon their experience.

Paradoxically, the unpromising prospects for psychotherapy often prove wrong, despite the initial rejection of the interpretations of early loss. But, whilst the young person concerned eventually becomes engaged with a psychotherapeutic process, change does not occur at a sparkling rate. Rather, progress can seem so slow that it can appear non-existent and the apparently stuck quality of their lives becomes replicated in the therapy. This can reinforce the impression of early emotional deficit or perverse resistance as the psychotherapist can wonder whether any meaningful resolution of the young person's difficulties will, or can, occur. The significance of this clinical picture is that progress differs markedly from a common clinical pattern where symptomatic change is assessed to occur in the first 6 months of treatment (Baruch, Fearon and Gerber, 1998). For the most part, the apparent rate of change in these cases can be imperceptible and there can easily be the thought that the initial decision to offer psychotherapy was a mistake.

These adolescents may seem to depart somewhat from the admirable distillation of the adolescent position described by Brenman-Pick (1988, p. 188). 'For while he ... [*the adolescent*] ... may consciously find it difficult to admit his need for guidance, he unconsciously desperately searches for objects which he believes will provide leadership.'

In contrast to the defiant 'don't help me' (Wilson, 1991) position of many adolescents, these young people appear to be saying in a despondent way 'you can't help me', and yet the paradox is that they come for help. One cannot refuse to treat them; hence the question becomes how to conceptualise theoretically this pattern observed in assessment and in treatment.

THE THEORETICAL PROBLEM

The central issue is the situation whereby the young person appears to be making little progress in their lives at a time when the normal pattern of development is that there is considerable change accompanied by conflict within the self and with others. All this is occurring within the confines of a newly maturing sexual body, which creates a new psychosomatic matrix within which relationships with others are experienced. It is as if these young people are doubly disadvantaged in that the ego strength they need to cope with the changes entailed in progress are being continually undermined by their lack of progress. Demoralisation increases and there seems to be a sense of giving up the struggle as futile.

This is readily experienced in the counter-transference in the early stages of the consultations. The point is that the common feature of these young people is not one of directed anger towards the self or others, as in a melancholic state of mind, as described in *Mourning and Melancholia* by Freud (Freud, 1917); but of apparent inertia. They can seem to the adult mind to be apparently motivated to defeat any structuring efforts. Sometimes I have been tempted to regard this position of emptiness as regressive and provocative. In some cases they may be but I have found that to assume it to be so immediately can be a mistake. The early phase can often be one of testing the psychotherapist to see if they can be trusted.

Once this is achieved, they do not markedly act out but make slow progress and appear frustrating.

Any enactment there is, therefore, is more of an *enactment in the transference*. The transference established is what I have come to think of as a *transference depression* and the likely duration of the therapy can promise to be endless. Themes can be repetitively worked over to the point that the treatment can begin to seem without point or object. To illustrate these general impressions I shall offer some clinical examples in the form of particular themes that can often occur in the treatment of these young people.

CLINICAL THEME: 'YOU CAN'T HELP ME'

The unconscious message 'you can't help me' can seem to be symptomatic of a passive–aggressive position. The young people have found themselves unable to study or engage in any meaningful way with their life. They seem demoralised and unable to explain what often has seemed to them a rather sudden onset of depression. They typically do not call this depression but describe a sense of self-worthlessness and sometimes a sense of feeling compelled to do the opposite of what others wish, which can be thought perverse.

In terms of their history, there is often some evidence of a family disruption either as a result of a bereavement or break-up of the parents. It seems sometimes that, within their immediate family, such young men can become the 'ghost' of their absent fathers, attracting the same antagonism as does the absent figure of their fathers. It seems that they seek to mourn their fathers but have no one with whom to mourn this loss because of other family members' antagonism to the father. Their response to this seems to be to identify with their lost father or, at least, with the image of the father in the minds of the remaining family members. Because this identification is with an object that is hated in the family, it becomes consistent to be antagonistic and possibly perverse.

In the course of working with these young people, the main focus of the work often becomes the pattern of their attendance, which can be unpredictable. This often creates a kind of enfuriation in the counter-transference. Because such young men are struggling to escape from an identification with a father about whom they have very ambivalent feelings, they even become that provocative figure in the transference. One way of enacting this can involve them behaving as if they can hardly be bothered to get out of bed to attend the session. This may be belied by the effort they seem to put in when they do attend. Sometimes they enquire whether the psychotherapist thinks he is wasting his time with them and wouldn't prefer to be helping others. This can be so persistent that the psychotherapist is introduced to an apparently impossible position, which perhaps reflects his patient's internal predicament. This impossibility arises from the young man's ambivalence towards their departed loved object, which means they hate what they deeply love. Their solution is often to be that hated object.

The transference situation frequently, therefore, seems to be one in which the young person believes that they are despised by their psychotherapist. This can provide the clue to the identification with the absent family member. This enables a forthright interpretation of the meaning of the young person's absence or sporadic attendance patterns in terms of his identification with a despicable object, which can appear to be in defiance of their common sense. But, when they begin to see that the purpose of the identification 'with the lost object' could possibly be a defence against their sense of abandonment, change can begin to occur. The trouble is that to seek to explain this intellectually will not help because it will have no emotional meaning for the young person. It has to be experienced by living it out through the young person's use of the therapeutic contact. In regard to these cases, the central point I wish to make is that these young people's difficulties are largely expressed in the pattern of their engagement. However, to engage them it is often apparent that the psychotherapist needs to be attentive to this pattern and not to concentrate on its apparent perverse destructiveness. The psychotherapist also needs to be open to all the potential meanings of the pattern of attendance. As we shall now see, a regular attendance does not necessarily reflect a picture free of psychopathology.

CLINICAL THEME: 'I DREAD WHAT YOU THINK OF ME'

The next theme I would like to consider may not necessarily apparently present problems of engagement. These patients commonly attend with great consistency and regularity. However, one can find that the dominant pattern of the therapeutic work is a display of a young person's determination to hang on to an explanation of their situation, when this so-called explanation is essentially self-defeating. In the last section I described situations in which young people are in identification with an absent figure for whom they, and their family, have very ambivalent feelings. However, it is often the case that the young person coming for help is in a family in which a parent or a sibling is either mentally ill or suffering from a physical illness which is disabling physically and mentally. It might seem at first sight strange that the young person should feel disturbed by such an illness.

It often becomes clear that, in these cases, an identification with the ill member of the family takes place either because of an unconscious guilt for failing to save them or a belief that whatever has caused the disabling illness will transmit itself to the young person concerned. There is often a great fear on the part of the young person of their being seen as identical to, or as ill as, the suffering family member. This can often lead them to suppress their symptoms or to believe that they do not need help. Alternatively, they may develop a theory for their ills to which they commit themselves with a great determination. As an example, a young person may become convinced that they have suffered a trauma and this then becomes the centre of their difficulties. This, whilst possibly true, then masks the more fundamental difficulty arising from their disturbed reactions to an ill parent. In the consulting room, it can seem to the assessing psychotherapist that an image of the suffering family member is presented by the young person from whom they are struggling to free themselves but the young person will be quite oblivious to this phenomenon.

Although one might expect that the details of their histories would be readily forthcoming, this is often not the case. The young person's childhood is described as unremarkable because, of course, it is the only childhood they have directly experienced. But this may not be the only reason. The truth of a young person's history may take some time to be revealed fully because they fear that they will be categorised in the psychotherapist's mind as identical to the person that they find so problematical. Or, there can be an irrational fear that if they think about it with their psychotherapist, they will develop these same difficulties themselves. This is because the psychotherapist is identified with the object who forced them into a disturbed state of being. Thus, in these cases, what takes place in the therapeutic sessions is strongly influenced by what the young person is afraid the psycho-therapist thinks of them. This, of course, will be a reflection of what they privately fear they may become.

If this is so terrifying, one may ask why they continue to come. I think the answer lies in the fact that they cannot reject their psychotherapeutic sessions, because that would leave them totally isolated and unable to prove that they are not what they unconsciously dread they are. These cases, therefore, enable us to see how a young person's disturbance becomes enacted in the relationship with their psychotherapist and in the psychotherapeutic setting. The theme of 'I dread what you will think of me' reflects a deep anxiety that they will be thought identical to the disturbed object, who is so important to them that they cannot easily separate from them. What is worse, they fear that thinking about their situation threatens to drive them deeper into this identification. Very often there is a re-enactment in the transference of the moment when they first realise the extent of the disturbed parent's illness. With the shock of this realisation, their emotional response comes to define its meaning and their possible complicity with whatever is imagined to be its cause. These re-enactments cannot be thought of as a repetition of a single instant but will inevitably be a condensation of many such moments. Clearly, it takes some time to reach this because of the profound anxiety which is then experienced.

As an example, I began to realise when treating one young man that he could experience his sessions as though they too could be as mentally disturbing as he found his ill mother to be. I came to realise that what terrified him was the moment when he looked at me and I looked at him. Eventually, I wondered with him whether this situation was connected with when he had first felt the full impact of the disturbing effect of his mother's organic disease on her state of mind. In that moment, he had experienced it through seeing a particular look in her eye. When he had first told me about this incident, he had cried for the first time. I thought that the eye or 'I' (i.e. part of his ego), representing his capacity to be in touch with his emotional reality, became conflated with my own eye, which threatened to see him as disturbed and thereby force him to feel he too was like his mother.

Some reflections on these themes

It has been customary to regard adolescence as a time of transition and change as the subject moves from childhood to adult status. As a result, there has been a tendency to regard a degree of disturbance during adolescence as in some sense 'normal' for which the only cure is the passage of time (Winnicott, 1961). These days the rate of morbidity in respect of psychiatric disturbance during adolescence is regarded as about 20 per cent (Smith and Rutter, 1995), which stands in some contrast to the earlier view. This paradoxical picture obscures the hypothesis that disturbance of a psychiatric order must be seen in adolescence against a background of 'normal' patterns of disturbance, which makes judgements about normality and pathology problematic but essential to try to get right because of the consequences of failures to treat at this age.

The next feature is that behaviour during adolescence can appear paradoxical because relating by identification is very pervasive (Brenman-Pick, 1988; Rayner, 1986). Because psychic structures are in a state of flux, what can appear as a representation of the adolescent's sense of self can turn out to be an identification with an ego ideal that will shift and change and return and disappear, being an indication of apparent morbidity. It may be but it may not be. The shift in the background or experiential frame of adolescence results from the changes in body function and the development of genital sexual functioning which challenges for-ever the sexual patterns of relating to others developed in childhood. As a result, adolescence is a time for both mourning lost childhood and eager anticipation of adult status, which can give it a paradoxical flavour of regression and progression. This antinomy presents the challenge and difficulty of treating adolescence.

In both situations described above, at least one of the child's parents was absent from normal daily contact as the child grew up. For these young men, we can say that as they reach adolescence they were not only mourning their lost childhood but also needed to mourn the absence of one of their parents as well, whether in sickness or in health. Green (1986) has suggested that, in adults, there is a form of *pathological mourning,* resulting from what he describes as psychic holes in experience. He terms this 'blank mourning' and this reflects an impression of blankness or emptiness in the patient's consciousness and presence in the counter-transference. In vernacular terms, these patients lack colour. He proposes that such a picture results when an individual's mother becomes depressed, or otherwise preoccupied, in such a way that she is perceived to be distracted or unavailable to the child. The mother cares for the child, but 'her heart is not in it'.

Green suggested that this creates a figure in an individual's internal world, which he called the 'dead mother'. The dead mother is the mother dead to, or dis-tracted from, the child because something, for example an absent father or indeed any preoccupation or disturbance, chronically takes her mind away from the child.

This distraction is experienced by the child as an emotional withdrawal from the child by the mother. It is important to be clear that this pattern is not specific to loss arising from actual death. Any separation or rupture in the relationship between the parents can lead to this pattern. The important feature is not the actuality of the loss but the preoccupying effect on the mother. *The result is that the child is plunged prematurely into a very particular Oedipal situation; or, in other words, the triangle created by the mother's impenetrable and unchanging preoccupation.*

Many of the observable features of the two thematic situations described above were very different. In one situation, there is an absent parental figure, that is the father. In the other, there is a significant family member who is ill in some life-threatening or disabling way. However, some essential features of the basic predicaments were similar. In both situations the patient is tied, in a very powerful way, into a web of identifications that binds them to their mothers, either an absent or an ill one. From this situation, they could not easily move or develop; and hence, not surprisingly presented as though they were dealing with something impenetrable and unchangeable. This reflected the nature of their Oedipal situation in which they were locked into a relationship with a powerful other with no *alive and independent third party* to mediate the intensity of this pairing.

In the first situation, the combination of the family constellation and their fathers' absence, I think, drives these young men into a situation in which they cannot mourn their father's departure. In the second situation in which a parent suffers from some form of physical or mental disability, the patient can feel either responsible for the disability or guilty for being healthy. When it is a parent who suffers the disability, the young person can feel identified with this parent and, at the same time, responsible for their predicament. It takes a great deal of courage for a family to help the patient escape from this identification because it entails sharing hostile feelings towards the disabled one, which can feel totally unacceptable to all concerned.

Of particular significance to the discussion of these situations is the conclusion that, in the first situation, the young person's engagement in the psychotherapeutic process was influenced by his seeming to be a representation, by identification, of his absent father. In the second, the young person dreads what the psychotherapist may think of them, e.g. that they are disturbed and seek to attribute his disturbance to something *inside* him (i.e. an illness) and not *outside* him from which he could conceivably escape; namely, an alternative traumatic explanation. Because of the absence of a figure capable of facilitating the expression of hostile feelings, we find a similar phenomenon stemming from absence. In this second situation, absence is as powerful in its effect as it is in the first.

In both of these situations, a paradox emerged in the pattern of engagement or the transference; but the young people nevertheless came to be helped and continued to do so. However, the experience of futile inertia in the psychotherapist's counter-transference that was mentioned earlier in the discussion of the first encounters with these cases is not entirely accounted for by the idea of a distracted mother *per se*. This seems to be because it does not take into account the possibility that the young person is engaging with the *imaginary* something in their mother's minds that distracts them. The paradox seems to be linked to the psychic withdrawal or emotional dis-investment (referred to above), which I will term a 'de-cathexis'. As described above, this de-cathexis is often experienced in the counter-transference at the outset, or during assessment, by a sense that the patient is not likely to engage. In fact, they do but there is always something, physical or psychic, apparently present by its absence. In these moments, the patient may be thought of as communicating unconsciously to the psychotherapist *their cathexis of a de-cathecting object from which they cannot separate, that is their efforts to be whatever it is that preoccupies their mother but which is hard for them to access. In other words, these young men are cathecting the fathers who are de-cathecting them in their mother's minds.* This imaginary figure cannot make up for the absence of an actual alive because it cannot provide the independent dynamic necessary for change.

However, what is apparent is that the distortion of the Oedipal process created by an absent parent has a similar effect to that stemming from a disabled parent in that it destabilises the young person's development of their own identity. Furthermore, if a particular set of feelings cannot be expressed within a family then this does not mean that it ceases to exist. Usually, it becomes an impenetrable and terrible secret that no one dare utter but which continually exists in the family's mind. In this sense, it is similar in form and function to the secret and distracting something in the mother's mind.

What we seem to have in these cases is a situation in which there is a distortion to the usual triangular Oedipal process re-activated during adolescence (Blos, 1967), which is compromised by the absence of the actual father and whose empty place is filled by the creation of an imaginary figure. However, this absence does not mean that the father is non-existent but that he is extremely present by his absence. What these young men presented to their therapist is their experience of this insistent presence of their fathers in absence, which condemns them to being trapped in their mother's and family's projections without means of perspective or escape. In these circumstances, development of the psychic structure of the child is distorted by the existence of an absent object, with which they will either identify or fill up the resultant psychic hole with a new identification, which then surrounds and seeks to conceal the psychic vacuum. This situation creates considerable technical difficulties but may help to explain the problems that some adolescents can seem to have in engaging with a psychotherapeutic process.

What was described earlier as the transference depression in these treatments reflects the experience of the psychotherapist as an endless quest to cut off the head of the many-headed hydra of the patient's depression. The temptation is to be distracted by the identifications filling the psychic vacuum created by the object that is present by its absence. This leads one to regard the inertia as destructive and aggressive which will be expressed in enactments, e.g. poor attendance; a sense of hopeless and despairing inactivity; a sense of very slow progress and, once they are established, a feeling in the therapist that the patient never wants to leave and refuses to budge out of the regression. However, this amounts to tackling the subject's *responses* to the problem rather than the problem itself, which is the blankness of the psychic hole caused by absence or a denial of feeling. This is created by the de-cathexis of the young person as a child by the maternal object and the child's unconscious identification with the dead mother and the contents of her mind. This means that the important level at which to work is on the relationship between the mother and her preoccupying object as it is expressed in the transference. It is through this route that the 'dead mother' gives up the secret that preoccupies her. Patients like this are locked into this relationship, and as a result the psychotherapist will be deeply involved and implicated once the initial engagement process has been survived.

In Green's view, which he acknowledges as a meta-psychological speculation, one of the central functions of the mother's 'good-enough' disillusionment of the infant is to create a frame or matrix for experience. He uses the notion of disillusionment from Winnicott. *It is about creating a matrix for experiencing.* It seems to me that if this is so then the containing matrix will be inevitably identified with the mother. Green is using Winnicott's (1963) distinction between the object mother and the environment mother. Such a conception is, I think, especially appropriate for thinking about adolescence and is confirmed by the importance now placed on the kind of setting that is necessary to be able to engage with adolescents satisfactorily (see Wilson, 1991). In addition to the structuring effect of the mother's mind, the presence of a preoccupying figure in the mother's mind that seems to take her away from the child creates, of course, a dynamic from which the child is excluded. The mother's preoccupation is what is responsible for expressing this exclusion from the dynamic. Hence, it is to be expected that absence will initially be an important experience in the process of engagement, which will be experienced in the counter-transference as a sense of being shut out. Once, however, an engagement is solidly achieved then the vicissitudes of this dynamic will come to dominate the transference in the consulting room.

In normal development, as these Oedipal experiences are felt increasingly to be the adolescent's own experiences, there seems to be an increasing sense of being 'real'; again, in Winnicott's terms. When the normal process of development becomes distorted by absence or illness in either the father or mother, ownership of the mind, experience and the body is much more problematic. It is quite common that such a situation leads to a feeling of a lack of confidence. To illustrate these issues, I turn to my third theme.

CLINICAL THEME: 'I CAN'T BE HELPED BECAUSE I'M USELESS'

Another theme, which is commonly mentioned in the assessment phase, is the feeling of a lack of confidence. Others are seen as being supremely confident, especially a member of the opposite sex, and this is the source of much envy. This feeling leads the young person concerned to feel useless and that this feeling is going to be permanent. There is no way out of it. Yet, associated with this position is a hope, indeed insistence, in some cases, that the psychotherapist gives the young person something that will deal with it. This will feel to have some material quality.

The young person may remain preoccupied for some time with how they are going to become more confident in relating to friends, colleagues at work, and young women. This experience can be despairing and repetitive and the young person can feel their life will never improve. In order to avoid feeling abandoned by their psychotherapist to the harsh realities of life the young person may harbour a fantasy of being with their therapist outside the session.

After a while, it becomes apparent that something very powerful maintains this lack of confidence. We have discussed, so far, situations in which a child after the break-up of his parents' marriage is left in the care of his mother. Of course, a child can also be left in the care of his father when his mother decides not to stay in the marriage. In therapy the shock of the loss of their mother can dominate the transference because the young person is extremely sensitive to any separation from the therapist including the ends of sessions as well as holiday breaks. The point is, of course, that the patient leads their psychotherapist to the importance of the impact of the end of the session and what it means to them. At the end of sessions, one young man would look at me with an odd combination of fear and hatred as he left with a slight air of contempt. I understood the combination of these feelings and enactment, in the one moment, as portraying his imagined angry, contemptuous mother leaving his father in a state of fear and helplessness.

Interpretation of the impact of their experience of being abandoned by their mother can pave the way for a young person to seek and find their mother again. In cases where the young person has had virtually no contact with his mother over a long period of time his picture of her will be substantially out of touch with reality. Their anger with and fear of their mother turns her in their mind into a violent monster. But in reality the mother is usually a much more benign figure. This can challenge the defences that have been evolved to cope with the profound psychic pain of the original loss of the mother. The gap between the fantasised mother, that is the picture of the mother as an evil monster and the 'real' mother, can be another profound shock because it upsets all the fantasies built up to rationalise what has happened. However, as this shock is worked through, the young person can be helped to understand that his imaginary creations stem from the violence of his feelings in reaction to the loss. The young person can also be helped to understand that his belief that he is responsible for driving his mother away is, in fact, an omnipotent fantasy.

I would like now to examine further the peculiar triangular Oedipal situation in which there is an insistent presence expressed by absence, which was discussed earlier. In the third situation, a situation is created by the absence of the mother. Her absence gives rise to a *preoccupying* rather than preoccupied mother in the patient's mind, who is an imaginary figure created out of trying to understand the fact of her departure and the reasons for it. I mentioned earlier how one young person seemed to experience the ends of sessions. If we consider this in the light of his fear of his object's contempt and the subjective certainty that he would be rejected without a thought, then I think we can see a similarly distorted Oedipal triangle. This time, however, the internal maternal object is not lost in a pre-occupation but, in fantasy, angrily and contemptuously turning away to another unknown figure. Therefore, in all three situations, one point of the Oedipal triangle is taken by an imaginary figure created out of the individual's unconscious under-standing of the reasons for the missing figure's absence. Hence, there is no separate and alive figure outside the control of the individual's imagination to mediate the relationship with the remaining figure and prevent the child being caught inextricably in a dyadic enmeshing with the remaining figure.

It is clear that the individual trapped in these distorted Oedipal triangles is in a very complex situation to which he/she has no choice but to respond. In younger children, severe disruption to the family constellation through death, departure or severe mental illness has been linked with the development by latency children of 'imaginary companions' (Nagera, 1969) because of the difficulties of mourning the losses caused by these disruptions. Older children and adolescents uncon-sciously create imaginary figures with which to identify, in order to account for the meaninglessness of events. These provide the bases for a self-representation based on an *imaginary* object. It is therefore not surprising to find such a person report-ing a lack of confidence, reminiscent of a false self (Winnicott, 1960b), because their self-representation is intimately linked to an identification with an imaginary object, which is constantly disconfirmed by reality.

At the clinical level, the false self can appear quite convincing, particularly as the only sign that it is a false self is the reported 'lack of confidence'. But this is not necessarily a 'compliant false self', although it may be, which is thought to arise from a premature *over-impingement* by the maternal object. Nor can it be said that it is intended to be deceptive. We are clearly concerned here with *under-impingement* by an actual object that turns into an over-impingement by an imaginary object. It combined the hostility of the subject and the absence of the object into the creation of the imagined hating mother.

At the technical level, there is a need for a fairly extended period of 'holding' before persistent interpretative work can take place. Only when the psychothera-peutic setting has been securely established can the psychotherapist tackle these 'false selves'. If interpretation of the young person's 'false self' is premature then they may feel so anxious that either they drop out of therapy or they may find another psychic solution to their internal predicament that is equally false. To do so is tantamount to interpreting a defence without taking account of the anxiety against which it is defending. Hence, it is important that the therapist is patient and allows time for the young person to engage and settle and not be put off by their inevitable early difficulties in engaging, which I have described.

Whilst it will be confusing when one enters an individual's internal world in which powerful figures exert their presence by their absence, one should not be discouraged or pulled into the belief that absence necessarily implies destructiveness. At a time in life when the adolescent relates by identification so powerfully, there can often be little meaningful option open to the young person other than to relate in the way we have observed; for example, by being absent. By these means, they unconsciously and involuntarily communicate the impossible experiences with which they grapple.

Once a treatment is established, it becomes possible to work more directly in the transference interaction, which will reflect the fantasies of what is occurring in the mind of the internalised mother. This will only be revealed by examination of the transference and will take time. This is not easy and there are many opportunities for error because of the pervasive and confusing influence of what is absent as well as what is present. But, with time and patience, progress can be made. In essence, the psychotherapist is operating as a live father who intercedes between the subject and the imaginary mother and who enables the young person to say 'good-bye' to their disturbed childhood, and the defences they created to cope with the conflicting demands of their adolescence, and move into adult life. It is therefore to be expected that the young person will feel threatened by the psychotherapist and will be cautious and mistrustful of the therapist when their defences are threatened at the outset of treatment.

However, as a psychotherapist working with such young people at the Brandon Centre, I have found it very rewarding to see them 'become subjects' as described by Cahn (1998) and develop a sense of being 'real' (Winnicott, 1963). What Cahn and others mean by 'becoming a subject' is the process by which a person appropriates their psychic reality and thereby differentiates their appreciation of the external world from that of the internal. In a sense, they can be said to have achieved a theory of their own minds. Another way of putting it might be that they have achieved a means of thinking about a relationship from a point of view outside that relationship. In other words a triangulated space has been achieved, making it possible to think about experience in a new way.

Despite the unpromising initial prognosis when working with such young people, it is essential to persevere when treating the young person who is apparently so bound to their defences that little change appears to occur. Ultimately, the young person may be seeking to make sense of an empty psychic space. It should not be surprising to find oneself as a psychotherapist experiencing this space in all its despondent futility in one's counter-transference. But the young person who persistently maintains the paradox by continuing to attend despite all the apparent evidence and the therapist's internal questioning about 'why do they come?' should be thought of as seeking a way out of the futility. As in the overcoming of all Oedipal dilemmas, their courage deserves our respect.

References

Baruch, G., Fearon, P. and Gerber, A. (1998). 'Evaluating the outcome of a community-based psychoanalytic psychotherapy service for young people'. In Davenhill, R. and Patrick, M. (eds), *Re-thinking Clinical Audit (The Case of Psychotherapy Services in the NHS)*. London: Routledge.

Blos, P. (1967). 'The second individuation process of adolescence'. *Psychoanalytic Study of the Child*, vol. 22. New York: International Universities Press, 301–24.

Brenman-Pick, I. (1988). 'Adolescence: Its impact on patient and analyst'. *International Review of Psychoanalysis* 15: 187–94.

Cahn, R. (1998). 'On becoming a subject'. In Perret-Catipovic, M. and Ladame, F. *Adolescence and Psycho-Analysis*. London: Karnac.

Freud, S. (1905). *Three Essays on the Theory of Sexuality Standard Edition*, 7, 125–243. London: Hogarth Press.

Freud, S. (1917). *Mourning and Melancholia Standard Edition*, 14, London: Hogarth Press.

Green, A. (1986). 'The dead mother'. In *On Private Madness*. London: Hogarth Press and Institute of Psychoanalysis.

Laufer, M. (1998). 'The central masturbation fantasy, the final sexual organization and adolescence'. In Perret-Catipovic, M. and Ladame, F. *Adolescence and Psycho-analysis*. London: Karnac.

—— and Laufer, E. (1984). *Adolescence and Developmental Breakdown*. New Haven and London: Yale University Press.

Nagera, H. (1969). 'The imaginary companion: its significance for ego development and conflict resolution'. *Psychoanalytic Study of the Child*, vol. 24, 165–96. New York: International Universities Press.

Rayner, E. H. (1986). *Human Development*, 3rd edn. Routledge: London.

Smith, D. J. and Rutter, M. (1995). *Psychosocial Disorders in Young People, Time Trends and their Causes*. Chichester: John Wiley & Sons.

Wilson, P. (1991). 'Psychotherapy with Adolescents'. In Holmes, J. (ed.), *Textbook of Psychotherapy in Psychiatric Practice*, 443–67. London: Churchill Livingstone.

Winnicott, D. W. (1960a). 'The theory of the parent-infant relationship'. In Winnicott, D. W. (1990). *The Maturational Processes and the Facilitating Environment*. London: Institute of Psycho-analysis and Karnac Books.

—— (1960b). 'Ego distortion in terms of true and false self'. In Winnicott, D. W. (1960). *The Maturational Processes and the Facilitating Environment*.

—— (1961). 'Adolescence: struggling through the doldrums'. In Winnicott, D. W. (1965). *The Family and Individual Development*, 79–87. London: Tavistock.

—— (1963). 'On Communication'. In Winnicott, D. W. (1990). *The Maturational Processes and the Facilitating Environment*. London: Institute of Psycho-analysis and Karnac Books.

Chapter 4

The process of engaging young people with severe developmental disturbance in psychoanalytic psychotherapy

Patterns of practice[1]

Geoffrey Baruch

INTRODUCTION

Many psychoanalytic writers are pessimistic about the prospects of psycho-analysis and psychoanalytic psychotherapy with troubled adolescents and young adults (A. Freud, 1958; Panel, 1972; Geleerd, 1957; Eissler, 1958; Gitleson, 1948; Anthony, 1970; Winnicott, 1966). Anna Freud suggests that the emergence and the intensity of the adolescent's sexual and aggressive drives lend 'a new and threatening reality to (Oedipal and pre-Oedipal) fantasies which had seemed extinct but are, in fact, merely under repression' (p. 268). Engaging in psycho-therapy or psychoanalysis may be fiercely opposed by many troubled adolescents since it propels them into the kind of dependent relationship with a therapist from which they are trying to disengage in relation to their parents. In characteristic style Winnicott states, 'There is only one cure for adolescence and this is the passage of time and the passing on of the adolescent into the adult state ... We hold on, playing for time, instead of offering distractions or cures' (Winnicott, 1966, p. 79).

Some psychoanalysts do not share this pessimistic view about therapy and maintain that, once engaged, the adolescent can form a workable transference and remain in treatment until an agreed termination with the therapist. In their view, successful treatment is contingent on the analyst understanding the complex impact of developmental changes on the transference but not on an alteration of psychoanalytic interpretative technique (Blos, 1980; Laufer and Laufer, 1987; 1989). Novick (1982) states that 'despite the undeniable disparities between adolescents and other periods of life, psychoanalytic principles and techniques are applicable and psychoanalysis is the treatment of choice for a much larger number of adolescents than is currently thought possible' (p. 147). Other analysts also take an optimistic view about the prospects of therapy but recommend changes in

1 This chapter is an amended version of a paper originally published in the *Bulletin of the Menninger Clinic* 67(3), 1997. The publishers, Guilford Publications Inc, have granted permission for publication in this volume.

technique. For instance, regarding making interpretations, Bloch (1995) recommends the therapist take 'a stand on the side of the patient's efforts to feel more comfortably independent from the pervasive influence of parents' (p. 269) rather than be 'too silent or too emotionally unresponsive' (p. 269). Eissler (1958) asserts that the psychoanalyst or psychoanalytic psychotherapist has to be alert to the constantly changing nature of adolescent psychopathology, the manifestation of many different clinical conditions and levels of ego capacity, and be able to adapt therapeutic technique to meet the troubled adolescent's varying clinical presentation.

Despite the optimism of some psychoanalytic writers, the frequency with which therapeutic contact quickly breaks down in the treatment of troubled adolescents would appear to support the view of those who, like Anna Freud, are pessimistic about therapeutic work with troubled adolescents. In the Introduction we noted the characteristics of young people who drop out of therapy compared to young people who remain in treatment. Of 134 young people who participated in a study of the pattern of attendance at the Centre, 41 (30.6 per cent) were early drop outs (that is dropped out before five sessions), 39 (29.1 per cent) were late drop outs (that is dropped out before twenty-one sessions) and 54 (40.3 per cent) were continuers (that is stayed in treatment after twenty-one sessions). The number of sessions of treatment differed greatly for the three groups. The mean number of sessions for early drop outs, late drop outs and continuers was 3.0 (SD 1.30), 11.87 (SD 4.16), and 38.09 (SD 15.02) sessions of individual once-weekly therapy, respectively ($F(2,131) = 165.7, P < 0.0001$).

The findings from a retrospective study of predictors of therapeutic outcome at the Anna Freud Centre by Fonagy and Target (1996; 1994) are similar to those of the Brandon Centre: attrition is highest amongst young adolescents and high for children with disruptive disorders. The engagement of troubled adolescents, particularly younger adolescents, remains a serious problem in delivering psychoanalytic psychotherapy to this population.

In the psychoanalytic literature this problem has been largely addressed in terms of the impact on the troubled adolescent of his drive for separation from the primary objects. However, in this chapter I shall explore the sources of the problem of engagement from a different perspective, using ideas which are a development of Anna Freud's concept of developmental disturbance. I would like to suggest that the difficulties some troubled adolescents have in engaging in psychoanalytic psychotherapy can also be understood in terms of them lacking some capacities, due to developmental disturbances, which are essential for resolving adolescent tasks. These capacities involve deficiencies in certain types of cognitive functioning, particularly the capacity to be self-reflective, which is crucial for engaging in the therapeutic process. This perspective has technical implications for the focus of the therapist's interventions with regard to the troubled adolescent. The idea of developmental disturbance and the way this changes the focus of treatment from the interpretation of conflict to the provision of developmental support for missing capacities has been elaborated in therapeutic work with children (A. Freud, 1965;

1974; 1978; 1979). Yet it has received less attention in therapeutic work with troubled adolescents.

To begin with, I shall describe the assessment process at the Brandon Centre. I will then describe how an understanding of developmental disturbance can assist us with the problem of engaging the troubled adolescent. I shall discuss the technical focus for therapeutic work in the engagement period. Finally, I shall present case material of work with hard-to-reach adolescents who present with severe developmental disturbance using elements of this focus which led to the young person and the therapist becoming engaged in treatment.

THE ASSESSMENT PROCESS AT THE CENTRE[2]

As well as referring themselves, young people are referred by family doctors, teachers, social workers, psychologists, psychiatrists and other professionals working with adolescents. I shall concentrate on the assessment procedure applied to the referred group since this is the clinical population with which this chapter is concerned. If there is no referral letter describing the reason for the referral then the referrer is contacted before the young person is offered an appointment by letter. The Centre's therapeutic approach is well known to referrers who are therefore unlikely to refer adolescents who they think require family therapy or pharmacological treatment. However, if the referral letter indicates that any of these treatments are preferable to psychoanalytic psychotherapy or in the case of pharmacotherapy as an adjunct to therapy then this is arranged at an appropriate clinic or with the patient's family doctor. Some referrals notably from family doctors or psychiatrists may already be receiving medication. The assessing psychotherapist usually treats the young person. Although the boundary between assessment and treatment is flexible, the first three to five sessions are used for assessment. Usually the psychotherapist explains to the young person that they can meet for three appointments in order to develop an idea of why the young person needs help. The therapist also explains that ongoing help is available and that the length of this can be decided and agreed upon with the young person during the period of assessment. However, as George Mak-Pearce's chapter shows, the line between assessment and treatment is often unclear in these early sessions because many young people, especially young people at risk from deliberate self-harm, adolescents in acute anxiety states, or adolescents at risk of being excluded from school because of disruptive behaviour or being in trouble with the police, require immediate intervention as well as being assessed. After five or six appointments most young people have engaged in a therapeutic process and a contract of treat-

2 The assessment process described here is the one used at the Centre before the introduction of the six-session intervention described in Chapter 1. This process is still used for young people who, at the point of referral, request long-term help.

ment has been agreed. Often this consists of open-ended therapy with regular reviews between the therapist and the young person. There is a weekly staff meeting at which the assessing psychotherapist reports the early encounters with the young person. Unless they meet specific exclusion criteria such as being psychotic, or being at severe physical risk due to an eating disorder, drug and alcohol abuse, or the threat of suicide, requiring immediate psychiatric or other specialist intervention, it is assumed that the therapist will seek to work with the young person in individual treatment.

There are formal assessment measures that inform the discussion of individual cases, for instance the Youth Self Report Form completed by the young person at the initial appointment and the Teacher's Report Form completed by a significant other chosen by the young person (Achenbach, 1991a; 1991b). With some young people who find it difficult to talk about their concerns, these forms can also be useful as an 'ice breaker' to help them talk about their anxieties. Parental involvement is rare in the treatment of young people aged over 16 years but can occur as part of the assessment of younger patients depending on the latter's circumstances and wishes. For instance, parents of adolescents subject to child protection investigations are unlikely to be seen and the wish of young people to keep their contact with the Centre confidential is respected.

DEVELOPMENTAL DISTURBANCE IN ADOLESCENCE

Recently some psychoanalytic writers in the field of child psychoanalysis have developed Anna Freud's distinction between childhood neuroses and primary developmental disturbances (Fonagy, 1991; Fonagy and Target, 1993; Fonagy and Moran, 1991; Fonagy, Edgcumbe, Moran, Kennedy and Target, 1993). They take the view 'that the greater the unevenness in development, the less effective will be a technique which relies solely upon interpretations of conflict, and the greater the need to devise strategies of analytic intervention aimed to support and strengthen the child's capacity to tolerate conflict' (Fonagy and Moran, 1991, p. 16). Edgcumbe (1993) has extended these ideas to the treatment of the troubled adolescent and shown the importance of the distinction between neurotic and developmental disturbances for treatment approach when assessing the nature and extent of the adolescent's progress in resolving adolescent issues. She contrasts two types of interference in the adolescent's development. First 'the stunting or distortion of a range of developmental processes earlier in childhood which result in the individual arriving in the adolescent phase lacking some capacities for resolving adolescent issues' (p. 107). Second 'currently active conflicts which may be specific to the adolescent phase, or may be revived from earlier phases of development' (p. 107).

The life-tasks of adolescence include mentally adjusting to the new experience of a sexually mature body and developing a mature sexual identity and orientation, separating internally and externally from the primary objects in order to establish a sense of identity as an individual in one's own right, as part of this process being able to be part of a group of peers before making choices about a sexual partner, realistically thinking about areas of achievement leading in some cases to extended studying and then to work and economic independence, living independently or with peers and eventually establishing a partnership and caring for offspring. 'There are many decisions to be made on these issues which crucially influence the course of the individual's future life, and which depend on the adolescent's view of himself and his objects' (Edgcumbe, 1993).

As the adolescent engages with these issues he should be taking responsibility for his inner life as well as making choices and decisions connected with his external life. In order to do this:

> a range of mental processes are required which should have been developing through earlier developmental phases ... Fonagy and Moran (1991) have stressed that one form of defence against conflict consists of the attempt to avoid awareness of it; and that in cases where this defensive denial of the very existence of conflict becomes extreme, developmental stunting or deviation results. Vital processes to do with creating mental representations, integrating affective experiences and developing a mature capacity for symbolic thought may be defensively inhibited in order to prevent the development of conflicting representations. The failure of these processes to develop properly then has repercussions on other areas of development (Edgcumbe, 1993, pp. 108–9).

Thus a vital part of assessment of the troubled adolescent is whether *due to conflict* the young person is unwilling to take responsibility for their internal and external life or whether *due to developmental deficiency* they are unable to take responsibility for their mental life and outward behaviour.

Recent longitudinal research on how representations of attachment relate to cognitive functioning in adolescence lends empirical support to the importance of assessing the troubled adolescent for developmental disturbance, particularly for certain poorly developed cognitive functions. Researchers from the Piagetian tradition have proposed that disruptions and disturbances in the child's primary emotional relationships may negatively affect the child's ability to regulate cognitive exchanges and hence the quality of the knowledge he constructs (Piaget, 1981; Schmid-Kitsikis, 1976; 1990). Inhelder states that emotional factors can 'cause a loss of self-esteem, and reduce the subject's [cognitive] performance' (Inhelder, 1968, p.289).

The work of Inhelder and Piaget (1958) has shown that the development of formal operational structures which begin to emerge at puberty are a major developmental feature of the adolescent period. In this period the adolescent, unlike the latency child whose thought is concrete operational, begins to reason abstractly without having to refer to concrete objects. Moreover he is now able to reflect on his own thought. Jacobsen, Edelstein and Hofmann (1994) investigated the relation between representations of attachment assessed at the age of 7 years and cognitive functioning in adolescence, and found that adolescents aged 15 years and 17 years with a secure attachment representation achieved better results in their cognitive performance compared to adolescents with an insecure-disorganised attachment representation who were particularly disadvantaged on deductive reasoning tasks. These adolescents had advanced little beyond their performance in the syllogistic reasoning tasks at age 9 years. They were anxious, insecure, lacking in self-confidence which interfered with their ability to reflect on their own thought, and were at risk of maladaption in their school environment. The study controlled for IQ and attention problems which were not found to affect the findings.

The capacity to reflect on one's thoughts and feelings involves additional and more complex aspects of cognitive functioning than syllogistic reasoning so it is plausible to suggest that they too will be poorly developed in adolescents with an insecure-disorganised attachment representation. Moreover young people who are also subject to traumatic experiences in adolescence will be additionally handicapped especially because this is a time of considerable cognitive growth. Adam, Sheldon-Keller and West (1996) suggest, from a study of attachment organisation and history of suicidal behaviour in adolescents, that young people who have not resolved traumatic experiences in childhood may be vulnerable to disorganised cognitive responses in circumstances that represent a repeat of the earlier trauma. Current adolescent crises, such as loss or rejection, the most common precipitators of suicidal behaviour in adolescents, may trigger acute cognitive disorganisation that contributes to the confusion and disorganised behaviour of the suicidal episode.

In summary, adolescents whose capacity to think and reflect about themselves is impaired due to developmental disorder may be totally unable to cope with an insight-oriented approach focused on the interpretation of unconscious conflict, hence the importance of the therapist being aware of missing developmental functions in the adolescent patient in order to implement an appropriate therapeutic strategy, particularly in the engagement period of treatment.

THERAPEUTIC WORK IN THE ENGAGEMENT PERIOD

Research on the concept of the therapeutic alliance testifies to the importance of the engagement process between patient and therapist. Luborsky (1976) divided the alliance into two phases: Type 1 at the beginning of treatment and Type 2 which is more characteristic of later phases of treatment. He described Type 1 alliance as 'a therapeutic alliance based on the patient's experiencing the therapist as supportive and helpful with himself as a recipient' (p. 94). According to Horvath and Luborsky (1993), recent research findings confirm this division and suggest that the initial development of the alliance occurs within the first five sessions and reaches its peak during the third session. In order for therapy to proceed beyond this phase, patient and therapist must establish a satisfactory level of collaboration and trust. Failure to accomplish this is likely to lead to premature termination.[3]

Certainly, in community-based psychotherapy with troubled adolescents there is a consensus amongst psychoanalytic psychotherapists and psychoanalysts about the appropriate framework necessary to facilitate engagement and to prevent premature termination. Bloch (1995), Laufer and Laufer (1987) and Wilson (1991) have described the appropriate therapeutic setting for fostering psychoanalytic psychotherapy with adolescents. This includes accessibility by allowing self-referral, confidentiality, pleasant, comfortable and welcoming premises, receptionists who are friendly without being intrusive, a recognition by the psychotherapist of the anxiety and the state of conflict experienced by the young person as to whether to accept help, and a readiness to mould the therapeutic approach according to the age and developmental level of individual adolescents. Bloch (1995) emphasises how 'the adolescent patient must sense from the therapist something equivalent to the sponsorship he requires from parents in his ongoing development' (p. 267). Even with younger adolescents, who are less ready to accept psychotherapy and are still dependent on their parents, Bloch asserts the need for the therapist to convey his awareness of the importance of privacy and independence to the young person and to communicate the intention that the therapy is for the benefit of the adolescent and not for the benefit of his parents or the therapist. He emphasises the need for the adolescent to feel that the therapist understands his problems from his perspective, including behaviour which is problematic. He also advocates the therapist focusing on the young adolescent's interests as part of the engagement process. I would also add to this list the psychotherapist being sensitive to issues concerned with the young person's culture and ethnic background.

This framework for facilitating engagement is of course relevant to troubled adolescents who can use an interpretative approach as well as those who are unable to do so. However, additional measures are required for enabling the latter to engage in therapy.

The therapeutic approach to troubled young people whose capacity for thinking about themselves is grossly restricted differs markedly from the technique traditionally used with young people who seek help because they are aware of their difficulties but are unable to resolve them. With the latter, the psychotherapist can take for granted their understanding of the therapeutic setting. When they act out in relation to the psychotherapist and the therapeutic setting this can be understood

---

3 Type 2 alliance refers to 'a sense of working together in a joint struggle against what is impeding the patient ... on shared responsibility for working out treatment goals ... a sense of "we-ness"' (Luborsky, 1976, p. 94).

in terms of their conflict about getting help and facing painful personal issues connected with their failure to meet the tasks of adolescence. However, with young people who reach adolescence poorly equipped with the mental capacities essential for resolving these tasks, such understanding cannot be taken for granted. Indeed creating an understanding of the setting with these adolescents is a major therapeutic objective which precedes traditional interpretative work.

The main objective of the engagement process is to enable the young person *to return at regular weekly intervals*.[4] We are familiar with this as a primary concern when working with adolescents who have attempted suicide or are at risk of deliberate self-harm. However, with young people whose capacity to reflect and think is restricted, regardless of whether they are a suicidal risk, it is essential for the psychotherapist to raise the issue of returning at every session until the young person has internalised the idea of the continuity of the relationship with the psychotherapist. The psychotherapist can also facilitate this process *by making a connection with the existence of the previous session*. For instance, I saw a 15-year-old boy, Robert, who had been urgently referred by his mother. He was in trouble with the police and at school. There was a history of conduct disorder, which was intensified after his father unexpectedly died. From the beginning, I was unsure of his commitment or interest in coming to see me so I asked him before the end of each session whether he wanted to come. I made it clear that I thought it would be helpful for him to return and he responded that it was good to talk about things. This surprised me because in the session he was extremely parsimonious in what he said and gave me the impression of coming only to satisfy his mother's wish.

There are young people who are unable to keep the next appointment in their mind however much this is discussed with them by the psychotherapist. In these circumstances, the psychotherapist has to arrange for them *to come with a relative or friend or an adult who is in locus parentis*, such as a social worker, until they are equipped to think in terms of more than one session at a time.

As part of the engagement process the psychotherapist should be prepared *to take responsibility for the direction of the session* and not leave the young person in silence. The psychotherapist has to do a great deal of thinking aloud about the young person before the young person can think for himself. This involves addressing:

• the difference between internal states and external states;
• having feelings and thoughts about oneself and others who also have feelings and thoughts;
• differentiating feelings;

4 If the sessions are of greater frequency then the aim is to enable the young person to attend accordingly.

- how external events can cause mental states and how mental states can cause action;
- the effect of the past on one's current life.

The psychotherapist has *to 'create' a mind* for the young person and may have to do this by asking questions which in simple terms suggest that a certain action, for example a suicidal gesture, is related to a feeling such as anger which may be linked to the effect another person has had on oneself. This suggestion can be made directly about the young person or can be put in terms of how young people in general may feel and act.

The psychotherapist often receives monosyllabic 'yes' and 'no' responses from the young person. But if these responses are tolerated there are rewards when the young person spontaneously describes an inner state. Robert found elaborating on the questions I asked him painfully difficult but at some point in the session would be touched by something I suggested and would spontaneously volunteer what was going on in his mind, for instance how, when he had been building shelves at home, he remembered he used to do this with his father and how he missed him. Paula, who was 13 years old and had taken a very serious overdose, found it difficult to describe her feelings. An uncle had sexually abused her. Paula's mother often had to travel abroad on work assignments. One Monday morning she tele-phoned the Centre wanting to speak to me but I was out. In the next session she told me she had telephoned because she had got upset in class when she had been asked to write a composition about saying goodbye to someone who you are close to. She thought about her and her mother and the times she had to say goodbye to her and needed to talk to me about how distressed she felt.[5]

The interventions I have described are, I believe, essential for the engagement period with troubled young people presenting developmental disturbances whose capacity to think about their own and others' mental states and behaviour is severely limited. The technique involves helping the adolescent to address missing aspects of his mental functioning and only later does the therapist take up the conflicts, which may have been involved in the stunting of the mental process. In some cases, this may eventually lead to a release of the young person's cognitive development so that they are gradually ready to face difficult feelings and the awareness of situations and events, which provoke these feelings. However, with others the work may not develop further than the young person being able to make connections between thoughts, feelings and behaviour. Yet this may be sufficient to help the adolescent substitute talking and thinking with the therapist about feel-ings for acting on them. As Bloch (1995) says, such strengthening of the troubled adolescent's ego 'is often responded to by improvement in young adolescents without much insight being shared or imparted' (p. 282). Even in these cases there are, as I described in my work with Robert, occasions when the therapist can make

5 I am aware that there were transference implications, which I shall not discuss.

contact with the adolescent's inner world. It is also important to emphasise how mentally the therapist is continuously engaged in a dynamic process whereby they are thinking about the adolescent's conflicts as well as their level of functioning, and how to frame his interventions taking account of both aspects of the young person. The following two cases, which are typical of adolescents who usually drop out very early in treatment, were able to engage in therapy.

CASE ILLUSTRATIONS[6]

John

John was aged 14 years when he started therapy. There was a great deal of anxiety about him. He had been charged with a number of sexual offences. The court had considered a custodial sentence even though he was under 15 years, or removing him from home and accommodating him in a foster home. Before his appearance in court he had an interview with a social worker which had gone very badly. Following the interview, the social worker recommended that John should be removed from his family and attend a treatment centre. He was extremely anxious about the prospect of leaving his family. When he came to see me, social services were still considering removing him from home and sending him to an inpatient treatment centre for young people. His parents had little control over John who was refusing to attend school. There were considerable concerns about whether the father was physically abusing him and his younger sister.

John had very little capacity to reflect and think about himself and how other people were reacting to him. It was easy to see how his uncommunicativeness, especially about the incidents for which he was arrested, could be interpreted as him deliberately frustrating any discussion. Soon after he started coming to see me at the Centre, the sessions were interrupted because he went with his family on a holiday. Before the holiday the only time when he talked freely was when he spoke enthusiastically about playing soccer with his friends and wearing designer label clothes. However, he did acknowledge that when he responded to any questions connected with the incidents with 'I can't remember' this could either mean that he couldn't remember or that he didn't want to remember. Despite the limited nature of his talk I felt, as with Robert, that he found it helpful to have someone who was interested in him and wanted to help him make connections between his thoughts, feelings and behaviour.

When he returned from holiday our sessions restarted. His social worker continued to bring him to the Centre. My interventions took the form of questions as I wondered aloud what the incidents were connected with, for instance whether he was emulating his friends. This made some sense to him. I then wondered whether

6 In these cases I shall consider the therapeutic approach rather than the complexities of their psychopathology.

he felt as though he was going mad when he made advances towards older women. He denied this but when I connected his behaviour with feeling out of control and asked him whether he felt out of control of his mind he agreed with me. He said he felt weird. He also added that he would never do these things again. We were also able to make a connection between sexually feeling out of control and feeling out of control when he got angry with his friends if they provoked him or if his younger sister provoked him. When I spoke to him about going mad and feeling out of control he gently hit his head with his hand as though he was confirming that a connection had been made with something that happened in his mind. I also had the opportunity to observe and show him how he stopped fidgeting when something I said made contact with him. He became quiet, pensive and anxious as though he was thinking about what I had said. Our work never progressed into being able to understand the deeper conflicts, which were connected with his deviant behaviour, but I think he found it helpful to be with someone who helped him to make links between his impulsive behaviour and his feelings. He was able to substitute talking with me about his behaviour and feelings for acting on them in so far as he never repeated the behaviour which had got him into so much trouble. He came regularly to weekly sessions for over 7 months when there was an agreed ending. By this time, social services felt the risk of him being a danger to the public had receded. He was allowed to remain in the community under their supervision and he knew he could come back to therapy if he wanted to.

David

David was aged 15 years when his teachers, because of disruptive and aggressive behaviour in the classroom, referred him. He was on the verge of being permanently excluded from school.

David's background was characterised by a number of upheavals and traumas. He immigrated to Britain under traumatic circumstances with his mother and sister when he was aged 12 years. Even after they arrived in England they experienced further upheavals and traumas. During his second academic year in England, David was transferred to another school closer to where he lived but was unhappy there because he couldn't get on with the teachers or make friends, and after only a few months he returned to the previous school. These moves coincided with a considerable upsurge in David's aggressive behaviour both at home and in the classroom.

The therapist's first meeting was with David and his mother. The meeting was stormy and chaotic and the therapist was given an understanding of how David's behaviour could be disruptive in the classroom. David took control of the meeting telling the therapist that he could meet with his mother this week and he would see the therapist next week. Although his mother spoke little English she was able to communicate to the therapist about David's aggressive behaviour at home. The mother was in despair because David had said he did not want counselling and he didn't feel he had any problems. David stared defiantly at the therapist as if to confirm what his mother had said. However, the atmosphere changed as David's mother described how beneath his bravado David was unhappy. The meeting ended with David being greatly embarrassed as his mother hugged him but he reciprocated this gesture of affection.

On his own in the second session, David became timid and anxious and appeared like a lost, dependent child. The therapist's enquiries about his life at home and at school were met with monosyllabic answers, with David saying that everything in his life was 'fine'. However, the therapist persisted and wondered whether David had trouble getting on with other students and his mother. He answered that he found them hard to speak to and had the same difficulty with his mother. The therapist noticed a scar on David's right hand and asked him about it. He explained that he had cut the top of his hand when his mother wouldn't let him stay out at night with his friends. The therapist asked David whether he wanted to meet the following week. He was non-committal but the therapist said he would be available to see David.

David returned and although it was clear that he intended to attend reliably he remained in silence for many sessions. The therapist adopted an active role. He would think out loud trying to link David's silence with how he might be feeling and sometimes initiated conversation by asking questions. When these questions were about David's interests he willingly talked, for instance about his friends and football. It was as though David had found an external object who was interested in him for his own sake. However, for the most part David would shake his head and remain unresponsive.

At times David was able to acknowledge his sadness and pain from losing part of his family and his friends from home. Especially during the first few months of therapy, an important aspect of the work seemed to be the acknowledgement of the difficulties and upheavals he had faced in the past 2 years. This involved the therapist assisting David in the process of mourning by talking about how he thought David might be feeling in relation to these losses and providing words for these feelings to build up an emotional vocabulary. The absence of this vocabulary was an indication of an inhibition of mental processes, which meant that he avoided experiencing painful mental representations connected with loss and mourning.

In turn, David was gradually able to make connections between what he was like in the sessions with other times that he was silent. He explained to the therapist that he was like this at home, when he was angry with his mother. Four months into the sessions, he told the therapist that he felt as though the teachers didn't understand him, and blamed him, and this made him angry, so he ignored them. The therapist linked this to his silences in the session, suggesting that maybe he wanted the therapist to understand what it felt like to be ignored, and perhaps he wanted his mother to understand this too when he was at home. David looked at the therapist with an anxious and uncomfortable expression, but seemed to take this in and went on to speak about how he liked to be on his own, in his room, when he was angry. In the remainder of this session, David was remarkably thoughtful and co-operative with the therapist and asked him questions in an unprecedented and spontaneous way. Although this improvement was not long lasting and David lapsed into being silent and unreflective in the next session, by this time he was fully engaged in the therapeutic process and able to respond meaningfully to the therapist's interpretation of some of his conflicts. Their work together fluctuated between him being silent and withdrawn and collaborative and understanding.

Despite some setbacks and relapses of minor 'delinquent' behaviour, David made significant progress during the 9 months he attended once-weekly therapy. According to his mother and his teachers, there was a marked decrease in his disruptive behaviour and he was more integrated into his peer group.

CONCLUSION

In this chapter I have focused on cases of developmental disturbance where the young person has suffered a near-total inhibition of thinking. These damaged adolescents pose a considerable challenge to our efforts to engage them in therapy. Their need for understanding is easily overlooked because they tend to drop out of treatment during the engagement phase. I have tried to show that, with a modification of technique, valuable work can be done on developing mental processes that have become stuck. In some cases, like David, it becomes possible for the emphasis of therapy to move towards the interpretation of conflict whereas in other cases, like John, such interpretation will be rare. With regard to these young people we should never underestimate the impact we can have on their development and how they value our efforts to understand them.

References

Achenbach, T. M. (1991a). *Manual for the Youth Self-Report and 1991 Profile*. Burlington, VT: University of Vermont Department of Psychiatry.
——(1991b). *Manual for the Teacher's Report Form and 1991 Profile*. Burlington, VT: University of Vermont Department of Psychiatry.
Adam, K. S., Sheldon-Keller, A. E. and West, M. (1996). 'Attachment organization and history of suicidal behaviour in clinical adolescents'. *Journal of Consulting and Clinical Psychology* 64(2): 264–72.
Anthony, E. (1970). 'The reactions of parents to adolescents and to their behaviour'. In Anthony, E. and Benedek, T. (eds), *Parenthood: Its Psychology and Psychopathology*, 307–24. Boston: Little, Brown.
Baruch, G. (1995). 'Evaluating the outcome of a community-based psychoanalytic psychotherapy service for young people between 12 and 25 years old: work in progress'. *Psychoanalytic Psychotherapy* 9(3): 243–67.
Bloch, H. S. (1995). *Adolescent Development, Psychopathology and Treatment*. Madison: International Universities Press.
Blos, P. (1980). 'The life cycle as indicated by the nature of the transference in the psychoanalysis of adolescents'. *International Journal of Psycho-Analysis* 61: 145–51.

Edgcumbe, R. (1993). 'Developmental disturbances in adolescence and their implications for transference technique'. *Bulletin of the Anna Freud Centre* 16: 107–20.

Eissler, K. (1958). 'Notes on problems of technique in the psychoanalytic treatment of adolescents: with some remarks on perversions'. *The Psychoanalytic Study of the Child*, vol. 13, 223–54. New York: International Universities Press.

Fonagy, P. (1991). 'Thinking about thinking: some clinical and theoretical considerations concerning the treatment of a borderline patient'. *International Journal of Psychoanalysis* 72: 639–56.

Fonagy, P., Edgcumbe, R., Moran, G., Kennedy, H. and Target, M. (1993). 'The roles of mental representation and mental processes in therapeutic action'. *Psychoanalytic Study of the Child* 48: 9–47.

Fonagy, P. and Moran, G. S. (1991). 'Understanding psychic change in child analysis'. *International Journal of Psychoanalysis* 78: 15–22.

Fonagy, P. and Target, M. (1993). 'Aggression and the psychological self'. *International Journal of Psychoanalysis* 74: 471–85.

Fonagy, P. and Target, M. (1994). 'The efficacy of psychoanalysis for children with disruptive disorders'. *Journal of the American Academy of Child and Adolescent Psychiatry* 33(3): 361–71.

Fonagy, P. and Target, M. (1996). 'Outcome predictors in child analysis'. *Journal of the American Psychoanalytic Association* 44(1): 27–78.

Freud, A. (1958). 'Adolescence'. *The Writings of Anna Freud*, vol. 5, 136–66. New York: International Universities Press.

——(1965). 'Normality and pathology in childhood'. *The Writings of Anna Freud*, vol. 6.

——(1974). 'A psychoanalytical view of developmental psychopathology'. *The Writings of Anna Freud*, vol. 8, 57–74.

——(1978). 'The principal task of child analysis'. *The Writings of Anna Freud*, vol. 8, 96–109.

——(1979). 'Child analysis as the study of mental growth, normal and abnormal'. *The Writings of Anna Freud*, vol. 8, 119–36.

Geleerd, E. (1957). 'Some aspects of psychoanalytic technique with adolescents'. *The Psychoanalytic Study of the Child*, vol. 12, 263–83. New York: International Universities Press.

Gitelson, M. (1948). 'Character synthesis: the psychotherapeutic problem of adolescence'. *American Journal of Orthopsychiatry* 18: 422–36.

Horvath, A. O. and Luborsky, L. (1993). 'The role of the therapeutic alliance in psychotherapy'. *Journal of Consulting and Clinical Psychology* 61(4): 561–73.

Inhelder, B. and Piaget, J. (1958). *The Growth of Logical Thinking from Childhood to Adolescence*. New York: Norton.

Jacobsen, T., Edelstein, W. and Hofmann, V. (1994). 'A longitudinal study of the relation between representations of attachment in childhood and cognitive functioning in childhood and adolescence'. *Developmental Psychology* 30(1): 112–24.

Laufer, M. and Laufer, M. E. (1987). *Adolescence and Developmental Breakdown*. New Haven and London: Yale University Press.

Laufer, M. and Laufer, M. E. (1989). *Development Breakdown and Psychoanalytic Treatment in Adolescence*. New Haven and London: Yale University Press.

Luborsky, L. (1976). 'Helping alliances in psychotherapy'. In Cleghorn, J. L. (ed.), *Successful Psychotherapy*, 92–116. New York: Brunner/Mazel.

Novick, J. (1982). 'Varieties of transference in the analysis of an adolescent'. *The Inter-*

national Journal of Psychoanalysis 63: 139–48.

Panel (1972). 'Indications and contraindications for the psychoanalysis of the adolescent'. M. Slansky, reporter. *Journal of the American Psychoanalytic Association* 20: 134–44.

Piaget, J. (1981). *Intelligence and Affectivity: Their Relationship during Child Development*. Palo Alto, CA: Annual Review.

Schmid-Kitsikis, E. (1976). 'The cognitive mechanisms underlying problem-solving in psychotic and mentally retarded children'. In Inhelder, B. and Chapman, H. (eds), *Piaget and His School: A Reader in Developmental Psychology*, 234–54. New York: Springer.

——(1990). *An Interpersonal Approach to Mental Functioning: Assessment and Treatment*. Basel, Switzerland: Karger.

Wilson, P. (1991). 'Psychotherapy with adolescents'. In Holmes, J. (ed.), *Textbook of Psychotherapy in Psychiatric Practice*. London: Churchill Livingstone.

Winnicott, D. W. (1966). 'Adolescence: struggling through the doldrums'. In Winnicott, D. W., *The Family and Individual Development*, 79–87. London: Tavistock Publications.

Part II

Services for high priority groups of young people

Psychotherapy with young people from ethnic minority backgrounds in different community-based settings

Rajinder K. Bains

INTRODUCTION

The main aim of this chapter is to identify and discuss how cross-cultural issues may affect psychotherapy with adolescents and young adults from ethnic minority backgrounds.

Evidence suggests that cultural issues influence mental health work with this population in a number of ways. These include cultural variations in the expression of distress; beliefs about causation and treatment of mental disorder; and the psychological effects of specific social phenomenon (e.g. racism and migration).

Many argue (Krause, 1989; Krause *et al.*, 1990; Bal and Cochrane, 1993; Littlewood and Lipsedge, 1987) that physical, emotional and behavioural symptoms resulting from mental health problems are expressed in a way that may be idiosyncratic to a particular culture. These specific 'culture bound disorders' are responsible for cultural variations in the expression of distress.

Studies on the relationship between lay theories of mental health and help-seeking behaviour have found that conceptions of mental illness are significantly correlated with the choice of treatment. This relationship was found regardless of whether participants had received psychological help in the past. Further evidence suggests a relationship between the effect of culture on beliefs about the aetiology and treatment of mental health problems (Chang, 1985; 1988; Leff, 1988; White, 1991). In one study by Kua *et al.* (1993) Chinese patients attributed their mental health problems to spiritual possession. Associated with this belief was the tendency to seek help from a traditional healer. For example, of those patients who sought treatment in hospital, Chinese patients continued to use herbal medicine prescribed by a traditional healer including the use of a talisman to ward off the spirits. In addition, the belief in spiritual possession in the causality of mental health problems was unrelated to gender, educational attainment and the type of psychological disorder. The second example describing the link between beliefs about causality and treatment is given by Jacobsson and Merdasa's (1991) work in Ethiopia. They maintain that Ethiopian traditions share a belief that mental disorders are caused by evil spirits or evil forces such as bewitchment and curses (particularly with neurotic disorders). The therapeutic techniques developed by the traditional healers fit well into the culture and tend to be the most favoured form of therapy.

Additional evidence from research findings (King *et al.*, 1994; Cochrane and Stipes-Roe, 1990) attempting to investigate the psychological effects of migration suggest that the psychological and social adjustment required from an immigrant population (for example learning a new language, establishing a new social network, acquiring new beliefs and values, dealing with racial prejudice/discrimination and other socio-economic factors) result in higher rates of mental health problems than in either the native-born population or the population in the immigrant's country of origin. Recent findings specifically focusing on the effects of 'perceived' racism (Clark *et al.*, 1999) suggest that a number of physical (hypertension, cardiovascular, low birth weight) and psychological (anxiety, depression and addictions) problems may develop as a consequence of this experience.

In the literature, very little attention has been given to explain how the effects of migration as well as cross-cultural issues affect second generation young adults from ethnic minorities. This chapter will attempt to identify the effects of these factors on the development of self-autonomy and self-identity in these individuals.

In this chapter I shall base my observations on my work undertaken with second generation young adults originally from the Indian and Bangledeshi subcontinents.

CROSS-CULTURAL ISSUES AND REASON FOR REFERRAL

Intra-familial and individual conflict as a result of cross-cultural issues appeared to be the main reason for the adolescent seeking outside help. The conflict was due to a number of cultural issues including the effects of and reason(s) for migration; young adult beliefs about the aetiology and treatment for mental health problems; and the process of accommodation to the host culture.

The effects of and reason for migration

Adolescents were referred for psychotherapy when there appeared to be a deepening and wider divide between themselves and family members (mainly parents). Socio-economic factors contributed to the development of problems. In the parents these included financial/employment difficulties, language barriers (leading to problems in communication) and small social networks consisting of other individuals from the country of origin rather than individuals from the indigenous population. In the young adults these factors included relationship difficulties as a result of having non-Indian friends and having to cope with the rules and responsibilities assigned to them by their parents.

There was conflict between the parent and young adult due to the failure or refusal of the young adult to comply with cultural norms adopted by their parents with respect to relationships with members of the opposite sex, choice in the style of clothing and engaging in social activities with peers from the indigenous population. This resulted in the young person having a mixture of Indian and non-Indian friends and having to keep them separate. In addition, young people experienced the roles and responsibilities assigned to them at home as very different from those assigned to their peers (from the indigenous population) with respect to having to care for younger siblings, performing household chores and acting as interpreters on behalf of parents to outside organisations.

The reasons underlying the parents' decision to migrate also have a major effect on the children and precipitated the referral. The second generation Indian young adult commonly believed that one of the main reasons for migration was to improve their career prospects through educational attainment. The young adults were very aware of the reasons as well as the difficulties the parents had experienced in accommodating to the host culture. They felt a strong desire to meet the parent's expectations through undertaking specific subjects at school, following specific career paths, etc. Problems arose when the young person was unable to meet their parents' expectations or if the young person felt that the expectations had been met at the expense of his/her other needs and desires.

A local school referred Amin to the Brandon Centre. He was at risk of permanent exclusion from school due to his involvement in inter-racial fights with peers. His parents had high expectations with respect to his educational achievement at school and did not want him to undertake a job that did not require a professional qualification. When settling in England his father had undertaken various 'manual' jobs and Amin's mother was unemployed. At the time of the referral Amin was acutely aware of his struggle to meet his parent's expectations. His gradual failure to do so was resulting in considerable conflict in his relationship with his parents.

Karim was an adolescent who self-referred to the Brandon Centre due to difficulties in her relationship with her boyfriend. In Karim's case, she felt she had met her parent's expectations with respect to educational attainments and choice of career. However, conflict had arisen as a result of her ability to meet other parental expectations with respect to her choice of boyfriend. Karim believed her parents wanted her to marry a man from the same caste and religion as herself. Karim had a boyfriend who met the criteria. However, the relationship was unknown to the parents due to her ambivalent feelings towards her boyfriend. Increasingly, she began to question how much of her parents' expectations overlapped with what she wanted (including her choice of career).

Adolescents' beliefs about the aetiology and treatment for emotional problems

Internal conflicts resulting from the process of acculturation were also apparent in the initial sessions when addressing the second generation young adults' understanding of the aetiology for emotional problems and treatment. The young adults may express beliefs in astrology, clairvoyance, palmistry and religion, which are closely identified with Indian culture.

Young adults' beliefs about causation affected their behaviour in that detailed astrological charts had been compiled by members of the community (in one case) and they regularly visited their 'traditional' place of worship (e.g. temple or mosque). Psychotherapy was perceived as a type of treatment that had its roots firmly planted in the host culture. To reduce the danger of the 'Indian' and 'English' self being divided, some discussion was devoted to the aim of psycho-therapy and, more specifically, how individual beliefs about the aetiology and treatment of emotional problems may represent underlying internal conflicts concerning the development of a more 'cohesive' sense of self (e.g. cultural identity) as well as the development of self-autonomy. Further consideration was given to explain how the process of accommodation and assimilation to the host culture might further complicate this development.

Difficulties in accommodating to the host culture: experience of racism

Adolescents have a strong awareness of the pressure to acculturate. This pressure appears to be equal to or even greater than that experienced by the parents. The need and pressure to acculturate is often further complicated by the negative experience adolescents and significant others (e.g. parents, relatives, close friends, community members, etc.) had in attempting to accommodate to the host culture. Adolescents frequently described difficulties they and significant others experi-enced according to racial differences and attitude. If a referral was first made or reinforced by an institution (e.g. school), it was often perceived by the young ado-lescent as another attempt by the dominant host culture to undermine and punish them. The resulting feelings of anger and hostility were dealt with in the sessions by attempting to understand the psychological effects of racism as well as to establish how the experience of racism may lead to the development of negative self-beliefs.

Therapeutically, it was important to ensure that the adolescent did not internalise negative self-beliefs. This was achieved by encouraging the adolescent to externalise the effects of racism and not to internalise them and to perceive specific responses arising from racist experiences as functional or appropriate (e.g. anger, hostility, helplessness) as opposed to dysfunctional defences. It should be noted that when dealing with the psychological effects of social processes (e.g. racism) it was extremely difficult to differentiate between whether a defence is dysfunctional (e.g. a result of underlying conflicts) or functional (e.g. appropriate) or both. However, perceived experiences of racism did require the attention from the therapist and appropriate intervention when necessary to engage the young person in the therapeutic process.

DEVELOPMENT OF A SELF-IDENTITY

Second generation young adults growing up in two very different cultures may experience conflict in developing a 'cohesive' sense of self due to issues about cultural identity. For these adolescents, the development of a self-identity arises from the conflict involving the integration of the 'Indian' with the 'English' self.

In second generation young adults conflict arose when the two ('Indian' and 'English') cultures were perceived as very different with respect to roles and responsibilities, religious beliefs/practices and cultural beliefs and values.

A Bangladeshi adolescent (Bal) came to therapy when her views about establishing a relationship prior to marriage were in increasing conflict with the views of her parents (from Bangladesh) who believed that a relationship should only be developed after their approval (through the arranged marriage system) and that their daughter should not leave home until after marriage. Bal reached a point in her relationship (with a Bangladeshi boy) in which she felt that any further attempts to make a greater commitment to the relationship would go strongly against social custom and practice as well the wishes of her parents. Both Bal's older brother and sister had had arranged marriages. Interestingly, at school, she had decided only to befriend 'white English' peers. A family arrangement had also been made for her to visit Bangladesh for a period of 6 weeks. In her sessions, Bal was encouraged to think about issues relating to her own self-identity and, more specifically, how the differences in beliefs and practices arising from two different cultures had complicated this process.

The psychological effects of migration on family members (or significant others) including the process of acculturation to the host culture also play an important part in the development of a self-identity in second generation young adults from ethnic minority backgrounds. Interestingly, the parents' experiences of migration appeared to have a major impact on the children. More specifically, the negative experiences in the accommodation to and assimilation with the host culture coupled with their disillusionment about the quality of life in England resulted in many members of the family spending long and frequent holidays in their country of origin. Considerable conflict concerning the development of 'cohesive' sense of self arose in the second generation young adults from ethnic minorities when they felt under considerable pressure to acculturate to the host culture (as a result of schooling) as well as to maintain a cultural identity pertaining to their country of origin.

For Karim cultural issues concerning the development of a 'cohesive' self were evident in her relationship with significant others. Her boyfriend was from the same caste and religion as herself. However, her sister had selected a boyfriend belonging to a different Indian religion and caste. She expressed angry and hostile feelings towards her sister for this reason. With time, it surfaced that her main reason for continuing what she presented as an unsatisfying and unhappy relationship with her boyfriend was the fact that he would be considered a suitable man by the parents and community. Karim felt under pressure from her parents to marry someone from the same caste and religion. Eventually, Karim made a decision to separate from her boyfriend. This decision coincided with an improvement in her relationship with her mother through addressing cultural issues concerning her choice of partner as well as addressing how her strong affiliation to both 'Indian' and 'English' cultures had complicated the development of a more 'cohesive' sense of self based on a more established cultural identity.

Issues connected to the development of a self-identity in second generation young adults from ethnic minorities were further complicated by, first, individual members of a family having different levels of affiliation to the host culture (see case example below) and, second, this process being further complicated if the host culture was perceived by the adolescent as hostile and rejecting. The resulting feeling of anger and hostility towards members of the host culture often raised issues of a cultural identity in the adolescents' minds, greater feelings of identification with the parents who may have experienced similar negative experiences (e.g. racism), and the need to protect one's 'Indian' identity which was perceived to be under attack from members of the host culture. Interestingly, the young adults from ethnic minorities had adopted the parents' religion and were eager to participate in cultural activities. However, cultural beliefs and values associated with development of a sexual self as well as the development of self-autonomy were more likely to be in conflict.

As previously mentioned, different levels of assimilation with and accommodation to the host culture by individual family members increased internal conflict associated with the development of a cultural identity.

Karim's parents were brought up in an Indian village in which there was a complex network of responsibilities, roles and duties which extended beyond the immediate family to kin and other villages. These were largely prescribed in accordance with the individuals' age, gender, caste, etc. The parents were introduced to each other through the arranged marriage system and their marriage followed shortly after the initial meeting.

Karim and her younger sister were born and educated in England. Karim described her sister as 'too Westernised' due to the fact she had selected her own boyfriend and had decided to establish a relationship with him against the wishes of her parents. Her parents were perceived as holding orthodox Indian beliefs and values. In the sessions, Karim began increasingly to focus on developing a more 'cohesive' sense of self, primarily by focusing on her cultural identity (integrating her 'English' and 'Indian' self) which was different from that of other family members.

With specific reference to the development of a self-identity in adolescents from ethnic minorities a number of themes were developed in therapy. These themes will be addressed in conjunction with the implications from therapeutic work with individuals from ethnic minority backgrounds.

First, feelings of confusion based on not knowing what they wanted from therapy was a very dominant theme. The feelings of confusion appeared to develop from internal conflict concerning the development of a cultural identity based on a more 'cohesive' sense of self.

Second, feelings of anger and hostility arising from not being able to accommodate strongly with either an 'Indian' or 'English' culture resulted also in marked feelings of isolation or possibly rejection. Young adults engaged in therapeutic work as if they were assimilating with and accommodating to another culture (e.g. the culture of psychotherapy). As such, internal conflicts arising from this process were more evident in the sessions. Common themes which arose included: feelings of confusion about how psychotherapy would help them; difficulties in engagement (as suggested by the difficulties they experienced in assimilating with and accommodating to two very different cultures); issues and questions arising from the beliefs and values underlying interpretations and the theoretical framework adopted by the therapist; as well as a strong emphasis, in the sessions on intra-family conflict arising from cross-cultural issues.

Finally, there was a growing awareness from the young adults that the establishment of a cultural identity was a dynamic process which involved a constant reassessment of 'self beliefs' arising from both their own life experiences and those of different members of their own community in adapting to the host culture.

THE DEVELOPMENT OF SELF-AUTONOMY

The psychological effects of migration and cross-cultural issues may play an important part in the development of self-autonomy in young adults from ethnic minorities. For those young adults from the Indian community, physical separation away from the family home appeared to cause the most individual, as well as family, conflict. Culturally valued concepts such as loyalty, duty and dependence were embedded in Indian tradition which had implications for what was considered culturally acceptable behaviour.

Second generation young adults from the Indian subcontinent often felt a deep sense of duty and responsibility for the elderly (e.g. parents) and younger siblings. They also experienced strong expectations from parents to leave the family home only after marriage and not to establish sexual relationships with the opposite sex until after marriage.

These beliefs and expectations suggested that assessing the development of self-autonomy is complicated if the use of specific behaviours (e.g. physical separation away from the family home, choice of partner, etc.) are used as criteria to determine the development in this area.

Other factors also appeared to affect significantly the attachment the young adults had to family members or significant others, which may have had implications for the development of self-autonomy.

First, a close attachment to family members (as well as significant others in the community) may be important for the development of an 'Indian' self-identity. This was achieved through having greater contact with first generation Indians, who held more traditional beliefs and values and participated in religious, cultural and social practices as adopted by the country of origin. The difficulties associated with the development of a cultural identity have been discussed in the previous section. More importantly, the young person's decision to maintain close contact with family members may have arisen for this reason.

Second, adolescents reported significant negative life experiences in their attempts to accommodate and assimilate to the host culture (e.g. racism). They were also conscious of the similar negative experiences of significant others as well as members of the community experienced in attempting to acculturate. The associated anger and hostility in the adolescents appeared to strengthen ties with the family and community members as well as 'protect' their cultural identity which was perceived to be rejected or under attack by the host culture. As such, close contract with family members or significant others may have served an important 'protective' function.

Finally, feelings of loss experienced by migrants clearly had an emotional impact on their children. Parents were frequently reported as feeling disillusioned with the quality of life in England and maintained strong feelings of attachment to their country of origin. Eisenbruch (1990) attempts to explain this response in her description of the term 'cultural bereavement' which describes a 'connection between disruptions at several levels such as health, interpersonal, social and community relations' that result in consequent feelings of loss. Parents often made long and frequent trips to this country of origin (as previously mentioned). These factors increased the adolescents' vulnerability to emotional problems as well as affecting the development of self-autonomy.

After their arranged marriage, Karim's parents moved to England. Her parents felt dissatisfied with the way of life in England due to considerable financial and family pressures. They had no close relatives living in England and were in frequent contact with relatives/individuals from their country of origin (this was partly due to business reasons). The parents had wanted their two daughters to be educated in England. However, to maintain ties with his country of origin, the father took long and frequent trips back home.

The father's absence had a profound effect on Karim. She expressed sad feelings of loss about the lack of emotional contact with the father. As the eldest child in the family she felt it was her duty to 'look after' her younger sibling and mother. The mother had not accommodated to the host culture to the same level as her daughters (e.g. she was unable to speak the English language; only socialised with a few individuals from the community and was unemployed). Karim felt angry and hostile due to the lack of social contact she had with her 'English' friends at work and from her college days. She was aware that her English peers had a very different lifestyle and associated this with the fact that she and her family were of Indian origin. She rationalised her decision to stay at home as representing her 'Indian' self. However, she was worried that in terms of her future existence she would be unhappy (like her mother) and be a 'burden' to others.

Karim had frequent arguments with her mother about relationships/marriage.

Her mother expressed her wish that Karim should marry a man from the same caste/religion. Karim also experienced considerable conflict in her relationship with her sister who she perceived as having an easier lifestyle (by not conforming to cultural norms which included making her own decision about a choice of partner).

In the sessions, cross-cultural conflicts and the feelings associated with them were addressed. In addition, her relationship with her parents was addressed in the context of her role as a 'surrogate father' whose duty it was to keep the family together and to maintain a specific set of Indian values and beliefs. Towards the end of therapy, Karim was increasingly tolerant of conflicting cultural issues and was able to concentrate more on developing a more 'cohesive' sense of self. Shortly after the welcome return of her father, Karim (with her work colleagues) found employment in another European country for a short period of time.

Cross-cultural factors and psychological effects of migration in the parents (in particular) affected the development of self-autonomy in young adults. As noted, cross-cultural factors suggest that specific indicators of self-development (e.g. physical separation from family environment, choice of partner, etc.) cannot be used as indicators to explain the development of self-autonomy in second generation young adults. The importance of cross-cultural factors and intrapsychic conflict in the development of self-autonomy suggest that it is extremely important to consider how decisions about achieving greater independence are made by the individual and to further determine how the complex relationship between cultural factors and intrapsychic conflicts affect the issue of separation in particular.

CONCLUDING REMARKS

Psychotherapy undertaken with young adults from an Indian and Bangladeshi background suggest that cross-cultural factors may have a significant effect in the development of self-autonomy, the formation of a self-identity and the acceptance of a sexual self.

Cross-cultural factors also contribute to an individual's beliefs about the aetiology and treatment of emotional problems.

Evidence from case examples provided in this chapter suggest that the specific experiences of migrant parents (or significant others) and the cultural beliefs and values adopted by family members have strong implications for the individual seeking help as well as the work undertaken with the individual.

Exactly how the internal conflicts resulting from growing up in two very different cultures affect the nature and development of intrapsychic conflicts requires more detailed and thorough investigation in order to improve therapeutic work with this client group.

References

Bal, S. S. and Cochrane, R. (1993). 'Asian parents, somatisation and psychological distress; a cross-cultural comparison at the primary health care level'. (Paper under review.)

Chang, W. C. (1985). 'A cross-cultural study of depressive symptomatology'. *Culture, Medicine and Psychiatry* 9: 295–315.

—— (1988) 'The nature of self: a transcultural view'. *Transcultural Psychiatric Research Review* 25: 169–89.

Clark, R., Anderson, N., Clark, V. and Williams, D. (1999). 'Racism as a stressor for African Americans'. *American Psychologist* 10: 805–16.

Cochrane, R. and Stipes-Roe, M. (1990). *Citizens of this Country*. Cleveland: The Asian-British Multilingual Matters Limited.

Eisenbruch, M. (1990). 'Cultural bereavement and homesickness'. In Fisher, S. and Cooper, C. L. (eds), *On The Move: The Psychology of Change and Transition*, 191–205. Chichester: Wiley.

Jacobsson, L. and Merdasa, F. (1991). 'Traditional perceptions and treatment of mental disorders in Western Ethopia before the 1974 Revolution'. *Acta Psychiatrica Scandinavia* 84: 475–81.

Krause, I. B. (1989). 'The sinking heart. A Punjabi communication of distress'. *Social Service and Medicine* 29: 563–75.

—— Risser, R., Khiani, M. and Lotay, N. (1990). 'Psychiatric morbidity among Punjabi medical patients in England measured by general health questionnaire'. *Psychological Medicine* 20: 711–19.

Kua, E. H., Chew, P. H. and Ko, S. M. (1993). 'Spirit possession and healing among Chinese psychiatric patients'. *Acta Psychiatrica Scandinavia* 88: 447–50.

King, M., Coker, E., Leavey, G., Hoare, A. and Subine, E. (1994). 'Incidence of psychiatric illness in London: comparison of ethnic groups'. *British Medical Journal* 309: 1115–19.

Leff, J. (1988). *Psychiatry Around the Globe*. London: Gaskell.

Littlewood, R. and Lipsedge, M. (1987) 'The butterfly and the serpent: culture, psycho-pathology and biomedicine'. *Culture, Medicine and Psychiatry* 11: 289–335.

White, G. (1991). 'Attitudes towards mental health problems in Tanzania'. *Acta Psychiatria Scandinavia* 83: 59–75.

Chapter 6

The developmental and emotional implications behind the use young people make of family planning services

Mellany Ambrose

The medical service at the Brandon Centre has been providing family planning services to young people for over 30 years. As well as attending to their contraceptive needs it has always practised a counselling approach, offering the time to listen to young people in order to help them understand relevant personal issues. This model of medical counselling which focuses on both the physical and emotional aspects of the young person's request for contraception is a particular feature of the Brandon Centre's approach to the contraceptive needs of young people.

THE SETTING

A family planning service for young people needs to be approachable, accessible and respectful of confidentiality.

The setting is a terraced house in Kentish Town which does not have the appearance associated with a family planning clinic. This helps young people who may be worried about being seen accessing such help. They like the comfortable, non-clinical feel of the building. The waiting room is shared with the therapy clients, and reception staff deal with both the medical and therapy sides. They aim to be approachable, helpful and non-judgemental. The doctor collects the patient from the waiting room. Patients are seen in the 'surgery'. This room tries to provide a relaxed atmosphere with carpet, curtains and pictures. The doctor sits at a desk, with two comfortable chairs at right angles for the patient and anyone else they wish to be present. Next door is a small examination room where the contraceptive supplies are kept and examinations or smear tests can be performed if needed.

Two female doctors run the service, each working half time. Both are trained in family planning and have an interest in working with young people and counselling. One doctor sees patients on Monday, Tuesday and Thursday, the other on Wednesday and Friday. This means the centre is open every weekday, unlike some clinics, which are only open once a week. The hours are convenient for coming after school, and it is open late two evenings a week for people who work or find it hard to come during the day. There is no separate family planning nurse or counsellor; the doctor performs these roles as well. This helps build a trusting relationship with the young person and helps provide continuity of care. The two doctors meet weekly to communicate information about any people they are worried about, and for mutual support.

We see people between the ages of 13 and 25 years. In 1999/2000, of 559 young people who used the service 22 per cent seen were under 16, 45 per cent were 17–20 and 33 per cent were 21–25 years. Most people who use the service live locally and hear about it from their friends. Some people travel from other parts of London and beyond, and hear about us through leaflets or helplines. The people we see are a self-selected group and may differ from those seen at other clinics. Kentish Town has areas of high social and economic deprivation; young people from these areas use the service.

We operate a self-referral system. Young people can telephone or drop in to make an appointment. If someone comes to the door wishing to be seen we will try and fit them in. Most people can be seen the same day if they wish. Ideally half an hour is allocated for each patient, although this may be less on a busy day. Importantly, once contact has been made the doctor can arrange a longer appointment in the next few days if more time is needed. We try to make the system flexible as we know young people often want to be seen straight away and may find it hard to wait or may lose courage to come for help.

Very few boys are seen, which is a weakness for most clinics offering young persons family planning. Boys are free to make an appointment or ask to see us, and we do see a few. If boys under 16 years ask for condoms we see them to check they know how to use them and discuss any concerns. Since boys might find it embarrassing seeing a female doctor to obtain advice about using condoms, the director who is male is available to help them. Some boys come with their girlfriends and are seen with them.

Services offered by the Centre are: emergency contraception, routine contraception (e.g. condoms, the pill, the injection), pregnancy testing, and pregnancy and abortion counselling with referral for ongoing antenatal care or abortion. We also advise on sexually transmitted diseases including HIV, with referral to a sexual health clinic if needed,[1] smear tests and psychosexual counselling. The service also offers a place and time for young women to talk about any worries and anxieties about themselves, their bodies, periods, sex, relationships, family, school, etc.

Most new patients come for emergency contraception or a pregnancy test. These are services young people want and will come for. Hopefully if they have a good experience at the Centre they will return for further help with contraception. 'Old' patients, that is those who have been before, are more likely to come for routine

---

1 Since 1 April 2000 the Centre has been offering a limited sexual health service.

contraception. Some patients come back regularly, others move on to GPs or other family planning clinics.

Confidentiality is discussed with all new patients. Everything they tell us is confidential, unless we feel they or others are at risk of serious harm. In such cases we always discuss our views with the young person and try to get them to agree to us telling the appropriate people. To break confidentiality is extremely rare and only done after a lot of consultation and discussion with the director, other staff and a medical defence body. Young people under 16 are especially worried about confidentiality. We follow the guidelines issued jointly by the BMA, GMSC, HEA, Brook Advisory Centres, FPA and RCGP. All young people under 16 years are encouraged to tell their parents they have been to the clinic. If they feel they cannot the reasons for this are explored. If they still feel unable to talk to them, they can be treated confidentially without parental consent if we believe:

- they are mature enough to understand the risks and benefits of any treatment and advice given;
- they are likely to have sexual intercourse without contraception;
- their physical or mental health is likely to suffer if they are not given contraceptive advice or supplies;
- it is in the young person's best interests that they receive advice or methods without parental consent.

I would like to clarify how I am using the term 'counselling' in relation to the medical service. We use a 'counselling approach' with every patient we see which means allowing time, listening, trying to understand, talking about feelings, being aware of emotional factors and being aware of feelings aroused in ourselves. For some consultations, for example a repeat of contraceptive pills, this may be a small part of what is discussed. In other consultations, for example someone deciding what to do after a positive pregnancy test, this will be a major part of the consultation. We try to support people having abortions, or those with other contraceptive, sexual or relationship difficulties and see them again to do this. They may be offered regular 'counselling' sessions with us to discuss these issues. If a young person's problems are complex and less focused on psychosexual areas of functioning we then explore with them more formal therapy. They may decide to begin treatment with one of the Centre's psychotherapists for more regular, in depth, long-term work.

DEVELOPMENTAL CONSIDERATIONS IN YOUNG PEOPLE

Young people may come to the family planning service for an apparently simple reason but often the underlying situation is much more complex. Adolescence is a time of great physical and psychological change. Puberty brings about enormous physical changes, resulting in a sexually mature body. Psychological changes take place in thinking and emotional changes happen in the areas of identity and separation. However, there is often a gap between the reaching of physical and emotional maturity. This is very confusing for the young person, and creates many difficulties. Their bodies are capable of a sexual relationship and can have a baby, but they are not emotionally ready to cope with this. This gap puts them at risk of physical and psychological harm.

Adolescence is a time of transition from child to independent adult. It involves finding an identity as a person separate from one's parents. It is also a time of conflicts. Sexuality and sexual relationships are one area in which problems may be played out.

I want to look at the above in more detail, with examples from working in the family planning service.

Bodily changes

Young people may have worries and fears about their bodies that they feel unable to discuss with their parents or teachers. Peers are an unreliable source of information. Despite sex education and a good knowledge of some areas, ignorance and misinformation are common. Although it is unusual for girls to come out directly with these worries they often arise in discussing contraception, and can be talked about. Worries about breasts, periods, vaginal discharge or just what is normal are common. Questions such as can you still have periods if you are pregnant, and the 'safe period' often come up. Discussing possible side-effects of contraception such as breasts increasing in size on the pill or periods stopping on the injection can reveal problems girls have in accepting their bodies and their femininity.

Tina, age 16, first came with some friends who were very giggly and laughing and joking about the effects of the pill or injection on breast size. Tina later came back on her own. She was a very small girl and had only just started menstruating. Her breasts were very small and this worried her as she felt her boyfriend did not find her attractive. She wanted to start the pill as she was thinking of having sex with her boyfriend, but also knew it might increase her breast size. The doctor prescribed the pill but was also able to talk with her about her worries about her body and lack of confidence.

Psychological changes

Many changes in thinking and reasoning take place in adolescence and will affect young people's sexual behaviour and the use they make of the family planning service.

Adolescence is a time of *experimentation and risk taking*. This is particularly so in the areas of sex, alcohol and drugs. Trying out new experiences is important but harm can result. Having sex without contraception may be part of this but exposes the young person to the risk of pregnancy and sexually transmitted diseases. Often no contraception is used the first time a young person has sex. Alcohol and drugs are often involved; the young person gets drunk and is less inhibited so has unprotected sex.

> Kelly, age 14, confided in her school nurse that she had got very drunk at a party a few days ago and had unprotected sex with a boy she hardly knew. It was the first time she had had intercourse. She was very worried and distressed. The school nurse sent her to the Brandon Centre, where she was in time to get emergency contraception to allay her fears of pregnancy. She also felt able to talk a little about her experience and how bad she now felt about what had happened.

We often see younger adolescents coming for the emergency pill or a pregnancy test who have not used any contraception. There may be factors involved such as lack of information, misinformation, not knowing where to seek help, fear of confidentiality, but often they know about contraception from school and are aware of our confidential service so why do they not come earlier? An important factor is *cognitive immaturity*. In early adolescence the young person has not moved from concrete to abstract thinking. They have trouble seeing the consequences of their actions and planning ahead. This means they cannot make the link between sex and pregnancy and have trouble planning to use contraception. They usually know facts from sex education classes but do not see these apply to them. Even when they see their friends become pregnant or pick up an infection they may not be able to generalise that the same could happen to them. They have trouble learning from experience and may have unprotected sex even after a pregnancy scare. Even when they develop cognitive maturity it is likely to regress under new or stressful situations.

> Sarah, age 15, came to the centre for a pregnancy test as her period was 2 weeks late and a friend said she should come. She had been having sex with her boyfriend for 3 months but not using any contraception. When asked why she replied 'I didn't think about it. I knew I should from what we learnt at school but that didn't seem to have anything to do with me.' Unfortunately the pregnancy test was positive. She was very shocked and found it hard to take in. She was seen a few days later to discuss her options. She had managed to tell her mother and decided to have a termination.

Cognitive maturity develops throughout adolescence. Older teenagers do seem more able to connect sex and pregnancy and plan ahead, but still regress at times. They are more aware they've taken a risk and more likely to seek help early to rectify it.

> Zoe, age 18, came for the emergency pill. Normally she used condoms, but she and her partner had run out and had sex without. Luckily she was aware she'd taken a risk and came for the emergency pill.

Some people never seem to develop cognitive maturity due to learning difficulties or severe emotional problems.

> Jasmine, age 22, had learning difficulties. She had irregular periods and often came for pregnancy tests, having had unprotected sex. She seemed unable to link sex and pregnancy. After a lot of discussion she decided to have the contraceptive injection, which gives 12 weeks' contraception from one injection. She seemed relieved after this.

In adolescence there is great *ambivalence about being sexual*. The young person experiences biological drives and the wish to experiment. There is much external pressure to be sexual from society and peers. However, if they have sex they may be seen as sluts or whores. Many are unable to cope with this conflict, and denial takes over. If they plan ahead to go on the pill or carry condoms they have to admit they are sexual beings, so it is easier to ignore contraception. Also planning ahead to use contraception or discussing it with their partner may be seen as unromantic. Excuses are common, e.g. we ran out of condoms, I meant to come and get the pill, we got carried away, I didn't expect it to happen. These all make sex sound exciting and take the responsibility away from them.

> Three friends came for the emergency pill and wanted to be seen together. All were age 15 and had had unprotected sex at the same party, at the same time. They were unable to stop giggling and talk or think seriously about what had happened. The doctor felt a great contradiction that they were acting like children but had had sex. She did feel they were mature enough to understand the risks and benefits of treatment and were at risk, so she prescribed this. They seemed to be denying any sexuality and taking protection in numbers. The doctor hoped a good experience at the clinic would enable them to return in the future.

Despite sex education there are many *false beliefs* about sex such as you can't get pregnant the first time. It won't happen to me. I've got away with it before. Sometimes not using contraception and not becoming pregnant means the young person worries they are infertile, leading to an unwanted pregnancy just to make sure.

> Barbara, age 16, was shocked when a pregnancy test was positive. She had had unprotected sex for 6 months with her boyfriend so thought she would get away with it.

It seems hard for many young women to be *assertive* about sex. They may find it hard to say no or to insist their partner uses a condom. This may be because they feel they have no control over their own lives, so how can they be expected to feel they have any control over their bodies? Low self-esteem may also be important. They may be worried their boyfriend will leave them if they don't have sex with him.

> Jade, age 16, came for a pregnancy test. She had split with her boyfriend 3 months ago but was still having sex with him. She felt so bad about herself that any attention was better than none.

EMOTIONAL CHANGES, SEPARATION AND FAMILY PROBLEMS

The gap between physical and emotional maturity, and its potential for harm, has already been mentioned. As well as changes in thinking, many *emotional changes* take place in adolescence. Most young people live in a family, with one or both parents, and support and conflicts happen within it. Parents may have problems coping with their child growing up and leaving, and their daughter's emerging sexuality. Family disruption and new relationships, e.g. step-parents, affect the young person. The move from child to independent adult, forming new relationships outside the family, involves *separating emotionally from the parents*. This is not a quick, simple process.

There may be great ambivalence about pregnancy, and this means contraception is not used. Often this is unconscious, which makes it harder to address. If the young person is having problems with their development or is depressed this can be evident in the desire for a baby as a solution to this.

Unresolved feelings about a previous pregnancy or abortion can stop the young person moving on. Often several of the above factors will apply to one person.

The parents and family are an important source of support for young people. If this *support is disrupted* or simply not available, adolescents may look towards sex or a baby as a solution, or act irresponsibly because of feeling let down, angry, or on their own.

Lucy, age 13, came to the centre for a pregnancy test. Her mother was in hospital having a major operation and Lucy was staying with her grandmother whom she did not get on with. Since this change to her normal routine she had started staying out late and having unprotected sex with her boyfriend. She said she did not want to get pregnant and the doctor prescribed the pill. However she was unable to swallow the tablets, which the doctor thought was a sign of her ambivalence about taking it. During several consultations the doctor was able to get a picture that she felt angry and rejected by her mother. When her mother came home again and had convalesced, Lucy returned home. She decided she was too young to have sex and stopped seeing her boyfriend. Two years later she returned to the centre requesting help with contraception as she now felt ready to have sex and wanted to be prepared.

Michelle, age 15, came to the centre for a pregnancy test. Over the past few months her mother had become increasingly depressed and unable to cope with Michelle's wild behaviour. Michelle was very distressed by her mother's depression but felt unable to talk to her about this. She kept coming in for emergency pills or pregnancy tests. One day the pregnancy test was positive and she made the decision to have an abortion, which was very painful for her. Also she felt unable to tell her mother. She came for several counselling sessions with the doctor afterwards for support. Her mother improved with treatment and Michelle even managed to tell her about the abortion. She seemed to settle and started using regular contraception.

Many patients we see are, or have been, *in care or are homeless*. They do not have the family support described and often have to cope for themselves when they turn 16. Even if they have spent some time with their parents they have often had an upbringing deprived of love and feeling cared for, maybe even involving violence or sexual abuse. Often the wish to have a baby represents a desire to create a new family to make up for what they have missed. They want to be the perfect mother and give their baby everything they lacked. They also see the baby as someone who will love them.

> Laura, age 16, was pregnant and came for support as she felt everyone was saying she should have a termination. She had run away from home after family violence and was now living in a hostel. She wanted a baby to create a new family as she felt her own was so awful.

> Farah, age 15, had been born in Africa but moved to the UK when young. Her mother had not come with them and she had not seen her since. She lived with her father but was taken into foster care because of difficulties at home. She had a boyfriend, also from Africa, and had sex with him. She came to the centre asking for a pregnancy test. The test was negative, but she came to the centre several times for more. It turned out she was unhappy with her boyfriend, but since she was Muslim felt she had to now marry him. Their families were against this, but she became pregnant so they could get married. She could see no other way out of her difficulties. Her wish for a husband and a baby seemed to represent all her longings for her original family to be together again. Unfortunately her solution did not work and she still felt unhappy.

Changes to the family structure such as divorce, remarriage, step-parents and a new baby in the family can have profound effects on the young person.

> Ella, age 15, lived with her mother. Her parents had separated and she missed her dad. When dad's new partner became pregnant Ella felt very jealous and excluded and began having sex with no contraception.

A young girl's *sexuality* can create problems in the family. If the parents have their own problems this can be hard to cope with. The mother may feel uneasy at the daughter's attractiveness and sexuality at a time when she is getting older. A mother may have a baby herself as a reaction to this. A daughter may be sexually provocative, making the father feel uneasy.

This is also a time of separating from the parents and conflicts over independence, identity and control may arise between *mother and daughter*. The mother wants to protect her daughter, who still seems like a child. The daughter wants to be treated as an adult but does not yet have enough resources to cope on her own. If there are problems in the mother–daughter relationship the situation becomes even more complicated. These issues may be seen in the area of sexuality and pregnancy.

> Zoe, age 17, had a termination at age 14. She had felt forced by her mother to do this, not part of the decision making. When she became pregnant again she decided to have an abortion but felt this was her own choice, even though very painful.

> Sarah had felt forced to have an abortion 6 months ago by her mother when she was 15. She became pregnant again quickly and was determined to keep the baby. She ran away from home to live with her boyfriend. She felt her own family was too controlling and never let her do what she wanted.

> Linda, age 14, was brought by her mother. She was pregnant. Her mother had told her she had an abortion at the same age, and thought she should do the same. Linda wanted to keep her baby. There was a great emotional struggle in the room between the mother and daughter.

Separation usually involves physically *leaving home* as well as emotionally leaving. This is very difficult for many young people, particularly if they are very enmeshed with their mother. They may be scared of coping alone. A gradual loosening of bonds may be too difficult and pregnancy may be a way to leave. It may be seen as a way to leave home, separate, be seen as a grown up, independent, different. Alternatively, since pregnant teenagers often stay with their mothers it may be a way not to leave home, solving the dilemma for the young person. The boyfriend is unimportant in this case. Pregnancy avoids painful choices about the future.

> Helen, age 17, had been to the centre for the pill then did not come for several months. She came in for a pregnancy test which was positive. She was asking about abortions one minute and antenatal care the

next. She had been feeling very low after several rows with her boy-friend. She'd left school but had been unable to find a job. Part of her wanted to leave home and become independent, but another part could not manage this. She decided to keep the baby, despite saying she did not want to stay with her parents for ever. They were understand-ing but this meant she was trapped at home. It solved her dilemma about leaving home.

Caroline, age 16, came to the centre but refused to use contraception. She seemed very unhappy and complained her parents were very strict and did not care about her. She was not doing well at school. She eventually became pregnant and went into a hostel. This seemed the only way she could leave home, whilst having a baby meant someone to love her.

Sexual behaviour the parents would disapprove of may be used as a way of *rebelling* against them.

Sita, age 18, was a refugee from the Middle East. Her parents were very strict and forbade her to see boys. She came to the clinic for the emergency pill, very scared. She felt she could not take regular contra-ception in case her parents found out. One day she came in for a pregnancy test, which was positive. She felt she had been having sex as a rebellion against her parents. She felt it impossible to continue the pregnancy, because her parents could not know but also because she wanted to finish her education and do something with her life.

Often the young person is *depressed*. They feel their life is empty and see a baby as filling that space and making them happy. The baby is also seen as someone to love, who will love them back. They may have nothing else in their lives, no job, and no continuing education and see a baby as the solution to their problems.

Marie, age 14, came to the centre for a pregnancy test. She was not doing well at school. She lived with her mother and had not seen her father for many years. She seemed very cold and cut off and the doctor felt unable to reach her. She wanted a baby for someone to love, plus something to give her boyfriend. He was older and very much wanted a child. One day she came in looking more grown up. The doctor was able to talk to her more easily and she looked sad while talking about how depressed she felt. She hoped a baby would help with the emptiness she felt inside. Counselling was discussed but she was scared it would be too painful.

Fiona, age 16, came for a pregnancy test. She wanted a baby to love and care for, but also wanted to finish school. Her parents were separated and Dad had a new baby. She came for counselling with one of the therapists and decided to start the pill and stay at school.

Sheila, age 19, wanted a pregnancy test after the emergency pill. She was talking as if she was pregnant and when the test was negative looked upset. It turned out she felt down and worthless, not valued by her boyfriend, and wanted a baby to help her feel better. The doctor pointed out she seemed to see a baby as solving her depression. She became very thoughtful and said she realised this would not actually solve her problems, and decided to use contraception and explore finding a job she enjoyed.

Unresolved feelings about a previous pregnancy or abortion may mean the young person becomes *trapped by their guilt* and continues to be at risk of repeating.

Deirdre, age 19, came for the emergency pill just weeks after having an abortion. She had not used a condom then panicked. She had wanted to keep the baby but felt unable to due to financial worries. Everywhere she went she seemed to see newborn babies, which reminded her of her loss. The doctor was able to help her explore her ambivalence and guilt. When she returned she chose to have the injection.

Nadia, age 20, had become pregnant despite being very careful. She was waiting to have an abortion when she was rushed in with an ectopic pregnancy (a pregnancy in the tube, which is not viable, so has to be removed by an operation). The doctor picked up in follow-up visits that she was not coping well. In her mind she felt guilty as if she had had an abortion. During several counselling sessions with the doctor she was able to talk about the deep emptiness she felt having lost the baby.

Moira, age 17, became pregnant soon after an abortion, despite taking the pill. She wanted to keep this pregnancy as she felt she had killed the previous baby, but her mother changed her mind. After the second abortion she became very anxious about becoming pregnant again but was unable to use any contraception regularly due to side effects such as feeling sick. Over several consultations the doctor tried to help her explore her feelings about the abortions and whether these might be contributing to her feeling sick.

Which factors are most important?

I have discussed many factors that are relevant in working with young people in a family planning service. We feel the emotional factors are the most important and so should be looked at, although there is no research evidence that this improves outcome. Some people might argue unwanted teenage pregnancies can all be explained by lack of knowledge or cognitive immaturity, but all adolescents pass through this stage so why do only some become pregnant? Surely this cannot be the whole story and a young person's background, relationships and feelings about themselves are of major importance.

IMPACT ON THE DOCTOR AND SUPPORT

The work I have described can be very stimulating, rewarding and fulfilling for the doctor. However, it can also be frustrating, distressing and disheartening. The nature of the problems dealt with, particularly when a young person requests or chooses an abortion, and the close relationship that is often formed with a patient can be emotionally draining. The doctor needs to be able to tolerate the patient's feelings and possible feelings of sadness, hopelessness, frustration and irritation that are aroused in her. It is vital to be able to take a step back and analyse what is happening between patient and doctor.

A young girl may come for contraceptive advice, and the doctor may spend a lot of time discussing various methods and exploring her feelings about sex and relationships. She may turn up for a subsequent appointment requesting a pregnancy test, not having used any contraception as though the doctor's advice had made no impact whatsoever. The doctor may then feel all her efforts were a waste of time. A patient may have an abortion then decide to use the pill afterwards. All seems well until she returns a few months later saying she ran out of pills, is now late for her period and turns out to be pregnant. Some young women may keep presenting with unwanted pregnancies requesting abortions, but reject all methods of contraception for one reason or another. Such apparently 'mindless and meaningless' behaviour may produce in the doctor feelings of helplessness, frustration and anger.

At the Brandon Centre each doctor has weekly supervision with one of the therapists to discuss such situations. They also attend weekly meetings with all the clinical staff where complicated cases can be discussed. Meeting the other doctor weekly is another source of support. Having the opportunity to discuss cases with a therapist is a luxury for doctors but incredibly useful and supportive. It offers a new way of thinking about family planning work that goes beyond the physical aspects. Maybe I feel angry with a young girl who is taking many risks because she is angry at feeling unloved by her parents. Perhaps I feel I am being used and degraded by the girl who has repeat abortions because that is how she feels inside and it is the only way she can communicate her distress. Perhaps I feel sad after seeing a girl who seems very organised in requesting an abortion because I am picking up the sadness it is too painful for her to acknowledge.

Sometimes it may be possible to use these insights in work with the patient. Sometimes this may be impossible, but understanding one's experience of the patient can help the doctor cope with these difficult situations. It means the doctor can be more objective rather than feeling the situation is a personal failure and acting upon the feelings aroused in her. Ideally a patient who has many problems can then see one of the therapists. When working with these patients it is helpful for the doctor to have a therapy service at hand and she can facilitate a transfer. However, often the people we see are unable to commit themselves to regular therapy or do not feel ready to do so. They can continue to see us when they wish to, which might be less anxiety making for them. Sometimes a young person who has come to the family planning service at a young age will feel more able to use therapy when they are older especially if they have had a good experience at the Centre.

CONCLUSION

Work with a patient that feels difficult, painful and emotionally draining at the time can feel the most rewarding afterwards. Sometimes it is as if we only see our 'failures', as our 'successes' are able to move on to other services and do not keep returning misusing contraception, pregnant or dissatisfied. On the other hand perhaps it is not a failure if such young people are able to return and talk to us, seek our help, and communicate their painful and distressing feelings.

Chapter 7

Working in a school for severely physically disabled children

David Trevatt

INTRODUCTION

In this chapter I shall be looking at the work I have conducted in a special school over the last 2 years. I hope to show how there are significant advantages and some drawbacks to offering a psychotherapy service which is school based. I shall describe the school in its physical and organisational forms and I shall try to draw out the lessons I have needed to learn about working as a therapist in school. I shall also describe the contribution I think I have been able to make over this period of time.

Let me begin by saying that I do not consider myself an expert in understanding disability, or the needs and wishes of disabled people. I am aware that there are many strong feelings held by disabled people and by others working with disabled people who are more or less informed on the subject of disability.

I respect the views of people who have different experiences. This chapter is an account of my experience and some of the thoughts that have emerged as a result of my contact with young people in particular circumstances who have 'additional requirements'. I hope this account will contribute to a discussion which enhances our understanding of the work being carried out in this area.

My experience as a psychotherapist has been divided primarily between working individually with children of all ages in therapy and listening to parents and whole families in various therapeutic settings. As well as working and training in clinical settings I have worked in several day and residential special schools including one other school for children with severe physical disabilities. I know what busy and complex places these schools are and the daily challenges they face which require careful thought, and sometimes prompt action when there may be an emergency needing attention. The school referred to in this chapter is no exception and I would like to acknowledge the sensitivity and hard work that is done by a committed staff group led by a compassionate and resourceful head teacher.

THE SETTING

The area in which the school is situated is on the edge of the commercial and business district of the inner-city area. There is not much evidence of a local population but there are substantial residential premises behind the more notice-able shops and offices. The school was purpose-built in the early 1970s. It is mostly all on one level with a large forecourt for school buses to park.

The school premises are not clearly visible from the street. There is a perimeter wall to the front which encloses a fairly unremarkable building. The forecourt has some space for staff parking but this is not encouraged because space outside is just as scarce as space inside the building. There is also a priority need for the school buses to have clear access to the school entrance.

The school has been designed with a raised 'promenade' at the front of the building. This means that the buses that most young people use can reverse up to the promenade and open their back doors on to the same level as the school entrance. This is much easier and quicker than the use of tail lifts when loss of heat to some of the young people is a critical factor. Looking at the front of the school it is clear that the priority is for the students arriving in buses. Ramps at the sides of the school building are there for other forms of arrival.

FIRST IMPRESSIONS

It is interesting to compare first impressions with the experience born out of familiarity. On my first visit to the school (which was during school hours) I remember the sight of the vacant wheelchairs, walking frames and other equip-ment immediately in sight on entering through the front door.

There is, I think, something evocative about entering a school for the first time that may bring to mind strong feelings and memories. There were for me memories of early schooldays; the fear of becoming lost, or not finding one's place in a strange new world. I had a feeling like being the 'new boy' and, for some time, not wanting to stray far from the limited area I knew of the school.

There was and continues to be plenty of activity in a school where so many different professions offer services. There are the various therapists (speech, occupational and physiotherapists) who use the school as their work base. There is a constant flow of trainees, students and various observers. Children are coming and going to such people at different times of the day while class lessons continue without them.

I soon had the thought of being part of a minority of able-bodied people in an environment geared to the needs of people who had different abilities. Here overt disability was the norm. There always seemed to be activity in the corridors. Many staff and students greeted each other when passing, mostly by first names. The corridors were used as extended walking practice areas for those receiving physiotherapy. The atmosphere was positive and the differences imposed by the special needs soon became ordinary in their familiarity.

MY ROLE IN SCHOOL

The Brandon Centre established its work in this school because most of the students would not physically be able to reach the Centre by themselves. In this sense the service is taken out to young people who are in need of it. My role is to offer psychotherapy on one day per week to a number of young people attending this school.

It is not my role to work with the staff or with the families of the people I see. I do meet briefly with some members of staff, and I have had some formal meetings with parents and contact on the telephone. Often there is some discussion needed for parents to give informed consent for their child to be seen. Generally I try to limit the contact I can be seen to have with staff and parents. The staff have such different roles with the young people. They can be very closely involved with personal care or the more formal role of teacher. I have some liaison with external agencies, although once again this has not needed, so far, to be very extensive.

I would explain the need for distance as an important feature of the setting for confidential work to take place. I do not think it is helpful to be seen talking openly to staff who have quite different kinds of relationship with the students. They can allow themselves to be much more open where confidentiality does not have to be central to their role. I am often conscious of the very close community that exists in school and the proximity of students and staff. I imagine that students may sometimes wonder, when they see staff talking, whether they themselves might be the subjects of discussion.

I believe that I have an accepted place in school where relations with all staff are cordial. I am aware that there are many ways in which fantasies may arise about 'counselling' and 'counsellors' and I do depend on good working relationships with a staff group I have found helpful and friendly.

BACKGROUND TO THE SCHOOL SERVICE

There has been a child psychotherapist working in this school for more than 4 years. I am aware of benefiting from the good working relationship that has been built up between my predecessors and the head teacher and staff. Hence, a reasonably smooth transition was possible when I took over this position. I was able to meet with the colleague I was to replace and visit the school at the end of term. I was also introduced to some of the staff and students I would be continuing to see in the new term.

There were a number of young people who had already been seen in regular once-weekly therapy for a period of time. Some of the students were therefore familiar with the setting of regular and confidential counselling.

Continuity in supervision at the Brandon Centre has contributed to a reasonably smooth transition between therapists. Knowledge of the previous work with the young people, and familiarity with the setting has kept a perspective that is so often lost when there is a break between therapists.

STUDENT PROFILE

Students are referred to the therapist by the head teacher. She may confer with particular members of staff before discussing a referral with the young person and their parents. There may also be other agencies to inform or to give consent. I should like to acknowledge that whilst I may be treating a child in therapy at school I am aware of the many unmet needs of parents and siblings.

There are a few children looked after by the local authorities but the majority are living with parents. There are many single parents and step-parents looking after the young people attending school.

I do not know of any children who come to the school from the immediate area. Most children come from the funding borough or the neighbouring ones, with a few travelling in from outlying boroughs at some considerable distance. There are over fifty children on the school roll and attending on a regular basis; this includes nursery, infants, junior and secondary departments.

More than half the children attending this school have an identifiable minority ethnic origin. Efforts are made to address the specific needs with regard to religion, culture, diet and language and these provisions are kept under review. However, there are no members of the teaching or therapy staff who are obviously from an ethnic minority. There are, however, some people from an ethnic minority on the care staff. This is surprising in an authority that has had clearly established policies in this area for a considerable length of time. There are people with disabilities on the care staff and teaching staff.

Sometimes child protection concerns arise. I have always followed these matters up, first with the child, by encouraging them to speak to the head teacher who has the designated responsibility. If the child is reluctant to do this by themselves I have offered to accompany them, with their agreement, or to speak on their behalf with the head teacher. Issues which have come up in therapy regarding 'child protection' include inappropriate touching between young people and hostility between siblings. However, some of the children I see have previously experienced physical, emotional and sexual abuse which has been investigated on disclosure.

NEGOTIATING WORK: PSYCHOTHERAPIST AS COUNSELLOR

Working with the school and around the school timetable can be quite difficult. There are particular lessons that a child or a teacher would prefer not to be missed. There are some students who would be only too happy to miss some or any lessons! There are young people who only want to come to see me outside all lesson times, particularly in their GCSE year. There is no convenient time for therapy. Something is always being missed whilst coming to see me. Changes to the timetable are frequent which means that the difficulties about finding suitable times for some young people can be repeated several times a year. It is hard to achieve a settled rhythm to the work especially as school terms dictate the beginnings and endings of contact as well.

I understand that the intention of the school is to offer as much of the curriculum as possible and there is no deliberate attack on the functioning of therapy. There is a high degree of co-operation with the staff and therapy times are found for everyone I see with little disruption normally.

Some young people would not make it to their session if I did not go and find them and collect them. Sometimes this means they need to be pushed in a wheelchair or standing frame, or escorted in some form. Others are rigorously punctual, or early in their eagerness.

In school the child psychotherapist is referred to as the school counsellor. I believe this is felt to be the most acceptable and understandable form of address. I have wondered whether the desire was for a person who would seem more appealing and accessible in some way and the title of psychotherapist could be in some way discouraging to young people and their parents.

One might look at the meanings that 'counsellor' and 'psychotherapist' might hold for school staff both consciously and unconsciously. I believe there are some very real worries sometimes in the network of family and professional services about the powerful feelings that may be stirred up in young disabled people involved in emotional work. 'Counsellor' has, I imagine, something more approachable and accessible associated with it. Perhaps it has an air of something more manageable to it also?

I have been introduced to the school by my first name which also has a meaning in how I am to be seen by staff and students. Again, I believed I had little choice in this and it would have felt hard to insist on a change without setting a precedent I did not wish to set. Staff can be referred to by their first names or their last names, including the head teacher. These changes are subtle and yet fundamental to one's identity and how work in the transference may take place. I believe there is a wish to set a precedent of friendliness which tries to offset the fantasy of harm that could be done to vulnerable young people in personal therapy. I need to remind myself that in other places I am uniformly referred to by my last name without any actual damage to the therapeutic relationship.

In clinical work I am used to a more formal setting which keeps a respectful distance and security for the emotional work I learned during training. The school setting suggests to me a wish to keep the contact informal and friendly. What fantasies might abound otherwise? What is it that one might be asked to agree to unconsciously? It suggests that formality is not friendly. This is not necessarily the case but it does help to ensure there is a seriousness to the process of counselling and therapy which is first identified by the clear structures of time and place.

So much work is undertaken in school that is an attempt to alleviate pain and suffering. There is a reality that also says that in some ways this attempt is not going to stop the pain. What we as professional people find so difficult to deal with is our helplessness in the face of children's pain. That is not to say our work is futile or without benefit. It is to say that often at the end of the day we cannot give children the legs that walk, the arms that lift, or the means to clearly articulate their words.

THE COUNSELLOR'S ROOM

In my experience in other schools I know how difficult it can be to find and pre-serve a space to see students which is private. Pressure on space in school is always great and I know that one cannot underestimate the space that a school gives up for counselling, and which the therapist must safeguard as much as possible – against even the friendliest of intrusions from passing children!

The room I see students in is the occupational therapist's office. This is a room full of 'papers and parts'. It is a typical working office and not the deliberately empty therapy room I am accustomed to in other places. The OT kindly vacates her room for the day I am in school but she frequently needs to come back for additional items.

As one enters this room there are two signs. One picturing the work of the OT and one picturing the counsellor, with the words for these two professions under-neath. All around the school there are similar symbols describing objects in symbol and word form. The counsellor is depicted as two 'matchstick' people sitting opposite each other at a table.

In my room I have kept a minimum requirement of two chairs and a table despite whatever else might be happening there in the way of other things coming and going. However, I cannot evade the impact and allure that some of the mysterious packages and articles that appear from week to week have on some of the students I see.

Each student has half an hour. This is partly to accommodate as many as possible in the time available and to fit around the school timetable. I need to remember who I am seeing in what is a rapid turnaround from one student to another and who may need a space made for a wheelchair or to sit next to the radiator for extra warmth. It feels like a small but important matter to have remembered who is expected and that I have made the appropriate space for them physically as well as emotionally.

Some children seem to be oblivious of the changes in the room environment. Others are drawn to every small or large addition or removal.

DAILY LIFE

It is true that in school with other young people challenged by severe physical difficulties there is not the same emphasis of standing out as the 'disabled person' with all the unwanted attention this may bring. In school the majority of people are disabled. So here perhaps is more of an opportunity to put all that to one side for a few hours and know that others have done the same.

The attitudes to the young disabled are neither soft nor indulgent. A lot of extra effort is called upon to walk that extra step or make disobedient and recalcitrant muscles do what they have been instructed to perform. Staff can be very demanding and sometimes the students complain that they are too hard on them. It is very difficult for me to know the truth of this, but it sounds like the sort of thing anyone might say or have said about their experience of school.

The students in this school are familiar with many kinds of changes in their environment that might affect them to a greater or lesser degree. They have many more routines than able-bodied young people because of their special needs. They have feelings about their dependency. In many ways they express regret and frustration for what they would like to do for themselves. Yet there is an acceptance for the importance of the help that is at hand. Behaviour problems arise more often at home where families may be struggling to meet the needs of younger children as well as the disabled young person in school.

Classrooms usually have their doors open and children may require classroom assistants to help them go to the toilet or attend to some other function as well as directly helping in work tasks with individual children.

It becomes clearer how the psychotherapist is likely to be regarded in the transference with these working arrangements. There is less of a stigma in seeing the counsellor in a school where so much help and attention are being given as a matter of daily and sometimes hourly need.

School for most of these young people is not the place to shun and shy away from. It is the main source of stimulation and social intercourse. It is the time and place where many of them are in their most conducive environment. It is a place where they can feel wanted and accepted whatever their difficulty might be. It is, perhaps, the place where they can feel most 'normal'. It is where they can move with more freedom in an environment specifically engineered to address their needs and abilities.

Some of the students I do not see appear to take an interest in looking at me curiously either when passing my room and looking in, or going to fetch someone from class. But they tend to keep their distance in an attitude that conveys to me some understanding or acceptance of my presence as something different from the staff who are so very 'hands on' in their relationships with the children.

It is hard to keep things private in school. Respect and privacy appear to be exercised appropriately. However, it is not hard for personal matters to be generally known. I have demonstrated my understanding of confidentiality by refraining to comment at all on whom I see and whom I know whilst explaining why I do this. Even when I can be seen picking up from classroom or playground some of the children I see who need escorting I keep absolutely focused on the young person in question. I think this practice usefully shows the young person how I shall be treating anything they themselves might say or do.

Working in a school means working with the school. Nothing happens without the active support and consent of the staff and head teacher. I have wondered about the question of what kind of working relationship best suits the development of psychoanalytic psychotherapy. If the children could attend therapy in an ordinary outpatient clinical service then that would be the most appropriate place for them to be seen. The nature of their difficulties requires a service to be taken to the school.

The service that is established in school is not a part of school and not a part of the curriculum. The therapist is not a member of staff although nominally answerable to the head teacher.

On Monday, before the school buses arrive, there is a staff briefing meeting for 15 minutes. All the activities in the school and outside are announced and prepared for. Staff who are to be out on activities or absent are identified. Everyone, including the expected visitors to school, are noted in a weekly diary sheet that is circulated and amended during the meeting. It is extremely helpful for me to gain an idea of the life of the school through the staff meetings. The range and diversity of the plans for students are impressive and the level of commitment shown by the staff group is high. The enthusiasm of the staff gives a very positive feel to the environment. Furthermore, in sports and activities it appears there are few barriers to what the young people are encouraged to participate in even when their ability to employ physical control is apparently minimal. There is a different standard used in school to denote involvement when the range of movement that many young people have is severely restricted.

With the universal presence of wheelchairs, motor- or self-driven, and children of all shapes and sizes, on crutches, supports, or walking in their own unique and characteristic way, the corridors are often full and even blocked at break times. Yet there is a feeling I have that collisions rarely occur. These children appear to have developed a dexterity in their movements that might have otherwise been thought to be ungainly. But there can be scenes of purposeful colliding in incidents reminiscent of any ordinary schooltime show of playful bravado.

THE WORK WITH YOUNG PEOPLE

The primary aim of the service is to offer a counselling service to adolescents who, it is understood, are experiencing the difficulties of adolescent development and the impact their disability presents to them in this phase of their lives. When most adolescents are struggling with the physical and emotional demands of rapid growth and change, the teenagers at this school are undergoing similar processes with the additional factor of physical and learning problems that are likely to impede their progress.

There are many young people at this school who enter puberty at the same time as other young people and there are some who have developmental delay which can affect adolescent growth and sexual maturity. The work that I undertake individually with adolescents in school takes account of their abilities to communicate. Where there are difficulties because of physical or learning problems I have had to adapt my technique accordingly.

At one end of the continuum there are adolescents who can think and talk with an adult in an age-appropriate manner. At the other end there are some moderate to severe learning problems that require a different approach that includes an emphasis on communication through play and dramatic enactment of roles and circumstances. Whilst this may appear to be similar to techniques of therapy with younger children it is important to bear in mind the differences that are present in an older age group and how physical, psychological and sexual maturation are expressed through these alternative means of communication.

A developmental delay is not necessarily global and one should not assume a young person who has limitations in their range of communication is at the same stage of development as a younger child. They are not necessarily without the means of perception that those of the same chronological age possess.

A further technical issue arises in the treatment of young people with communication difficulties. I have seen adolescents who have little or no means of using their voices. They can be regarded as having learning problems that may be more social in origin as a result of this particular form of problem. I feel that their restricted means of communicating may contribute to a misperception of their ability and lead to a passivity in them and a consequent under-stimulation.

Young people with these restrictions communicate with electronic keyboards which voice the words tapped in by the student. Additionally they may have a specially compiled book with pictures, words and phrases they can point out. These devices need to be familiar to the 'listener' as well as the user. The selection of odd words and phrases tends to leave much room for interpretation and mis-interpretation that can easily lead to frustration when meanings are not picked up and understood.

When seeing a young person with communication difficulties I am aware that the chosen word may be full of meaning for the student. However, it is not always easy to discern the intention and emotion behind it, as well as the grammatical construct implied but unexpressed in the selection of a word by pointing in a book.

Young people with speech impairments can be very sensitive when their expressions in words are not immediately understood. When they are asked to repeat themselves for clear comprehension and the meaning of their words remains unclear, frustration can occur very quickly.

The awareness that the emerging adult has of their own identity can be difficult to determine. There are always limitations to abilities and adolescence is a time when physical and emotional competence can be tested by each individual to their own perception of the limits. For the young person with a severe disability one can imagine there being emotional reactions to the realisation that their disability may impede them in a way that is significantly different from before adolescence, and impede them significantly more than less challenged, non-disabled adolescents. This may be as much in the manner in which the young person perceives their own difficulties as it is the way in which their difficulties continue to present problems.

The presence of sexual feelings in some of the young people I see is, I believe, very clear as they are in most people at this age. However, the expression of these feelings is often quite muted or apparently absent.

The teenage years are primarily the ones where there is usually a distinctive move away from the influence of parents and towards the peer group. During this period, group approval can be very strongly sought or imposed demanding conformity to its own principles.

The families of the students at this school perhaps remain more directly involved with them where physical difficulties often make exploration and independence more difficult to achieve. There is a response I have had from several students who do not look forward to the weekend in the same way that another child might. There is often more activity and socialising potential in school than there can be at home. If the young disabled person is in a large family with the competing interests of younger siblings and working parents they can be left in a less stimulating environment at home than at school.

DISCUSSION

Can a school-based psychotherapy service be effective? In the USA some research has shown that students have benefited from an increase in school-based mental health services. There is little evidence in the scope of this research that one particular theoretical approach is more effective than another (Weiss *et al.*, 1999). As a psychoanalytically trained psychotherapist I have found that the students I see can benefit from counselling based on the understanding of feelings through analytical concepts that would not be available without a specific training.

I would like to consider the relationship between physical ability and disability in the emerging adult. Usually adolescents have some degree of difficulty as they experience the physical, mental and emotional changes of the teenage years. The drive for growth completion can be periodically rapid and vigorous. Some adolescents are alarmed by these changes over which they have little or no control. Some are pleased with developments and the newfound powers and abilities they bring. The familiar image of volatile and labile emotional states in the adolescent is a very real experience for some. Briefly, we know that the adolescent person is seeking his/her adult identity consciously and unconsciously. They may experiment with different ideas and behaviours in pursuance of this goal. But what happens to the severely disabled adolescent?

Many of the same changes occur physically and mentally. Disabled adolescents are interested in the same things as other adolescents. They are subjected to the same influences; they have the same heroes and watch the same television programmes. They listen to the same music and support the same football teams. So where are the differences?

As I have said, it seems that the disabled young person in some respects may need to mature very quickly. However, additional help from parents and organisations may result in more physical dependence that implies greater emotional dependence. Disabled young people have had to adapt to physical conditions, usually from a very early age, that directly affect their daily lives. They will have some realisation regarding their differences in ability and how they need to learn specific skills to compensate for this difference. Nevertheless, with all the forms of help available, and the modification of some public attitudes in favour of awareness and acceptance of disability, there is not a great amount of personal emotional help available for these young people. There seems to be a feeling of helplessness about the ability to help those with a disability. There is a tendency to ignore the disability in a wish to accept the person with the disability as normal and equal. With such a move to promote positive attitudes it might become more difficult to be in touch with feelings underlying the inability to perform as one would wish to.

Adolescence has been defined as a separate stage of development, separate from childhood and adulthood (Leffert and Petersen, 1995). Research also shows how adolescence has changed, beginning earlier in some countries and under greater pressure from external factors such as parental separation and peer aspirations. Negative life events are associated with an increase in psychosocial disorders.

'Going through a phase' is one of the most common explanations in general usage applied to adolescent behaviour. There is an attempt in this statement to reassure and normalise incidents of behaviour that might otherwise be considered more worrying and alarming by adults who hold responsibilities for adolescents. The worrying behaviour is expected to stop of its own accord when development has finished. Sometimes adolescents resort to extreme or 'out of character' behaviour without consciously knowing why. Perhaps they are testing out how such behaviour makes them feel or whether it makes them feel 'something', rather than the 'nothing' that more normal behaviour produces.

Sometimes the more extreme 'out of character' behaviour can be seen as a way to preserve psychic structure that otherwise might give way, in this period of turbulent change and development, to regression and fears of dissolution. It is like standing on the edge of the parental nest and trying to gird one's personal resources for a jump into the unknown when the thoughts of comfort and security in the nest behind them are enticing the adolescent to further inaction, safety and 'anti-development'.

In adolescence individuation occurs through development. Part of that development is progressive and part is regressive as the objects of childhood are left behind and then revisited before the greater challenges of adulthood are attempted (Blos, 1967).

How does this apply to the disabled young person? The stages of development are already challenged by the severity of the specific disability, to whatever degree each young person has physical and learning problems. The history of the adolescent with a disability may have been marked with incidents of failing to reach some of the targets and standards that other young people without severe disability have attained.

It is worrying that so many young disabled people seem to have ambitions which appear to be unrealistic. But it is also quite usual for young people to have far-reaching plans or fantasies about the future. Why should the ideas of disabled young people be seen any differently? I believe they should be encouraged to achieve to their greatest ability but I do not think this should incorporate illusory thinking.

Then who is to say what is illusory? Adults are often surprised and confounded by young people in particular. After all, it is the primary task of the young to question and modify the world they inherit even if this may sometimes appear to be turning something upside down.

It may be more appropriate to consider illusion as imagination and therefore something which is to be encouraged, especially in the young, and particularly in the school setting where so much work depends on developing a creative frame of mind. But the mind also depends upon fantasy as a precursor to action and communication. I would like to describe some impressions I have received in this area of work.

I have seen disabled adolescents who appear to hold very firm ideas about what they will do after they leave school that seem quite unrealistic. I have also encountered young people who seem to live more in a fantasy world to the extent that they appear to need me to believe that their fantasies are true. I am thinking that these fantasies are usually counter to the physical reality. They are communicating a desire that they are competent to perform in accordance with ordinary adult expectations.

It seems that the strengths of these fantasies may be linked to anxieties about death. Many of these young people will never achieve full adult potential. Many will die young and some do not even have a clear diagnosis and therefore have even more uncertainties about their future. Parents, teachers and other concerned adults, far from wanting to take away these fantasies, may find themselves supporting them, or at least not challenging them. Some parents fight for their children's rights and for services that the children may have difficulty using. In these cases the important factor may be the acknowledgement of the rights of a group who have been marginalised and discriminated against. It also allows parents to devote their energies to a 'worthwhile cause'. In some circumstances parents may feel they can be useful and seek to overcome some of their own fantasies about having damaged their children. Parents can feel overwhelmed with the feeling that they are responsible for the disability their child has suffered.

Children too have an awareness of this being someone's fault, theirs or someone else's. I have heard many angry feelings expressed towards parents and doctors. Doctors tend to be easier and safer to blame for mistakes that lead to disability. There is often an uneasy relationship between parents and health and social services. The anger and frustration felt towards professional services for not caring enough, or not being competent enough to prevent disability and all that ensued from this event, can prevent a much-needed partnership from being effective.

When the ex-England football manager Glen Hoddle was quoted for saying that disability may come as a punishment from God, he was severely criticised by the media and many others. But what he said is also what some people believe, even what some disabled young people and parents believe. It makes me think it is a very dangerous area to express views in. There is much denial in young people who do not want to think about something painful that may not be healed, such as a lifelong disability. But we are all in danger of colluding with an unhelpful untruth about disability, our own feelings about it, and our helplessness in the face of it. There is something outrageous about seeing children in this state and whether we wish to include them or distance ourselves from them.

SUMMARY

I have tried to show the way in which work with young people in a school setting can take place and that, within some limitations, there can be many advantages to this setting. There are adaptations needed for therapeutic work to take place but I feel that it is necessary for the needs of the client group and that enough of the basic requirements can be preserved to enable useful work to be done. The school setting would not suit every therapist nor every young person.

There are different opinions concerning what kind of a service is best suited to the emotional needs of young people in a special school setting. Different approaches may all have something to contribute. I can say that in over 2 years most of the young people referred have attended regularly and they have seen their therapy time as very important to them.

I would like to emphasise the need for understanding of the institution when attempting to conduct emotional work on the premises. The impact of institutional processes is central to the success of this kind of work. I feel that it is necessary to develop the therapeutic space as a temporary institution within the host organisation and that work always needs to be done to ensure the relationship between the two is perceived to be benign.

There is no assumption in this chapter that every young disabled person needs therapy because of their disability. But research has suggested that developmental delay may increase the likelihood of psychosocial disorders in adolescence and adult life (Graham and Rutter, 1985). The purpose of the outreach service is to provide to a client group that would not be available to them otherwise because of practical reasons. The primary aim of the project is to address the emotional needs of young people faced with the challenges of adolescence. However, the service also recognises that physically disabled young people have feelings to express and among those feelings they will have some about their particular abilities and their limits, however they may perceive them.

References

Blos, P. (1967). 'The second individuation process of adolescence'. *The Psychoanalytic Study of the Child*, vol. 22: 163–86. New York: International Universities Press.

Graham, P. and Rutter, M. (1985). 'Adolescent disorders'. In Rutter, M. and Hersov, L. (eds), *Child and Adolescent Psychiatry: Modern Approaches*, 351–67. Oxford: Blackwell Scientific Publications.

Leffert, N. and Petersen A. C. (1995). 'Patterns of development during adolescence'. In Smith, D. J. and Rutter, M. (eds), *Psychosocial Disorders in Young People: Time Trends and their Courses*, 67–103. Chichester: John Wiley & Sons.

Weiss, B., Catron, T., Harris, V. and Phung, T. M. (1999). 'The effectiveness of child psychotherapy'. *Journal of Consulting and Clinical Psychology* 67(1): 82–94.

Chapter 8

Psychotherapy with bereaved adolescents

Suzanne Blundell

INTRODUCTION

The bereavement service at the Brandon Centre was started in 1994 for adolescent boys and girls aged 12 to 18 years. Mourning in childhood and adolescence can be a natural response to loss that does not require professional intervention. However, in some cases, loss can trigger a maladaptive reaction and make existing problems worse.

The bereaved adolescents who come to the Brandon Centre for psychotherapy often have years of emotional suffering behind them before the actual bereavement and are therefore ill-equipped for 'healthy mourning'. Their mourning process does not follow an ordered structure as described by Worden (1991). For instance, help the young person to first accept the reality of the loss, then work through the pain of grief, then adjust to an environment in which the deceased is missing, so that they then will be able to move on with their lives.

Even though all the young people using the bereavement service at the Brandon Centre have in common the death of a close relative or a friend, they in fact grieve differently. They seek professional help following their bereavement because there are anxieties about a serious disorder occurring. They are referred because their emotional life and their external life are seriously at risk. The referrer recognises that the young bereaved person will not grow out of their problems. Typically they come from backgrounds where a parent was depressed, violent, deprived or, in a minority of cases, was psychotic. They have not been able to form a secure attachment with their parents. The absence of this makes grieving very complicated and excruciatingly painful, especially if one or both of these parents dies. When the young person suffers loss in adolescence they have to mourn the external loss of a close relative at the same time as having to deal with internal losses such as the loss of their childhood. Such losses create feelings of vulnerability and are stressful for every adolescent.

Adolescence is a time when some young people may find themselves increasingly alone as they leave their family for the first time to go to university or college. An actual bereavement just before or at this time can make such normal developmental steps much harder and more painful.

According to some experts on adolescent development, adolescents are especially vulnerable to breaking down (Laufer and Laufer, 1984). Bereavement counselling can make the difference between averting a breakdown and one occurring. Many bereaved adolescents seen as part of this project have a range of disturbances that point to the danger of a developmental or emotional breakdown. The most common disturbances are eating disorders, drug abuse, school phobias, depression, learning difficulties and an inability to make friends or socialise. Many of these disturbances have been there for years. However, a serious bereavement allows these adolescents to feel that they can ask for much-needed help since emotional upset due to the death of a loved one is considered to be an acceptable reason for feeling depressed and upset.

DESCRIPTION OF THE SERVICE

The bereavement service is available on one day a week. As the only therapist working on the project I am able to offer six appointments per week. This is sufficient to meet the actual demand for the service. There is a waiting list but waiting time is short.

The referrals to the service come from teachers, social workers, doctors, psychiatrists, foster-parents, elder siblings and of course the surviving parent. Some older adolescents refer themselves.

As the case examples in this chapter show, the exact timing of the referral and its process are often important and can help to understand the conflicts of the young person as well as the referrer's conflicts.

Deciding the appropriate therapeutic intervention is not always easy and depends mainly on what the young person and the primary carer are able to manage. Some adolescents only come for a very short period, up to five sessions. Others come for long-term help. With younger adolescents I have found that it is important to see the surviving parent as the death of their partner can stir up unbearable feelings and they may be finding functioning as a parent extremely difficult. The same may apply to foster-parents. They may be faced with a foster-child who, because of the death of one or even both parents, is unable to form a meaningful attachment to their new foster-parents and may even act destructively because of much unresolved anger towards the dead parent(s). Supporting the foster-parents as well as the adolescent in these situations can be vital to the recovery of the young person.

I would like to illustrate this and other aspects of the service.

CASE MATERIAL

Bereaved boys

There are gender differences in the way bereaved boys and girls react to loss.

For example, boys can find it harder to return to school after a bereavement than girls can. They are more likely to show their feelings in delinquent behaviour whereas girls tend to be more depressed and turn in on themselves.

Paul

Paul was aged 13 years when his mother referred him to the Brandon Centre. She was worried about him because his 12-year-old brother had died in the school playground, 1 month prior to the referral, suddenly collapsing of a brain haemorrhage. When I met Paul, together with his mother and father, he came across as a very thoughtful and sensible boy who was obviously trying to come to terms with what was an unbelievable and shocking death. Paul's mother was upset and weepy whereas his father was angry. Paul felt confused.

Initially I thought Paul's main problem was being unable to return to school and face his peers. How could he show how upset he felt yet carry on with life in an ordinary way when everything seemed to have changed because of his brother's sudden death? Boys do not talk easily about emotions and feel more pressurised by peers, especially in adolescence, to be strong rather than weak or even to 'cry'. Paul had an added difficulty about going back to school because his brother actually died at school. School for him meant an unsafe and frightening place, which he needed to avoid.

Before this tragedy happened Paul was finding school difficult and, being very sensitive, he was prone to feeling different, easily hurt and criticised. In summary, the tragic loss of his brother made Paul feel increasingly isolated, different and vulnerable.

He often came to me confessing that he had not managed to go to school. I felt he was full of guilt not only about not managing to go to school, but also unconsciously about not having managed to protect his brother from dying. He felt terrible about the rivalry with his brother and arguments and fights they had had in the past. Obviously there were times when he wished his brother had died. He felt equally responsible for all the fights his brother had had with his own peers in the school playground. His worst fantasy was that people at school would say behind Paul's back that his brother was horrible and it was no great loss that he died.

Paul also worried greatly about having to be the only child in the family from now on. He felt more responsible and more pressured to be a 'good' boy. Paul did not dare to tell his mother he was not going to school for fear of getting her worried and upset.

He constantly felt he had to protect her as she was already very upset and weepy. He did not dare to tell his father either, because he would get angry, which was his father's way of showing upset.

Therapy was important for Paul. It gave him a space to think independently on his own, without having to deal with his grieving parent's feelings. It also gave him a safe space to realise that his feelings were normal. This made him feel less confused and guilty. Finally therapy gave Paul the strength to face going on with life. He went back to school and increasingly felt less isolated and more part of the school community.

James

James was a 12-year-old boy who was also referred to the Brandon Centre by his mother who had lost her own father, James's grandfather, only a few weeks before the referral. James was an only child with no father and his grandfather had been a substitute father. His father had left the family when James was 2 years old because of marital rows.

When I saw James and his mother, I observed why James according to his mother did all his grieving 'wrong'. She was very emotional, anxious and crying all the time, which seemed quite intimidating to her son. James showed little emotion. He was uncommunicative and wished he was not at the Brandon Centre with his mother or me. His mother felt the whole world was collapsing as her father, who had acted as a replacement 'husband' for her, was dead. She could think of nothing positive. Unlike his mother whose mind was full of unhappy thoughts, James preferred thinking about all the nice things that had happened when his grandfather was alive. He was even hoping his grand-father would come back soon and he certainly did not want to talk to his mother about his feelings or cry with her. He did not like the word 'death'. I thought that James was desperately trying to hang on to life while his mother appeared to be 'dying' together with her dead father. James seemed unable to talk to his mother because understandably she was very emotional. James said in an angry voice that he could not see why his mother had to cry all the time and that there wasn't anything wrong with him. Research has shown that young people often avoid revealing thoughts and feelings to a parent who is 'too emotional' for fear of upsetting them even more (Christ, Siegel and Sperber, 1994).

I pointed out to James and his mother that they were very different and that James may grieve in his own way which does not involve tears. In my opinion the two were indeed very different, not only regarding their feelings and the way they dealt with them, but also in other ways. Mother had very black hair and James was blond. James felt very worried about what would happen to him and his mother, living together on their own. He missed his grandfather who would take him out for the day and on holidays away from his mother. Andrew Samuels (1985) in his book *The Father* writes that the role of the father is to be active and insert himself between mother and baby as a reminder of the world outside. James lacked a father or grandfather who acted as a male role model and a buffer between him and his mother. He felt, like many fatherless boys do, stuck to his mother which was frightening for him.

He felt intruded upon by his mother's grief and controlled by the demands to cry with her. Unconsciously his mother may well have increasingly clung to her son now as her own father had gone, as well as her previous husband 10 years ago. I wondered whether she would be able to let James be an adolescent and emotionally separate from her.

I suggested to James and his mother that there was no right or wrong way to be sad when someone you really loved dies. He wanted to come with a friend from school who had lost his grandmother and apparently 'didn't cry' either. His mother was initially not very keen on the idea saying that the Brandon Centre was not a 'playground' but after some discussion understood James. I felt that James's wish to share his grief with a friend rather than his mother was quite healthy and whilst in general I see bereaved boys individually or with their parent(s), I encouraged James to come with his friend. Whilst I agreed with James's mother that the Brandon Centre was not a playground, I also felt James needed to think of his grandfather in perhaps a more playful, positive manner to start with, rather than losing all his defences like his mother. She appeared to have very different and more difficult feelings about the death of her own father than James. I have often noticed that bereaved boys (and men) do in fact grieve in a different way from girls (and women). They tend to be more stoical and prefer to talk about positive ways of dealing with a crisis rather than cry. This mechanism, to stay in control, I felt in James's case, needed to be respected. James felt coming with his friend, who had had a similar experience, made him feel less different from other peers, less stigmatised and isolated. For James, being an only child coming to the therapy with a friend felt very important and supportive. Deep down James was frightened of being controlled by adults, be this his mother or me, his therapist. Like most adolescents, he had a wish to preserve his autonomy. Having someone of his own age helped him with this (Wilson, 1982).

Sometimes it is not easy to come to an arrangement regarding a child's therapy that suits both the child and the bereaved parent. However, it is important to respect the parent's feelings and wishes and ideally increase not only the communication between the child and the therapist but also understanding between the parent and the child. After all, they have to live together daily and not just spend 50 minutes a week in each other's company, as is the case in therapy.

Alan

A boy who loses his father who has been absent in his life even before he dies is bound to find mourning additionally difficult, that is the difficulty of mourning someone close to one who one has never actually been that close to. How can one mourn someone one has never had?

Alan was a 13-year-old boy whose father died drowning whilst on holiday in another country. His father had left the family when Alan was 5 years old. Alan had had very little contact with his father until he was 12 years old, which was just 1 year before the father's death. Alan had lost his father just at the age when he had started to bond with him for the first time since early childhood and at the beginning of adolescence. It was a cruel and untimely interruption. Alan like many 13-year-old boys was bewildered and defensive about his grief and talked little. I therefore encouraged him to draw, which he felt was less threatening and which he liked and was good at. Alan's drawings were interesting because they revealed a great deal about his internal world and particularly his thoughts and feelings towards his father.

He drew a man with strong muscles on his arms and legs, broad shoulders, a stiff collar around the back of his neck to protect him and a mouth that turned up on one side and down on the other, which gave him an air of superiority and ambivalence. When I asked Alan what sort of a man he had drawn he explained that it was 'a forest man'. He explained that the man was saying: 'I am stronger than you, I can fight bears'. I understood his picture as a drawing of a fantasy father. Alan wished he had a strong father who was unbeatable and could survive even the most dangerous situations in life's jungle instead of drowning in the sea. Alan needed to create a strong internal father in order to survive himself and to find his own male identity. The reason why Alan's internal father was so idealised and imaginary was to do with the fact that as a boy Alan had very little notion of what a 'real' father was like and therefore of a real role model. Bettelheim (1976) writing about the meaning of fairy-tales elucidates the meaning of a 'forestman' as a 'hunter'. He writes: 'In the unconscious, the hunter is seen as a symbol of protection. It is a suitable image of a strong protective father figure … The hunter is an eminently protective figure who can and does save us from the dangers of our violent emotions and others.' (Bettelheim, 1976, p. 205)

Alan, like other bereaved boys who grow up without their father, showed in his drawings that he missed a protective shield to modify his own aggressive and violent emotions. In my work with bereaved boys who have lost their fathers I have observed how difficult they find working out their aggressive feelings with the caretaker of the opposite sex, i.e. their mother, grandmother or sisters. They may act out these feelings pretending to be strong and tough by becoming delinquent. It is interesting that a recent study of bereaved children has revealed that single mothers and sons had more psychological disturbance than other bereaved children did (Dowdney *et al.*, 1999).

Eventually, as Alan felt safer in therapy, he was increasingly able to change his idealisation of his father for more realistic feelings. He was able to express anger with his father for abandoning him early in his life and again at the age of 13 years, as well as keeping some affection for him.

BEREAVED GIRLS

Cara

Cara referred herself to the Brandon Centre when she was 17 years old because of depression. She had lost her mother when she was 10 years old. Her mother had died of breast cancer after an illness that lasted a year. I wondered why it had taken Cara so long to seek help. Cara's elder sister had already gone to university. Cara was going to leave school after completing her A levels. She would then be faced with the possibility of leaving home too. However, Cara felt very anxious about leaving home because there would not be anyone left to look after father. Cara, as the only remaining woman in the house, felt responsible for looking after her father. However, I also thought Cara was much more worried that if she left home there would be nothing and nobody left. Unconsciously, perhaps, she feared her father would literally not survive without her. Like her mother he might just die. Because of the death of her mother, which Cara had never come to terms with, she did not regard a separation like leaving home and going to university as a natural step. Instead she believed it was catastrophic, like death. Cara's wish for therapy in late adolescence emerged from her need to come to terms with her mother's death and to help her with separations past, present and future.

Cara often said that she felt confused and did not remember anything about her mother except when she was ill and dying of cancer. Like any healthy adolescent, she tried to analyse, understand and criticise her parents and her family in order to find her own identity. However, an important link, her mother, was missing and inhibited this process. Her mother's death undermined this process. She said that she wanted to know what her mother was really like but somehow it was really difficult to talk to her father about her as he also had much unresolved grief himself.

I thought that the death of Cara's mother when she was 10 years old had a profound influence on her emotional development. Edelmann (1994) has suggested that this is the hardest age for coping with the loss of a parent because 'the children are cognitively and emotionally advanced enough to feel profound loss, but their resources for managing their emotions haven't yet reached a level of mastery' (p. 38). I often wondered whether Cara had postponed dealing with her mother's death because she had found her feelings unmanageable and overwhelming with no adults around her who would help her with her grief as a little girl. When Cara's mother was ill and before she died, the adults in her life would not tell her what was happening. She often said to me: 'I always thought mum was going to be alright because everyone told me that she wasn't going to die. Sometimes I feel the whole world lied to me.' The feeling of not knowing the truth left Cara with a deep sense of mistrust, loneliness and fear. It was an infantile fear of a 10-year-old girl who had no 'mummy' to help her moderate her fears, which seemed unresolved even now as an adolescent.

I found it hard myself to get a realistic picture from Cara of what her mother had really been like. Sometimes I forgot, together with Cara, that in fact she did have a mother for the first 10 years of her life. I often thought that Cara must in fact have been identified with an ill and a dying mother as she could only remember her when she was ill. It was not surprising that Cara often had great difficulties in seeing herself as healthy. At times she suffered from a slight eating disorder, which may well have been connected with fears and insecurities about her own body, originating from seeing her dying mother who was not in control of her body, and who had lost her fight with her own body. Cara was often controlling regarding her eating habits. She may well have unconsciously felt a need to control her body rather than eat naturally and see what happens.

Part of my work lay in helping to bring the image of a 'well' mother into Cara's life. After about a year of therapy Cara did manage to have some normal and happy memories of her mother. Her relationship to her own body became healthier as she was increasingly able to 'mother' herself in a more adult way. After leaving school she went to college near London which made it possible for her to stay at home. Finally, after another year of therapy, she was able to leave home as well as therapy in order to stay in college with friends of her own age.

Anna

Anna referred herself to the Brandon Centre just before she was 18 years old. Her mother died suddenly in a car accident 2 months before the referral. Anna wanted help because she was so depressed that she feared she would not be able to keep up her training as a teacher or get up in the morning to do anything else. She had already moved away from home a year before her mother's death. She made the move, as many adolescents do, to get away from home and try to start a new and better life in a place with better educational facilities. She told me that she used to quarrel with her mother, that they used to shout at each other until Anna would either go up to her room or leave the house. Her move away from home was also an attempt for her to renegotiate her previous, often inharmonious, relationship with mother by gaining some physical and emotional distance, as many adolescents need.

When I first met Anna, it was obvious that she felt not only depressed but had also been feeling lonely, angry and not understood many years prior to her mother's death and before she had finally left. She looked heavy and was thinking a great deal about her bad relationship with her mother. She was missing her and felt much guilt. She talked little and often seemed unable to use my presence, going off into a world of her own and leaving me sitting there as if she had left me too and 'gone up into her room' as she used to do at home. This situation no doubt increased her already strong sense of loneliness and would often make me feel like giving up on her.

Anna seemed to be stuck in a state of never-ending mourning. I wondered how to help her out of this paralysed, depressive state.

When Anna spoke, which was not very often, she was very negative. According to her, no one cared about her, no one listened to her, no one liked her and no one was interested in her. This hopeless state pervaded her relationships, for instance at work, at her flat and with her family.

The therapy became stuck and I felt disheartened. However, I was able to understand my feelings of hopelessness and anger towards Anna as a counter-transference reaction, that is as a form of communication about Anna's state of mind. Bolwby (1975) makes the distinction between functional and non-functional anger. He suggests that whenever a loss is permanent, as it is after a bereavement, anger is necessarily without function. Even though Anna knew that her mother was dead, she still continued to act and feel as though it was possible to find and recover her lost mother. However, she also reproached her mother for dying and hence abandoning her.

These feelings were accentuated because she lived away from home. There was a bit of her that was not in touch with how much things had changed at home without her mother, for example she was unaware of how her siblings now had to live differently as their mother was no longer alive. Bowlby describes how non-functional anger can be expressed against the lost person and others who are thought to have played a part in the loss including that person's family and friends. Non-functional anger hinders grieving and can have a destructive impact on the bereaved. On the other hand functional anger has an unconscious goal of assisting the individual in making a reunion and discouraging further separation. Therefore, when expressed towards a living person, such anger can act to promote, and not to disrupt, the bond and thus it can be constructive (Bowlby, 1975).

After much thought about how to help Anna move forward I said to her that I thought her real problem was not only that she did not feel anyone loved her, but that she did not seem to love anyone either. She reacted with tears for the first time. She was also thoughtful as though we had reached an important insight. When I asked her why she was crying she said that she was thinking of her mother. At home she never got on with her mother but then, after she had left home, she started to be able to communicate with her on the telephone. They started to have a closer relationship and then, a few months later, Anna's mother died. This happened just as Anna was about to renegotiate her relationship with her mother into a mature, more equal adult relationship. The timing of the mother's death was particularly tragic for Anna. What might otherwise have been a temporary separation with the hope of reconciliation became for Anna an irrevocable physical and mental fracture. Her guilt was great and contributed to her depression. She wished she could say to her mother: 'Wait a minute, I didn't really mean all the anger and shouting, come back!' (Edelmann, 1994, p. 45). Anna was mourning a 'bad mother' and felt she had only had the 'good mother' for a few months, after she moved away from home. I felt she had not had enough time to learn to love her mother as well as 'hate' her and I think my observations made her realise this tragic fact.

During 2 years of therapy Anna learnt increasingly to feel less angry and less depressed about the loss of her mother. She started increasingly to value what she did have instead of constantly being angry about what she didn't have. I tried to help her by building on her strengths such as the fact that she was doing exams and she was also living in a flat with people her own age. She also had a father and siblings who had a common fate, namely the loss of their wife and mother. I tended to interpret the functioning part of her. By the end of her therapy she talked more about people who were alive than were dead. She even had a boyfriend for the first time in her life who she felt cared for her. She was less isolated and more willing to relate to life. She passed her exams as a primary school teacher and was then able to function as a mature young adult.

CONCLUSIONS

Some thoughts on violent and sudden deaths: suicide and accidents

In my work with bereaved adolescents I have noticed that the most difficult and traumatic deaths to deal with for both adolescent girls and boys seem to be parents or siblings who die because of suicide, violent accidents, sudden deaths or because of war.

It is also the most distressing work for the therapist who often has to deal with intense projections coming from very traumatised patients. All children and particularly adolescents are desperately trying to struggle with key issues such as the predictability of events, a sense of fairness and justice and a mastery of control.

A violent death will affect adolescents particularly badly, leaving them feeling very helpless and out of control and maybe making them wonder whether it is worth their while trying hard to make sense of the world when unpredictable and unfair things are happening to them. For instance a 15-year-old patient whose mother tragically died from a car accident repeatedly asked what the point was of planning the future, doing exams, etc. when one does not know what will happen from one day to another.

A sudden death in adolescence, particularly of a parent, can leave a young person in an unmanageable, conflicting relationship. Death freezes difficult times they may have had with the dead parent. The result is that it is forever conflicted, forever unfinished and unsatisfactory. The guilt and rage can be overwhelming. The young person keeps on saying 'if only I had …'. A sudden death leaves no time to say goodbye, to prepare for life without the deceased and also leaves too much unfinished business. A trusting therapeutic relationship can help the young bereaved to come to terms with all the complicated feelings of guilt and rage in a safe, non-judgemental relationship.

Young people who have a parent who has committed suicide are also particularly prone to feelings of helplessness, anger and bitterness. They find it very hard to come to terms with what ultimately must seem like a total rejection by their parent who could not bother to stay alive for their child. All feelings of being cared for or loved come under attack which can pose difficulties for the therapist who inevitably wants to try to establish a helping relationship. The adolescent, however, is often compelled to transfer his or her feelings towards the dead parent, who so cruelly left him or her, to the therapist and turn the therapeutic relationship into an uncaring, weak and rejecting experience. The demand on the therapist to repair the unrepairable and extinguish the suffering caused by such tragedy can be very strong. But this urge has to be carefully watched so that such an impossible task does not overwhelm the therapist or, worse, get enmeshed with the adolescent's expectations of a magic cure, which can be counter-productive. Supervision is essential for very difficult cases. It gives support and much-needed objectivity when transference and counter-transference feelings are powerful.

Deaths that occur as a result of war also need thoughtful handling. This is particularly so when adolescents from other countries and cultures come for bereavement counselling. For instance a 13-year-old girl who came to the Centre for help because she lost her parents and other relatives in her country of origin constantly felt that I did not understand her culture or her country. Whilst feelings like these are very common in adolescents who have suffered a serious bereavement and express loneliness, helplessness and anger, they can also be painfully true. When dealing with bereaved adolescents from very different cultures, who have suffered serious war traumas, the therapist has to be very honest about the fact that she may well not have the necessary political, cultural or emotional knowledge to deal with such cases. I think it is always important to verbalise to the young person the fact that often one may not understand aspects of their life. In such cases a person who shares the same cultural backgrounds or with a great deal of specialised experience in dealing with war trauma can be more helpful. Children from war-zones often make better use of group therapy than individual therapy. In a group with other young people who have gone through similar experiences the members of the group identify with each other and immediately feel less alone and better understood.

Is working with bereaved adolescents worthwhile?

Many bereaved adolescents who come to the Brandon Centre carry a hope of finding with the therapist a new relationship that might make up for the deficiencies and frustrations of the past, as well as the current life. Bereaved adolescent girls, who have lost their mothers, particularly are looking in me for a 'replacement' mother who will help them to grow up into healthy adult women. Whilst this hope and wish can inevitably lead to frustration and disappointment because the therapist can never be an 'all-embracing saviour' or a 'real' mother, the therapist can in fact be of enormous help. She can represent a safe and reliable 'object' to an adolescent girl who has no mother left to model herself on or exchange ideas and feelings with.

It is easy to assume that when the work of mourning is over and when the bereaved adolescent has sufficiently detached himself or herself from the dead relative to resume a functional life again, the work of therapy is complete. However, what makes working with the adolescents I described in this chapter extremely worthwhile is that many of them, because of the therapy, are able to find more meaning than before their bereavement, in more fulfilling relationships with friends and family as a result of a substantial amount of personal growth. They may also learn to make better use of the present rather than postponing important decisions about their life to the future.

Mothers usually refer adolescent boys who come to the Brandon Centre. As we saw, in many cases they have not had regular contact with their father before his death. Their grief is often not only about the loss of their father, they may mourn for other losses in connection with their own life. They seem to be less hopeful than girls about getting help. The fantasy that I would be able to replace the father is not applicable. However, if they manage to come regularly and over a long period, they too can benefit from a therapeutic relationship which often feels much safer to them than their remaining relationship with their bereaved mother. Ideally they would be better off with a male therapist. Nevertheless the work with these boys is important and worthwhile. In the transference I can become like their father and sometimes like an ideal father they may never have had. I can also appear to them as a strong mother when their mother is distressed and unable to function properly. If therapy is successful, these boys are able to live with an 'internal parent' or voice that helps them to find a personal identity and perhaps even helps them to distance themselves from their mothers. They may be able, as Worden suggests, to find a new and appropriate place for the dead father in their emotional lives rather than giving him up – one that assists them to live meaningfully (Worden, 1991).

References

Barker, P. (1988). *Basic Child Psychiatry*. London: Blackwell Scientific Publications.
Bettelheim, B. (1976). *The Use of Enchantment: The Meaning and Use of Fairy Tales*. London: Penguin Books.
Blos, P. (1965). 'The initial stage of male adolescence'. *Psychoanalytic Study of the Child*, vol. 20, 145–64.
Bolwby, J. (1980). *Attachment and Loss*, vol. 1–3: *Separation*. London: Penguin Books.
——(1980). *Das glück und die Trauer: Herstellung und hösung affective Bindungen*. Stuttgart, Klett-Cotta.
Christ, G., Siegel, K. and Sperber, D. (1994). 'Impact of parental terminal cancer on adolescents'. In *American Journal of Orthopsychiatry* 64: 4.
Dowdney, L., Wilson, R., Maughan, B. *et al.* (1999). 'Psychological disturbance and service provision in parentally bereaved children: Prospective case-counted study'. *British Medical Journal* 19: 354–57.
Edelmann, H. (1994). *Motherless Daughters*. London: Hodder and Stoughton.
Flemming, S. J. and Adolph, R. (1986). 'Helping bereaved adolescents'. In Corr, C. and McNeil, J. (eds), *Adolescence and Death*. New York: Springer.
Laufer, M. (1982). 'Developmental breakdown in adolescence'. In *Adolescence*. Monograph No 8. London: Brent Consultation Centre.
Laufer, M. and Laufer, M. E. (1984). *Adolescence and Developmental Breakdown: A Psychoanalytic View*. New Haven and London: Yale University Press.
Pynoos, R. S. and Nadil, K. I. (1990). 'Children's exposure to violence and traumatic death'. *Psychiatric Annals* 20: 334–44.
Samuels, A. (1985). *The Father, Contemporary Jungian Perspectives*. London: Free Association Books.
Wilson, P. (1982). ' "Don't help me". The troubled adolescent's dilemma in accepting help'. In *Adolescence*. Monograph No 8. London: Brent Consultation Centre.
Worden, W. (1991). *Grief Counselling and Guilt Therapy*. London: Routledge.

Chapter 9

Providing a psychotherapy service in a school for the emotionally and behaviourally disturbed child

Caroline Essenhigh

INTRODUCTION

There are significant differences between working in a clinical setting and working in a school. Whilst some of these pertain to the particular setting, it is possible to generalise and consider how the service is altered by the differences. The single most important question to my mind is 'Has the therapeutic process been compromised by these changes?' In other words, do the drawbacks of working in such a setting outweigh the advantages? My view is that many children who would not otherwise get psychotherapeutic help are now given the opportunity. There are various reasons why these children cannot access NHS provision, the most significant being the absence of a parent or carer who can support the treatment emotionally and practically. However, the advantage of providing therapy in school must be weighed against the greater risk of superseding the parents. Clearly, the younger the child the more important it is that parents are involved in the treatment though limited resources may prevent the ideal of having a colleague work simultaneously with the parents. It is therefore an important question to consider whether time and money might be better directed, for example, in helping families access NHS provision.

The kind of help offered in school is also an important consideration. Individual psychotherapy does not suit everyone nor is it always the right treatment. Sometimes a more structured and diluted contact is needed. It can be an uphill struggle with little profit to engage a recalcitrant adolescent in individual psychotherapy where a group experience might have felt far less threatening. Unlike most of the young people who turn up at the Brandon Centre, few in the school consider that they need help.

There is something in a clinic assessment process that promotes the beginning of self-reflection. Sometimes the therapeutic process gets under way during these preliminary stages because of the sense each member of the family has of being heard and thought about especially if family therapy is the treatment model. It is not really possible to recreate the same atmosphere within the school. This is partly due to the lack of parental involvement but also relates to the nature of the emotional disturbance. Many of the young people in this particular school have borderline features. Delinquency at the more neurotic end of the spectrum is rarer. Ego defences and deficits contribute to the perception of the outside world as dangerous. As a part of that outside world I am viewed with suspicion. Being part of the school can be both helpful and a hindrance to gaining trust and entry to the child's inner world. How to be part of the system but providing a very different experience from within is a challenge and is the main theme of this chapter. The school is an inner-city special school for boys who cannot cope with or be managed in mainstream school because they present with severe emotional and behavioural problems.

My focus and concerns have changed over the 3 years of being in this school and many of the starting-up problems have lessened. But there remain larger political, ethical and theoretical questions that concern the practice of psychotherapy at one step remove from parents or carers. For example, what is the role of parent, teacher and therapist where referral, assessment and treatment are provided within school and what are the aims of the treatment? How is the task of educating separated from the aims of psychotherapy in the child, parent and teacher's mind? It has been unfortunately easy for psychotherapy to be seen by parent and child as a punishment when it is recommended following a spell of 'bad' behaviour no matter how well intentioned the referrer might be.

A BRIEF DESCRIPTION OF THE SCHOOL

The school is located in a small Victorian schoolhouse in a quiet residential street. In all there are about fifty young people attending the school. The teacher–pupil ratio is two teachers[1] to a class of five pupils. In spite of the high ratio of staff to boys and the small size of the school there is a constant and high level of tension which needs managing. The tiny football pitch is in constant use but even so one has at times the feeling of sitting on a powder keg with limited ways of diffusing the blast. Whilst being secondary, younger referrals are on the increase. Nine and ten-year-olds present staff with different kinds of management problems to those of 11- and 12-year-olds who are different again to 13 plus. There are marginally more black young people than white and most are second generation, or more, British. There are a small number for whom English is not their first language. Occasionally new arrivals to the UK include those with refugee status. At the time of writing there is no ethnic minority representation among qualified teachers but the school is trying to redress this. The gender and colour of the psychotherapist is also a matter for consideration. While issues surrounding racial and sexual identity are extremely wide and cannot be usefully simplified, it is a fact that many black families have been, or feel themselves to have been, discriminated against. A psychotherapist who can more easily allay parents' anxieties about the stigmatising of their son by white professionals can make a difference between success and failure

1 'Teachers' includes assistant teachers and class assistants.

in getting psychotherapy started. Similarly, a psychotherapist who can become an alternative role model may on occasion have an extra string to his bow.

Being based in the school inevitably means that one becomes part of the system and affected by how the system operates. It is difficult not to feel frustrated by rules and regulations which satisfy administrative, financial or political needs but which do not always have the best interests of the child in mind. For example, one consequence of the extensive closure of such schools is that the young people travel from all over London, some travelling nearly 4 hours a day. The younger boys arrive in minicabs or special buses which must add to the cost. The distance and cost for parents also does not facilitate good parent/teacher relationships. The logistics for getting the boys home at the end of the day is such that after-school activities are impossible. For many, the school is the main source of friends and links to the child's community tend to weaken. It is also true that the stigma attached to attending such a school is alive and thriving. Few of the young people I see have friends in their own neighbourhood; they tend to gravitate towards boys who are on the edge of exclusion.

The shortage of special schools also means that there are many more referrals than places and constant pressure to take more than the teachers feel able to manage. Referral follows the permanent exclusion from mainstream school, usually from more than one school. The reason for exclusion is generally to do with the child being beyond the control of the teachers and his subsequent failure to respond to help offered whether in school or through the local mental health services. The kind of help that might be offered within the school tends to be educational though many large comprehensives now have counsellors. NHS provision usually breaks down due to the inability of these vulnerable families to make use of the help offered.

All the boys arriving at the school, with the occasional exception, have been statemented, that is undergone an assessment of educational and psychological needs. The majority of boys are diagnosed as having some kind of learning delay or difficulty such as dyslexia. Attention Deficit Hyperactivity Disorder is also commonly diagnosed. The difficulty with these assessments is that in a large number of cases so many awful life experiences have occurred which make it difficult to know what is primary in considering the emotional and cognitive problems. It does not take long before a minor perceptual problem becomes major as a result of a poor environment. Anna Freud's concept of developmental lines is particularly helpful in thinking about the interrelation of genetic, biological and environmental factors. It helps in assembling a picture of a child's development by conceptualising the following processes: maturation, adaptation and structuralisation of the personality. For example, a difficult-to-settle infant, becoming a child with low frustration tolerance, may provoke certain responses in an overburdened mother leading to a cycle of battles. The pattern of relating may lead to maladaptive defences in the developing psyche of the child. These in turn interfere with his cognitive and emotional development. Further negative experiences may then consolidate the difficulties and lead to even more detrimental ways of coping.

Another factor that is common to this group is the emotional unavailability of either parent often due to mental illness. Maternal depression is frequently found. Drug and alcohol abuse among parents is high and with it comes an increase in aggression and violence. Most boys appear to have witnessed some level of violence at home. A few have fathers who have received prison sentences for assaulting the child's mother. Physical punishment of children is ubiquitous within this population and many of the boys have been placed on child protection registers at some point in their lives for physical abuse. Although some boys have disclosed sexual abuse there is probably a higher number who have not disclosed this, but one suspects there has been some kind of sexual abuse. Emotional neglect is also ubiquitous.

Absent fathers is a tremendously important factor contributing to these young peoples' emotional difficulties. It is a factor that does not decrease as the child gets older but has a different impact at each stage of development. The powerful yearning for a father figure frequently underlies rivalrous and acrimonious relationships with male staff. Often it seems that the rage with absent or frightening fathers is displaced on to mothers. This too distorts the relationship between the child and female members of staff. The powerful projections take their toll; one teacher told me that when feelings of hatred arose in her she knew it was time to take stock and to think about what the child was trying to achieve with the provocation, by which time she generally felt free of the 'pull'.

A HOLDING ENVIRONMENT

A 'holding' environment is one that facilitates rather than undermines the treatment process and it can be seen from the perception of treatment as a punishment how this might be disrupted in such a setting. It is also in the nature of delinquent adolescents that they will exploit any weaknesses in the system. This exploitation is often the result of paranoia and projected aggression; the adult is all too easily seen as the enemy. It may also reflect a maladaptive struggle to achieve a sense of safety by rendering the adult ineffective and powerless.

The first therapy room, an under-used library, was not ideal but it was surprising how little damage was done to the books. The toys brought by me received most attention. The new room was far better and had a little corridor and second door so that there was a slightly more private and separate feel about it. A bolt on the inside of the door is essential. It is not possible for teachers to prevent boys intruding into sessions. This does not prevent sabotage by the client who invites all and sundry to share his session. Another popular use of the room is to treat it as a safe base from which to hurl insults or launch attacks on those passing by. Working with staff to devise strategies for dealing with these situations not only helped with containment but also demystified therapy for staff. There is no magic: we struggled together.

On the whole, such excessive acting out is the province of the pre-pubertal group. The 13 years plus group tends to stage a more manageable protest, although there were notable exceptions and these generally did not manage to stay in the school. Puberty is a very difficult time, as one would expect, but in several cases boys have resurfaced and come back into therapy after a year's break. One great advantage of being in the school is the possibility of maintaining some contact and being available when the young person feels able and ready to start again.

One consequence of puberty is the growth spurt that leads to the possibility of the young person becoming stronger than an adult. Knowing that one can be physically stopped affords a sense of safety to the latency child, which is frequently tested. Discovering new strength seems to herald a realisation that new controls are needed. Pent-up frustration is more likely to be directed to objects rather than people. Again, the exceptions include those whose self-perception and reality testing are distorted and those with severely disturbed super ego development.

The following is a typical beginning but for purposes of confidentiality is not an actual client.[2]

Ben, a very lively and well-built 13-year-old, has been at the school a number of years. He joins his classmates in deriding therapy, something for 'psychos' but he is relatively good-natured when in conversation with me. I have observed him around the school and seen a volatile, immature young person given to bullying but also occasionally generous. During one lesson Ben, at the back of the room, started to show pictures of naked women. A large and unpopular boy tried to peer over his shoulder. Ben turned on him viciously calling him a 'fat cunt' to which the boy responded by calling Ben's mum 'a slag', making some reference to the picture. Ben began punching this boy and did not stop until physically restrained by teachers. After the event Ben was taken to the head and remained unrepentant. All he can remember is that his mother had been insulted which felt justification enough. Outraged at being sent home he delivered more verbal abuse and stormed out of the office sweeping desks clean on his way. Such events were escalating and the staff worried about being able to keep Ben. When Ben begins punching he seems unable to stop himself and is unconcerned about the injuries he might inflict. Moreover, he refuses to acknowledge that he is ever in the wrong. His divorced parents are at their wits' end and also preoccupied with their new families. Ben goes back and forth between the parents but usually to father for punishment. It has been difficult to get their co-operation, they will not come to meetings with staff and certainly not together. Under threat of permanent exclusion Ben agrees to come and see me. His parents agree to psychotherapy whilst remaining aloof and resistant to working with the educational social worker at the school.

Ben arrives to his first session and falls silent. He doesn't really have a problem,

2 Throughout this chapter references to individuals are fictitious.

he tells me. He is only coming in order to get everyone off his back. I say, 'It must feel as if I too am here only to make you behave'. He gives me a sullen nod. He stares at the toy tray and touches nothing. Touching anything might look like wanting to stay, it might also threaten his strong wish to be seen as grown up. I try engaging the reasoning part of him, what did he think was going on, how was it that it was always him that got into trouble? A string of invectives about those who are against him comes out. I feel quietly jubilant that he hasn't left the room yet. At the end I try to make him feel less pressured and free to come back by saying that we will meet for five sessions to get to know each other and see if we both think it will be helpful. He agrees and leaves. Next week I have to hunt high and low, he slouches in looking defiant. I think over the previous week, had my final words made him feel uncertain and rejected? Had the outpouring made him anxious about consequences? Has the pressure to come receded so swiftly? I end up trying very hard to make contact and he realises that he is in the driving seat and that I want him to come. At this point there are various options: he might come back but only on his terms, which means that if I say anything uncomfortable or it gets 'boring', he will leave; or he won't come back at all.

I have frequently found myself working terribly hard, coming up with all kinds of possible feelings that a young person might have about seeing me. I dither between the idea of trying to 'make friends' or maintaining a more objective stance. Whatever their view is of this strange adult pretending she has no hidden agenda, they often do stay. With teenagers like Ben, however, there is such a fear of not managing and of someone seeing the stupid, mad or childish bits that they do not come back.

Another difficulty is with the more borderline young person who is unable to manage his anxiety in the room. Alex immediately began with a perverse game. He poured out sexual insults then ran, hoping I would give chase. I felt responsible for his whereabouts and would unwisely try and keep track of him. It was soon agreed that a member of staff would register his movements, I would stay put. It is a frustrating but rather common happening to find oneself being the immediate cause of manic flights around the school and not in any position to address the anxiety. There are times when I have talked with the young person during break time about what has happened and verbalised the anxiety at staying in the room. It is interesting how a split way of relating can be maintained, friendly and reality based outside the room, full of fearful projections in the therapy room. It has often seemed to me that the possibility of touching base outside facilitates therapeutic contact by challenging their belief that I have been hurt or driven away.

Adam illustrates the difficulty of trying to engage teenagers who are in the sway of the adolescent process and wanting to separate from parents but terrified of being alone. His mild criminal activities and indifferent manner remind me of Aichhorn's statement that 'manifest dissocial actions are fully determined as the result of emotionally charged mental processes' a statement easy to forget when faced with mindless acts that appear born of boredom. The wish of the young person to present himself as some kind of 'rebel without a cause' reinforces the stereotyping. The ability to charm adults whenever necessary also hinders recognition of the depth of the underlying emotional difficulties. Adam's mother was deeply depressed and needy. His violent father disappeared when Adam was very young but lived on in mother's vivid recollections. Separating from his mother meant identifying to some degree with his father. Superficially the destructiveness looked like father's behaviour. In the course of 10 months of irregular meetings it appeared that Adam was fighting a more primitive battle. He was struggling to stay alive and not succumb to a depression that felt to him like dying. Suicidal thoughts were hinted at but denied. It was not uncommon for him to be phobic about the room and then we would talk outside.

It is hard for such a teenager to allow a new attachment to occur but also very hard to analyse a defence that is so gratifying. Acting the 'rebel' provides a kind of identity and sense of belonging. The delinquent acts may also represent perverse or fetishistic fantasies that are unlikely to surface outside intensive treatment – if then.

Sometimes, in agreeing to changes in the setting I feel manipulated and at other times it is clearly needed. Occasionally I have begun therapy in the teacher's room with a trusted teacher present. This is particularly helpful with sexually abused boys who are understandably frightened of being alone with a stranger. Even when one knows that as the fear recedes manipulation takes over it seems important for the child to have the experience of being in control so long as it is eventually interpreted. But sometimes the gratification of having two people for 40 minutes[3] proved too attractive. On one occasion it was quite possible to have the teacher leave but premature moves towards my room led to total withdrawal. There is a fine line between making contact and colluding with the pathological part of the personality. Knowing that everything else has failed with this particular young person and that time is running out for him, he may be on the verge of permanent exclusion, one feels tempted to stretch the boundaries of treatment and keep searching for a point of contact. If he is still attending sessions then there is still hope. But there are others waiting to take his place and there is the nagging suspicion that one is feeding a narcissistic need and nothing more. There are also the omnipotent rescue fantasies of the therapist to disentangle.

REFERRAL AND ASSESSMENT

A well-managed referral and good assessment dramatically improves the chances of getting psychotherapy off the ground. But here I found myself falling between two models and in a dilemma that I have not resolved. To initiate a clinic system requires much more time from staff. There would have to be meetings with the

---

3 It became very difficult to have sessions of different length to class times but one advantage of the shorter time was being able to see more children.

teacher who wanted to refer a child, with the deputy head who is an educational social worker, between teacher and parents and possibly three-way meetings with all of us. There would also have to be someone, probably the child's teacher, to help him think about coming to see me. There are just not enough free staff hours in this school for this to happen regularly. Occasionally it worked.

The other approach is for me to be proactive, for example talk to children in the playground, follow up any indications that a child would like to come and talk, pick up on likely candidates in staff meetings. This means being available, having an open door when not actually in session and running a kind of counselling service with the hope that out of these visitors some may make the transition to psychotherapy. It is always surprising to discover that some of these early chats are well remembered some time on and may have played a part in their return months if not years later.

In the end I continued to use both approaches and perhaps, looking back, the different ways of starting had something to do with different pathologies. There was a certain kind of visitor to my room who I would almost ignore, continuing with whatever I had been doing. I might answer his questions but would ask none. My observations of him around the school remind me of Hoffer's description of the imposter. There is nothing genuine in his communication and he is clearly out for a little diversion. The theft of a toy or rapid graffiti on his way out belies his frustration but rather than verbalise this I merely ask him to return the toy and spell out that this is my room and he may only remain so long as he treats it with respect. But I might then engage him in conversation if we meet elsewhere in the school. It was not thought out on my part, but in retrospect a response to feeling manipulated. Words are empty of meaning, merely a tool for exploiting. Speaking when I choose and not when he decides perhaps in some way lets him know that I have a mind of my own and that I have noticed and thought about him. It might also lead to a more conscious curiosity about what it is that he isn't getting.

In contrast, one 10-year-old who had come in for a chat two or three times made an effort to engage me. He wanted something from me and was delighted when I offered a regular time. Those who were particularly keen were particularly needy and looking for mothering. Some were well and truly stuck at a pre-Oedipal level; others had the appearance of taking flight from genital phase interests. The absence of an involved father suggests that one unconscious motive for coming might be to find an adult who can rescue them from an enmeshed maternal relationship whilst overtly seeking to repeat the intrusive pattern in order to feel safe.

It can be seen that the balance of engaging and assessing means that reaching a diagnosis can take some time. Yet assessing the young person's suitability for psychotherapy is an important part of the process. His inability to stay in a room with me would suggest that psychotherapy is not the right recommendation. I have to say that the lack of alternatives does make one persist. Referrals to other services have never succeeded with the exception of the Brandon Centre, in particular to the conduct disorder project (see Chapter 10). This has worked because of the proximity of the Centre and my connection to it. One other alternative, when a severely disturbed child refuses all offers of help, has been to work with parents, the usefulness of which has been hard to gauge.

The more structured referral was particularly important for the older teenagers. Those who have wandered in have tended to wander straight out again, although there were exceptions. Generally, those who wanted to come drew my attention to them in some way but would involve a teacher in the process. Again this is a generalisation but it seemed to me to reflect the stage of development they had reached. Their uncertainty as they grow into young men might be the motive to seek help but also be a strong disincentive – how will they cope with exposing their worries and self-doubts, especially to a woman? At the same time the wish to separate from their parents and the fear of their intense dependency wishes increases anxiety about the undertaking. Sometimes the whole conflict is played out in the process. A passive youth provokes his parent/teacher to save him/ initiate the referral only to reject the help as it confirms their helpless dependency. Loyalty conflict and rivalry also enter the field, as the young person feels pushed out to make way for 'siblings'. Some solve this problem by continuing to confide in their teacher and to undermine the process by splitting the therapist and teacher into good and bad parent. The advantage of having a more formal referral process is that the involvement of a third person, usually the education social worker, can facilitate the transition. The parents, if they are brought in at this stage, are then reaffirmed as the primary carers who are handing over their child to a therapist for specialised help. They can be brought back in to the equation concretely. Even though there may be no ongoing contact with the parents there is at the outset clarification in everyone's mind that this young teenager has a problem, that it is not an educational one and that it is not being treated educationally.

Although, normally, the psychotherapist would want to limit parental contact when working with teenagers, or ideally have a colleague work with them, I think working in a school, especially a school for children with emotional and behavioural disturbances, complicates matters. By the time a child arrives at such a school there have been many meetings with parents the best of which will have been with the aim of forging an alliance, the worst a kind of 'telling off'. The statementing process may reinforce the sense of being 'done to' just as it does for the child, in spite of every effort to involve parents. For many there is a stigma attached to being in a special school. Some parents express this openly, sometimes directing their disappointment at the system sometimes at their child. It is an uphill battle to gain the parents' trust and a lost battle if they feel alienated. So, going against the developmental push may serve a purpose if it draws parents' attention to the needs of their child and how these needs are changing. In reality, one meeting and a quick chat at parents' evenings is the most that happens.

PSYCHOTHERAPY

Once psychotherapy is started, testing the boundaries of psychotherapy or my commitment to them is ongoing and the most popular moment for doing so is on arriving and leaving my room. Unlike a clinic population where a concerned adult brings the child I have to rely on the young person's desire to come to his session. It is very easy for him not to. Although some teachers may act *in loco parentis* and remind or escort him, this is not always the case. Having begun by trying to establish a routine discussed with teachers, I now have a variety of approaches depending on the young person I'm about to see. One young man likes to remember by himself but initially wanted me to just remind him at the beginning of the day. Another hates to be seen talking to me outside the room but again looks for the eye contact earlier in the day. The younger ones need to be collected. If I hear that they have failed to get back to their classroom afterwards I take it up next time. Again, the balancing of different aims makes me wonder whether to explore the meaning of such wanderings or rabble-rousing or else to talk about how to help him get back to his classroom. Generally the latter is opted for mainly because taking up a negative behaviour depends on having some kind of therapeutic alliance. It is clear that lack of structure is too anxiety provoking. However, there are some who do need 5 minutes outside before they find their way back.

It is not uncommon to feel that relatively good contact has been made only to find that one day they just do not want to come any more. I am then left trawling previous sessions for clues but unless they can be persuaded to come back nothing is certain. Occasionally one can assume it is linked to a significant home event that just does not seem to register. A move of house or a parent leaving that is not mentioned points to a marked degree of disassociation. Something may happen in school, which then triggers the pent-up anxiety. Refusal to come can be seen as acting out the rage but sometimes also a way of protecting me from physical attack and him from imagined counter-attack. It is easier if he can come back when he is ready although it may feel to his teacher that the need is greatest at that moment.

It is difficult to explain to staff, without compromising confidentiality, why some young people might need encouragement when they are reluctant to leave the classroom whereas others need plenty of space. I think that the process of testing the boundaries of therapy, the commitment of the therapist and freedom to come or not, without losing the option in this concrete way is a central part of my work and being in the school makes this possible. But it is also somewhat paradoxical to find that being so accessible increases the pressure on the young person to make a conscious choice and a rather public one. By the time he is taken to a clinic he is out of sight of peers and can passively surrender, a stance that can be taken up in the session. However, an advantage of the openness is that the sight of peers going to their sessions has created a culture of acceptance. In my third year at the school it is commonplace to hear boys explaining to teachers that X has 'gone to counselling' or Y being reminded that he has his session. Boys also come up in break time to tell me that Z ought to come and see me. There is always great interest in someone refusing to come or storming back from therapy in a fury and occasionally teachers will use the incident to talk generally about worries and psychotherapy.

It is not often that I feel in danger of being attacked but there are times when it seems that one is being pushed and harried into an explosive situation; the abused child certain that I am hiding a desire to hurt him. An overwhelming preoccupation with privacy and concern about what goes on in my room at other times alerts one to the abusing fantasies and fears. Such a child might feel particularly anxious about his own state of mind and work terribly hard at convincing me that he is sane whilst I am the mad one. Any interest I might have in his mind convinces him of my mad abusing intentions. My failure to answer his questions for example, 'Who has written on the wall?' or 'Who broke the fire engine?' might send him into a paranoid panic. At other times it is a device for provoking an explosion so that he can leave and I am responsible for his leaving. It is stressful working with children whom one fears are currently being abused and feeling helpless. It is a stress the teachers have to manage on a daily basis. Some choose to talk with me, others succeed in distancing themselves from the emotional onslaught. My support comes from the clinical group at the Brandon Centre and is essential.

There are few overtly depressed boys in the school. It is more usual to see manic defences keeping depression or despair at bay. As in most schools it is the disruptive child that gets the attention and in this school there is no shortage of volatile pupils. If a child can communicate his despair then action is taken. Those who cannot provoke such concern in others are also difficult to engage although it is rewarding to see a gradual coming to life even if it quite rapidly declines into a sterile, rigid mode of relating, as happened in one case. It was as if having found an object of his own, this particular 11-year-old boy would hang on to it in the only way he knew how.

One can see from these brief descriptions that clinically this is far from being a homogenous group. Descriptively, most have experienced some trauma but the nature, intensity and duration of the trauma is extremely variable. Few have had much to do with mental health services beyond assessment and nearly all view such help with great suspicion. The trust in teachers at the school greatly facilitated the move into therapy as well as helping to provide some protection from the drop out that occurs when parents are relied upon to get their child to the local child and family service. However, the family dynamics may continue to affect the child in such a way as to prevent therapy from getting under way. It may also reinforce the dependency of parents upon professionals to take over the parenting role. The lack of boundaries, structure or attention at home is evidenced by the anxiety that holiday breaks bring. School staff may be the only adults to converse with them. One young boy comes to school at 7.30 in the morning, and would come at weekends if the school opened then. One can see from this the added importance of establishing a working relationship with teachers, not merely being based in school but being part of the system.

SUMMARY AND CONCLUDING COMMENTS

This brief outline of child psychotherapy in an EBD school illustrates the kind of problems one faces and the adaptations needed to overcome them. These are not young people desperate for help but very damaged children and adolescents whose experiences have made them deeply cynical about offers of help. The mental health system has failed to reach them and an overburdened social services provides little support. The education department places a considerable burden on teachers to cope with a constant emotional, often physical, onslaught and to alter this behaviour and to educate the children.

It is, however, easy to criticise the system and not so easy to come up with answers. The current 'inclusion' policy aimed at keeping children in mainstream is in danger of failing due, to my mind, to the difficulty of integrating health and social services with education. Underlying this is a financial problem and also an ideological one. We find it difficult to move on from thinking about who is responsible, which leads to the unproductive 'state versus the individual' argument. 'Nature versus nurture' then reappears and imaginative solutions recede.

Being in the school has many advantages for the psychotherapist but one in particular has made an impact on my thinking. I am much more aware of group processes and the power of the group in affording a shared defence aimed at defeating adults' authority. For example, a client's invitation to classmates to take over the therapy room is not always a distortion of rivalry or other needs but sometimes a calculated and perverse attempt to rob the adult of authority and purpose. Fritz Redl, in 1945, describes with chilling clarity the psychology of the gang and points out the illogicality of trying to treat a young delinquent who returns to an environment that 'oozes gang psychological defence'.

Another thorny question underlies this point and that is whether segregation of a particular group, in this case emotionally disturbed children, is particularly helpful. One wonders whether policy is based on a thorough examination of the group's needs or society's. The EBD school reflects a significant move on from Borstal and detention centres but society is still in conflict over priorities as the allocation of resources shows.

Another model of working in a school like this would be as a consultant to staff. This was not my aim although I did find myself used in this way periodically by some members of staff but by no means all. Being based in the school gave me the opportunity to see how various psychological mechanisms of defence are employed to protect oneself from the strain of being with these demanding young people. It is also interesting to observe how the institution as a whole promotes these coping mechanisms, occasionally preventing better ones from being implemented. For instance, there is little time to reflect on the meaning of behaviour or one's response to it but much time given to managing behaviour. One feels that to stop and think in this way might leave the staff feeling overwhelmed rather than helped. Providing this space and allowing the pent-up frustrations constructive expression would be an invaluable service to staff.

A third model would be to concentrate on parents. I have on occasions visited parents at home but my aim, to help them access adult mental health services or support groups, was on the whole not successful. The school works hard at winning parents' confidence and support groups were run for a while, although attendance remained very low. I think there is scope here but as with the children it would take a strongly proactive approach to succeed. It would undoubtedly have helped the individual work to have a colleague working alongside with parents had resources been available for this.

I have enjoyed the challenge of trying to make psychotherapy accessible to a population of young people badly in need of it and have followed one way of working, but this is clearly by no means the only way and its effectiveness is hard to measure. My impression is that the experience of being heard or of having someone emotionally available has left its mark not only on the children who made use of the service but also on the school as a whole.

References

Aichhorn, A. (1951). *Wayward Youth*. London: Imago Publishing.

Freud, A. (1969). *Normality and Pathology in Childhood*. London: Hogarth Press.

Hoffer, W. (1949). 'Deceiving the deceiver'. In Eissler, K. R. (ed.), *Searchlights on Delinquency*. New York: International Universities Press.

Redl, F. (1945). 'The psychology of gang formation and the treatment of juvenile delinquents', *Psychoanalytic Study of the Child*, 1: 367–77.

Chapter 10

The treatment of severe antisocial behaviour in young people

Charles Wells

INTRODUCTION

One of the findings to emerge from a study of treatment compliance at the Brandon Centre was that adolescents who present with symptoms of moderate to severe antisocial behaviour are likely to drop out from psychotherapy (Baruch *et al.*, 1998). This would seem to indicate that the needs of a significant number of psychologically and socially vulnerable young people who are at risk to themselves, to others and to the community at large, are not being met through traditional psychotherapeutic provision. This finding is consistent with the findings from many studies of effective treatment for conduct disorder (see Lipsey, 1995; Andrews, 1996).

These findings from the study of treatment compliance and mental health outcome at the Centre suggest that therapeutic engagement with young people depends considerably on their level of development and cognitive capacities, so there is a need to match therapeutic approach to differing clinical populations. As will be discussed later in this chapter, characteristics associated with adolescents presenting with severe antisocial behaviour include difficulties in linking thoughts and feelings to behaviour, and in perceiving themselves as actually experiencing problems. For these adolescents, a psychotherapeutic approach that is insight-oriented and that depends on the client being able to reflect on their inner world would seem to be inappropriate.

The finding from the study of treatment compliance and mental health outcome at the centre encouraged us to search for interventions that might prove to be effective with this group of young people. Following an extensive process of research and consultation a model of treatment was identified that was pertinent to working with adolescents who present with severe antisocial behaviour and which was responsive to their particular treatment needs. This has led to the Brandon Centre piloting a randomised controlled trial comparing the effectiveness of two psychologically based treatments. The focus of the trial is persistent young offenders and pupils, permanently excluded from mainstream education or at risk of exclusion due to severe disruptive behaviour, who are aged between 13 and 16 years. The trial has been under way since 1997 and is expected to run until 2002.

This chapter will provide a description of the treatments. Drawing on case study examples I shall consider some of the difficulties that we have encountered in working with this challenging group. I will conclude by highlighting some of the lessons learned, and consider possible future directions.

The constellations of behaviour that constitute antisocial conduct can be grouped under the general rubric of delinquency, which has both a lay and a legal definition.

DELINQUENCY

Delinquency is sometimes used to refer to those child and adolescent behaviours such as lying and defiance that meet with adult disapproval. It is also a legal term referring to adolescent behaviours and activities that are illegal and are dealt with under criminal law. The latter definition specifically concerns young people who are above the legally defined age of criminal responsibility and who are not yet adult. In England this would mean a young person between the ages of 10 and 18 years. The definition necessarily excludes those adolescents who are suffering from mental disorder and solely refers to the criminal offending of 'normal' adolescents. When describing adolescent offending a distinction can be made between *status* crimes such as truancy and under-age drinking that will necessarily exclude adults, and *index* crimes which are serious offences such as rape, burglary and murder that are criminal acts whatever the perpetrator's age.

ANTISOCIAL BEHAVIOUR

Antisocial behaviour cuts across both legal and lay definitions of delinquency as described above, and is characterised by the transgression of social rules and the committing of violative acts against others, such as truancy, fighting, theft and lying. Antisocial behaviours can vary in severity, frequency and chronicity and there may be a case for distinguishing between adolescents with severe antisocial behaviours and those adolescents whose behaviour is less serious. There is some evidence that antisocial behaviour appears in varying degrees in most children over the course of normal development (Feldman *et al.*, 1983). However, whilst for the majority of adolescents antisocial behaviour will tend to decline over time, severe antisocial behaviour at childhood and adolescence remains a strong predictor of offending into adulthood.

The concern of the present study is with adolescents aged 13 to 16 years whose antisocial behaviour is sufficiently severe to warrant a clinical diagnosis of Conduct Disorder[1] or at least Oppositional Defiant Disorder (ODD).

1 This refers to a clinical diagnosis made on the basis of the symptoms and behaviour meeting the criteria for conduct disorder in the *Diagnostic and Statistical Manual of Mental Disorders* (4th ed., rev.; DSM-IV-R, American Psychiatric Association, 1994).

THE BACKGROUND TO THE STUDY

We decided to explore the possibility of developing a service that might work successfully with those adolescents with severe behavioural difficulties. The Brandon Centre embarked on a series of consultations with local professionals working in this particular field, drawing on the expertise of clinical psychologists, educational psychologists, educational social workers, teachers from pupil referral units, youth justice teams, probation staff and researchers.

At these meetings the issue of problem behaviour was explored in order to identify interventions that might be used with this client group. Participants would bring along individual cases for discussion, which allowed some useful themes to emerge – in particular how at-risk many of these young people were. A great many of those with moderate to severe antisocial behaviours came from adverse social circumstances and almost all were exclusively from non-intact family settings. Many were at risk from neglect, and from physical and sexual abuse. They were likely to be failing at school and have a history of learning difficulties. There was a high risk of school exclusion and placement into special-education units.

A senior social worker with the Camden Youth Justice Team, drawing on his experience of working with young offenders, suggested that there might be a crucial period when the young person 'crashes', during which time there would be an increased likelihood of therapeutic engagement. By this he was referring to a period when the young person realises the gravity of his or her situation and when a custodial sentence has become a very real possibility. At this time a 'window' on to reality is often created and there can be an acknowledgement by the person that their behaviour needs to change.

Certainly there was a perception that developing effective interventions with conduct-disordered young people was crucial. There is plenty of evidence to suggest these patterns of behaviour do not extinguish over time and persist, continuing across generations. Apart from the misery and distress caused to the young people themselves there are severe consequences for others and for the wider community. The victims of these young people can include family and peers, teachers as well as strangers who are the targets of their antisocial, aggressive and violent acts. Furthermore crimes such as murder, rape and robbery are significantly more likely to have been carried out by those with a history of antisocial behaviour (Kazdin, 1987).

One issue that was raised was whether any proposed programme should be voluntary. It was felt that attendance should be linked to the requirements of any supervision order that was given to the young person. Our audit and the experience of other professionals indicated that conduct-disordered adolescents would be insufficiently motivated to attend treatment sessions on a voluntary basis attendance unless it formed part of a supervision package. With younger children the participation of the parent(s) is an essential part of making the child available for therapy and can help with treatment compliance. Given the dysfunctional pattern of parental and family relations that often features in these young people's lives, there was a strong possibility that parental support would be lacking or even unwanted.

At this stage we had not resolved the question of what interventions should be adopted in working with this particular client group. Although some studies had shown positive results using cognitive, problem-solving and systemic approaches, these models of working posed a problem for the organisation. The Brandon Centre has strong roots in the analytic tradition, with the staffing structure of the Brandon Centre drawing heavily on professionals with training and expertise in this field. However, it became apparent that for the reasons stated earlier, the Brandon Centre would have to move beyond its traditional analytic orientation. It was therefore felt that a multidisciplinary approach would be the most appropriate, and that practitioners from the ranks of clinical and counselling psychologists (whose training offered competency in a variety of models of treatment, with an emphasis on cognitive behavioural interventions) would need to be sourced.

Before we could commit to a different model of working we needed to determine which would be the most effective. Our aim was also to develop and describe a treatment model that would inform practice in the field at a national level. The next step was to investigate the literature regarding offending and offenders with a view to identifying positive approaches to working with these young people.

The discourse regarding interventions with offenders has come a long way since the therapeutic pessimism of the late 1970s and the oft-cited 'nothing works' conclusion attributed in part to Robert Martinson based upon his review of treatments for offenders (Martinson, 1974). In fairness, the 'nothing works' statement was partly a plea for better-designed studies in which objectives were clearly defined and outcomes rigorously measured. More recent reviews have been less sceptical and more optimistic in their conclusions (for an overview see Andrews *et al.*, 1990). This optimism was in part due to the influence of emerging data from studies carried out in Canada and the USA. The shift from 'nothing works' to 'what works' has prompted renewed interest in identifying which practitioners in which contexts best treat which disorder in which client? There has been a corresponding shift away from traditional psychodynamic and non-directive therapies to cognitive behavioural approaches in working with young offenders.

Drawing on the findings from a meta-analysis of the outcomes of 400 studies of rehabilitation programmes for delinquents, Lipsey (1995) reported reductions in recidivism between 10 per cent and 60 per cent for cognitive behavioural approaches. The largest reductions were found in those programmes that delivered selectively to specific groups of juveniles with specific treatment goals. If the desired outcome of a programme is to reduce offending then there is a need for treatment programmes to target dynamic risk factors that are correlated with anti-social behaviour and offending and to delineate clearly between *clinical* and *criminogenic* outcomes (Hollin *et al.*, 1995).

PSYCHOLOGICAL FACTORS

There are many factors that are significantly correlated with offending and anti-social behaviour, and literally thousands of variables that differentiate significantly between offenders and non-offenders (Farrington, 1996). It is beyond the scope of this chapter to give a full and comprehensive account of the research findings and instead I will concentrate on those findings that inform the present study.

Some of the cognitive features associated with aggressive and antisocial behaviour are deficits and distortions in problem-solving skills. Young offenders tend towards concrete rather than abstract thinking, showing great rigidity in the way they deal with problem situations. The research evidence highlights the limitations they experience in conceptualising the consequences of their behaviour and their mostly impulsive response to problem situations. These young people have a limited capacity to identify problem areas and in conceptualising flexible responses to getting the results they want. Deficits in the ability to use means–end thinking in pursuit of a goal means that the young person's attempt to resolve a personal and interpersonal difficulty is often ineffective and probably counter-productive. Repeated failure to solve problem situations can then result in frustration and lead to illegitimate means of achieving goals.

There is a predisposition for persistent young offenders to attribute hostile intentions to others and a tendency towards viewing others, particularly adults and authority figures, with suspicion and resentment. Under these conditions confrontation becomes inevitable, with the young person quick to respond with anger and aggression.

Evidence also points to delays in the development of the capacity for moral reasoning as a correlate to delinquency and offending behaviour (Rest, 1979). Rest claimed that young offenders demonstrated reasoning abilities associated developmentally with young children, in that they were egocentric, self-serving at the expense of others, and with an immature understanding of social rules governing right and wrong. Consequently they are neither able to empathise with the thoughts and feelings of others nor anticipate the consequences of their behaviour upon others.

All these factors combine to give us a picture of the enormous impairment that is suffered by these young people and how this connects with their criminal or antisocial behaviour. There is a general consensus that programmes, which target these factors, are more likely to succeed in reducing offending behaviour (Vennard *et al.*, 1997).

There can be no doubt that underpinning delinquent behaviour is an interplay between socio-economic, environmental, psychological and perhaps genetic factors. What is more difficult to ascertain is the relative influence of each of these factors, alone or in combination with others. There is unlikely to be a magic bullet model of intervention, and the future for this area of work may well lie in a multisystemic approach that targets key systems in the young person's life such as peer and family relationships and schools. Evidence emerging from studies in the United States for instance (Bourdin *et al.*, 1995) report favourable outcomes using this level of intervention. As far as we know this innovative type of programme has still to reach the United Kingdom.

We felt it was necessary to move in the direction of research and policy and this clearly indicated using a cognitive behavioural approach that targeted problem solving, social skills and social perspective taking. A number of studies in the United States had shown the effectiveness of this type of programme with juveniles and adults with severe antisocial behaviours (e.g. Ross and Fabiano, 1985; Kazdin, 1993). However, the effectiveness of these programmes has not been tested with 13- to 16-year-old young offenders within a community-based setting like the Brandon Centre and it was this group of young people whose needs we wanted to address. Rather than assume that such programmes would prove equally effective with our target population we decided that once identified, a suitable programme would need to undergo rigorous testing.

We embarked on a search to identify a programme that could be used with our target population. Through the 1995 publication *What Works* and the Home Office study paper *Misspent Youth* we identified a programme 'Reason and Rehabilitation' (Ross and Fabiano, 1985). The publishers of that programme, the Cognitive Foundation, had also produced their own manualised programme aimed at the UK market *Offending Is Not The Only Choice* (1995). To begin with the controlled trial was based on this programme. Over the course of the pilot study the manual has been considerably revised and refined to make it much less mechanistic and more age-appropriate to the target group. Many of the examples of problem situations, for instance, have been altered the better to reflect the type experienced by adolescents. In addition the programme now includes a new module that provides a structured approach to tackling the problem area of developing capacities for empathy and moral reasoning. In our view this has resulted in a manual with content that has a tight focus on high-risk behaviours and is more relevant to the client. Moreover the manual is much more explicit about the method of delivery and draws upon lessons learned in engaging young people in psychoanalytic psychotherapy. To that extent the manual has a psychoanalytic influence; however, the model of intervention and the change targets remain the same

The randomised controlled trial

For the study, individuals are randomly allocated to either the experimental group or the control group. The treatment group receives the manualised programme, which addresses two key areas of functioning in the young person: those of problem-solving skills and social perspective taking. This consists of a programme of structured exercises involving the learning of primary skills in order to encourage alternative thinking and the ability to generate multiple solutions to personal and interpersonal problems. Each session builds on the last until the young person is able to plan a series of specific actions in pursuit of a problem solution. A key learning point is the ability to recognise the obstacles that need to be overcome when confronted with a particular problem. Participants are encouraged to anticipate the short-term and long-term consequences of alternative problem solutions and to use this in decision making. Once the young person has fully grasped the principles of problem solving, his or her offences are explored in detail, looking at the intentions behind their actions, what they had wanted to happen and the actual consequences for themselves and others of the actions.

The other key area that the programme targets is the development of moral-reasoning skills. The boundaries of the young person's morality are explored and the underlying beliefs and values are identified. Moving beyond simple definitions of right and wrong we look at the implications for them, for others and for the wider society. They are required to think about the feelings of others and in doing so to develop a greater ability to empathise. The goal is to develop in the young person a more sophisticated way of thinking about ethical issues and to provide a conceptual framework that can be useful in tackling moral dilemmas.

Young people who are allocated to the control group receive supportive counselling that largely focuses on their offending behaviour and family issues. The model of counselling used in the session draws on elements of the person-centred approach and emphasises practitioner qualities of warmth and genuineness as necessary conditions to create a facilitative environment in which client change can occur. In practice this means attending to the young person's concerns and allowing the space for problems to be aired and feelings expressed. However, the model of counselling used is directive rather than non-directive since its purpose is to address offending behaviour.

Both conditions consist of twenty sessions that are administered twice weekly with each session lasting between 30 and 50 minutes. At the end of each session the young person is provided with a nominal payment for their participation in the trial.

Once the twenty-session programme has been completed there are regular weekly follow-up sessions for up to a year to reinforce the skills acquired during treatment, and to support the young person in their efforts to behave prosocially. Where the young person has given permission, sessions are tape recorded in order to monitor programme integrity and to ensure the programme is delivered as intended.

After the initial twenty sessions have been completed the young person is re-assessed using the same measures administered during intake. Follow-up assess-ments are made at 1 and 2 years after completion of the programme

Initial sessions utilise assessment instruments that rate the young person's problem-solving skills and social perspective-taking skills. *A full inventory is taken of delinquent behaviour.* The young person is also assessed on their level of reading, writing and spelling in order to give an indication of their test age equivalent. This assessment will not indicate the causes of poor intellectual ability and is intended as a guide only.

THE CLIENT GROUP

Young people who are eligible to participate in the study must be aged 13 to 16 years at the time of referral. The entry criterion is persistent and serious offending that meets DSM-IV criteria for conduct disorder and for oppositional-defiant disorder. These offences are wide-ranging and include street robbery, burglary, grievous bodily harm and actual bodily harm, violent disorder and theft of motor vehicles. These young people are considered to be 'top end' or 'high tariff' offenders.

Tanya had a reputation as a tough girl who didn't back down. Her aggressive behaviour to fellow pupils and teachers had led her to be excluded from mainstream education and at the time of her referral to the Brandon no alternative placement had been found. On the estate where she lived Tanya was part of a group of youths that extorted money from younger children by using intimidation and violence. In the most serious reported incident Tanya had demanded £20 from a young girl; when this was refused she subjected the girl to a serious beating that resulted in the girl being treated for a broken jaw.

John was 14 years and the youngest member of a family that was well known to the local police. Both of his brothers had served time in prison for burglary and street robbery and John seemed headed the same way. Most of his previous offending involved the theft of mopeds and cars, usually when he was drunk. The most recent of these incidents involved a high-speed car chase down the wrong side of a main road before the police were able to arrest John and his friends. John was referred to the Brandon Centre after being caught attempting to break into his school to steal a computer.

Most of those attending the conduct disorder project do so as part of a supervision order in which attendance at the Brandon Centre is made a specified activity. By making attendance on the programme mandatory with non-attendance risking breach proceeding for the young offender, we are able to increase the likelihood of attendance and completion of the programme.

RUNNING THE PROGRAMMME: LESSONS LEARNED

In this section I shall focus on the work with young offenders receiving our manualised programme. However, many of the observations apply to young offenders receiving counselling.

Working therapeutically in a community setting with young people who present with severe antisocial behaviours brings its own particular dynamics and characteristics. This has had an impact on the other service users of the Brandon Centre and the centre itself. General recipients of services at the Brandon Centre by and large self-refer for the therapeutic and medical services on offer. The relationship between those young people and the Centre is essentially a private one and the young person will tend to arrive for therapy appointments unaccompanied.

However, for the young person participating on the conduct-disorder programme, the Brandon Centre may initially be perceived as simply one more court-mandated activity he or she is expected to attend. Whatever the reason, there were frequent occasions when a participant would arrive in the company of one or two friends who would remain in the waiting room or else would congregate in the centre forecourt. At such times the delinquent characteristics of the group would become salient, resulting in a great deal of noise and disruption.

This situation raised a number of concerns for us. There was a perception that youths loitering in the waiting room or in the Centre's forecourt would deter other young people from using our service and furthermore the risk of service users being identified by others would compromise the confidentiality and anonymity that the Centre offered. Young people attending the conduct-disorder programme were subsequently instructed not to bring friends with them to the Brandon Centre and would need to arrange to meet them elsewhere. In taking this action we also wanted to convey to them that participation on the conduct-disorder programme was a commitment to be regarded as a serious undertaking.

Often the motivation to change is poor and for many of the young offenders their offending behaviour is not seen as a problem needing to be rectified since it provides them with both tangible and social rewards. It is understandable how this perspective can develop given that many of these young people come from disruptive backgrounds with the overwhelming majority living within non-intact family situations characterised by disorganisation, instability and unpredictability. Most have failed, or are failing at school and have little sense of personal efficacy or control in their lives.

With their lives permeated by failure and a corresponding lack of social status, their belief in their ability to effect changes is correspondingly low. Given these circumstances a cornerstone of the work has been to encourage the willing participation in the programme of the young person.

In line with the research literature we have found that those with the lowest motivation are often those with the highest need and therefore poor motivation should not be an excluding factor for referrals to the programme. Instead of persuasion by 'expert' arguments the participants are encouraged to argue for change themselves. This, of course, is not easy nor is it always successful. A good first strategy is to explore with them those aspects of their behaviour that have caused them the most trouble or had the most negative consequence on their lives. The practitioner will refuse to be drawn into the individual's attempts to avoid accountability by attributing their antisocial behaviours to factors beyond their influence or by placing the blame on others.

The young people are expected to take responsibility not only for their offending behaviour and actions but also for change. Time is therefore spent in the initial session encouraging the young person to think of ways in which his or her life might benefit from ending such behaviour. For example we might ask, 'would you like to be the kind of person who is able to walk away from trouble and feel good about yourself?' We might also ask the young person to speculate what their life might be like in 2 years' time if their behaviour continued unchanged. The practitioner makes it clear that change is possible and achievable if the young person is willing to stay the course. If the young person has already made attempts to change their antisocial behaviours then this needs to be acknowledged. Note will be taken of the various strategies that have been employed and their relative success and failures.

The content of the programme has been devised to be of relevance to the young person and uses examples and problem situations that are likely to reflect the individual's experiences and needs. By making the goals of the programme relevant to the young person's life then we have found we are better able to engage his or her co-operation in the programme.

Whilst there appears to be no clear evidence that technical interventions rather than relationship factors are sufficient in themselves to produce change in the individual, a reasonable conclusion might be that both interact or work in conjunction with each other (see Beck *et al.*, 1979). The practitioner does have a role in educating the young person in skills that will help in stopping the offending behaviour; however, the programme is best undertaken as a collaborative enterprise rather than the practitioner taking the stance of an 'expert'. Within a spirit of collaboration the young person can come to see him or herself as effective and competent and this can challenge previously held beliefs. Similarly by demonstrating qualities of warmth and acceptance the practitioner is challenging the young person's view of how others are.

In the majority of cases the young person, with their agreement, has been ordered to attend the programme as part of a supervision order and often as an alternative to custody. Whilst the aim of the court may well be to try to rehabilitate the offender, the offender is just as likely to view the sentence as a punishment, albeit one preferred over custody. Furthermore the young person may well view the therapist (along with other authority figures) with suspicion and mistrust. Establishing a good rapport is an essential component of the work, but the process of building a good working alliance is extremely challenging.

The practitioner needs to be aware of his or her own attitude towards delinquency and authority. Any ambivalence on the part of the practitioner towards delinquent behaviour can become acted out in the relationship through an over-identification with the client. This will have the effect of colluding with the client's delinquency and will effectively reinforce the client's worldview, lending it tacit approval and opposing the values and goals of the treatment programme.

Similarly if the practitioner is overly disapproving and critical of the offender's behaviour then this will likely be experienced as an attack by the young person. The task is to model prosocial and appropriate behaviour avoiding the twin traps of bonding with the young person by collusion or by enacting a critical authority figure. It is of crucial importance to access those aspects in the young person that are non-delinquent and to strengthen and reinforce them.

One of the difficulties that we have encountered in working with young people, who present with severe antisocial behaviours and conduct disorder, is maintaining treatment protocols and service delivery. As outlined earlier, these young people are characterised by their transgressive behaviour, violation of social rules and lack of moral discipline. This is important to hold in mind when considering what is expected of the young people we treat. Our expectations of them need to be realistic and attainable. Running a treatment programme requires a considerable amount of organisation: meetings and appointments need to be scheduled and assessment forms sent out and collected. There will be calls to youth justice social workers, with teachers and with parents as well as with the young people themselves. A great risk to the therapeutic enterprise can occur if the energies of the practitioners and support staff become absorbed in the routine administration of the programme. If this occurs, the first casualty will be the therapeutic alliance, a point illustrated by the following case example from early in the trial.

Jackie at 15 years old already had a long history of offending by the time she was referred to the Brandon Centre. She was required to attend the conduct-disorder programme following her conviction for a particularly vicious robbery of a senior citizen. Jackie's home life was characterised by disorganisation and neglect. Her father had separated from her mother when Jackie was 8 years old and he had not stayed in contact with his family. Jackie's mother was a heroin user who spent frequent periods of time in hospital receiving treatment for hepatitis. At those times Jackie would stay with an uncle who made it clear that he did not welcome her presence in his home. Although initially Jackie had appeared interested in participating in the programme her attendance quickly became erratic, with her turning up late or missing sessions altogether. We became anxious that this behaviour would lead to a breach of her order and a possible custodial sentence. When Jackie did not turn up for her session we would attempt to contact her at home to find out the cause of her non-attendance and to offer another session at the earliest opportunity. Jackie began to miss her scheduled and rescheduled sessions more frequently and we were also aware that her attitude to the programme was changing. Where she had seemed involved at the beginning of the work, now she appeared unresponsive and obstructive. In the sessions Jackie would declare that she had nothing to say, and whilst not overtly hostile was defiantly uncooperative; eventually she dropped out of the programme altogether.

In trying to understand what had happened a reasonable conclusion might be that there had been a greater emphasis on programme-management issues than on thinking about the client and her situation. Experience tells us that adolescence is a time of great change and uncertainty, and of physical, social and emotional transition that is sometimes difficult to negotiate. Even within a secure framework of family and peer relationships this can be an uncomfortable period in the young person's life as well as a time of great excitement.

Jackie at 15 years was expected to organise her school and to keep regular weekly appointments with youth justice and the Brandon Centre. There was an expectation of her to remember the dates and times of court appearances and meetings with solicitors. *In other words to act like a responsible young adult.* For many of the young people that we treat this is not a reasonable or realistic expectation and allowance needs to be made for this fact.

Programme-management issues had clearly begun to interfere with the relationship between the practitioner and the young person and had obscured an understanding of Jackie's situation. We might speculate that she had come to feel persecuted by the Centre, perhaps even bullied. The responsibility for regular attendance had shifted from Jackie to us. There was a shift from her need to attend to our need for her to attend. Perhaps the practitioner became in her eyes another authority figure telling her what to do and in a sense she was being policed. In such an environment the work was unlikely to succeed.

This can be understood as role conflict between organisational and therapeutic aims. Our role was to remain consistent and to demonstrate respectful behaviour towards the young person. Wherever possible we try to elicit the co-operation of the young person, discussing with them any difficulties that they might have in attending appointments. Always we will avoid appearing too flexible or over-accommodating and try to be clear about our role. To do this involves understanding how the young person sees us and how they think we see them.

One aim of the programme is to encourage in the young person the development of empathy for others, an awareness of others' minds and the ability to imagine how others might think and respond in different situations and in different circumstances. These principles inform how we respond to the individual's *needs*, anticipate problem areas and plan appropriate action. In doing so we would hope to provide the young person with an experience of somebody who can imagine what it is like to be him or her.

Some of the young people seen as part of the study come with a range of problems that can impact the way the treatment programme is delivered or received. Those young people who show evidence of attention problems pose a particular challenge. The behaviours associated with this particular problem are restlessness and short-attention spans. These behaviours can range from mild to severe and some young people's hyperactivity is serious enough to classify as a clinical disorder. The difficulty is in balancing the targets for each session with responding to the needs of these young people. Each session builds on what has been learnt from the previous session.

There is substantial evidence that young people who present with severe anti-social behaviour will often present with a range of other behavioural problems. Fairly robust predictors of the development of conduct disorder in later adolescence are the disorders of attention and hyperactivity.

The following is an example illustrating the problem of inattention.

Leon was 14 years old when he was first referred to the Brandon Centre for psychotherapy before the conduct-disorder programme had been set up. He already had a lengthy criminal record and his behavioural difficulties at school had led him to be excluded from mainstream education. Leon found psychotherapy unsettling and was restless and agitated in the sessions, unable to articulate his worries and concerns. Midway through the third session he walked out and refused to attend subsequent sessions.

Once the conduct-disorder programme had been started it was decided to refer Leon to the Brandon Centre again. Leon had been in care since the age of 8 years whilst his brothers had remained in the family home with his mother. He felt immensely rejected by his mother and it was difficult for him to form close relationships with others. Leon showed clear evidence of attention problems and it was difficult for him to remain seated for any length of time without becoming angry and irritable. When Leon became distressed, particularly following arguments with his mother, his behaviour became manic and hyperactive and greatly increased his risk of offending. Initially Leon was reluctant to participate in the sessions, declaring them to be boring and becoming agitated after about 15 minutes. He would sometimes stand up and wander round the room or else start fidgeting with objects in the room. We were aware, however, that for those first 15 minutes of each session Leon was able to think about the structured exercises with a quality of attention that was thoughtful and engaged. A decision was taken to shorten the length of the sessions in order to lessen Leon's anxiety, and rather than deliver a reduced version of the programme we would increase the number of treatment sessions. Once the sessions were reduced to a level that could be tolerated by Leon he was able to participate more fully. Gradually the sessions were lengthened as his attention span increased until it was eventually possible for Leon to remain in the room for as long as 45 minutes.

CONCLUSION

At the time of writing this chapter the programme has been running for almost 2 years and will complete in another year. It is too early to say whether we have been successful in meeting our change targets although early findings suggest that a positive impact will be found. However, it remains to be seen whether this positive impact will be reflected in a reduction in self-reported and official reports of offending. We have had clear success in maintaining the treatment compliance of the young people we have treated; this is no small achievement.

Ultimately we are attempting to change the way the offender *thinks*, about himself, about others and about situations. In a very real sense there is a belief that underpins the structure and content of the programme. That is that if a young person is able to deal flexibly with problem situations, can identify short- and long-term consequences of their actions and has developed a level of empathy then they will reduce or cease their offending altogether.

References

Andrews, D. (1996). 'The psychology of criminal conduct and effective treatment'. In McGuire, J. (ed.), *What Works: Reducing Reoffending Guidelines from Research and Practice*. London: John Wiley & Sons.

——Zinger, I., Hoge, R., Bonta, J., Gendreau, P. and Cullen, F. (1990). 'Does correctional treatment work? A clinically relevant and psychologically informed meta-analysis'. *Criminology* 28: 369–404.

Baruch, G., Gerber, A. and Fearon, P. (1998). 'Adolescents who drop out of psychotherapy at a community-based psychotherapy centre: A preliminary investigation of the characteristics of early drop-outs, late-drop-outs and those who continue treatment'. *British Journal of Medical Psychology* 71: 233–45.

Beck, A. T. (1976). *Cognitive Therapy and the Emotional Disorders*. New York: International Universities Press.

——Rush, A. J., Shaw, B. F. and Emery, G. (1979). *Cognitive Therapy of Depression: A Treatment Manual*. Guilford Press: New York.

Bourdin, C. M., Mann, B. J., Cone, L. T., Henggeler, S. W. (1995). 'Multisystemic treatment of serious juvenile offenders: long-term prevention of criminality and violence'. *Journal of Consulting and Clinical Psychology* 63(4): 569–78.

Farrington, D. P. (1996). 'Understanding and preventing youth crime'. *Social Policy Research* 93. New York: Joseph Rowntree Foundation.

Feldman, R. A., Caplinger, T. E. and Wodarski, J. S. (1983). *The St Louis Conundrum*. Englewood Cliffs, NJ: Prentice-Hall.

Hollin, C. R., Epps, K. J. and Kendrick, D. J. (1995). *Managing Behavioural Treatment: Policy and Practice with Delinquent Adolescents*. London: Routledge.

Kazdin, A. E. (1987). 'Treatment of anti-social behaviour in children: current status and future directions'. *Psychological Bulletin* 102: 187–203.

——(1993). 'Treatment of conduct disorder: progress and directions in psychotherapy research'. *Development and Psychotherapy* 5: 277–310.

Lipsey, M. W. (1995). 'What do we learn from 400 research studies on the effectiveness of treatment with juvenile delinquents?'. In McGuire, J. (ed.), *What Works: Reducing Reoffending Guidelines from Research and Practice*. London: John Wiley & Sons.

Martinson, R. (1974). 'What works? questions and answers about prison reform'. *Public Interest* 10: 22–54.

Rest, J. R. (1979). *Development in Judging Moral Issues*. Minneapolis: University of Minnesota Press.

Ross, R. R. and Fabiano, E. A. (1985). *Time to Think: A Cognitive Model of Delinquency Prevention and Offender Rehabilitation*. Johnson City, TN: Institute of Social Sciences and Arts.

Ross, R. R., Fabiano, E. A and Ewles, C. D. (1990). 'Reasoning and rehabilitation'. *International Journal of Offender Therapy and Comparative Criminology* 32: 29–35.

The Cognitive Centre Foundation (1995). *Offending Is Not The Only Choice and Values Enhancement: A Cognitive Behavioural Programme*. Cardiff: Cognitive Centre Foundation.

Vennard, J., Sugg, D. and Hedderman, C. (1997). *The Use of Cognitive-Behavioural Approaches with Offenders: Messages from the Research*, Part 1. Home Office Research Study No. 171. London: HMSO.

Part III

The evaluation of mental health outcome

The routine evaluation of mental health outcome at a community-based psychotherapy centre for young people

Geoffrey Baruch and Pasco Fearon

INTRODUCTION

The Brandon Centre introduced a programme evaluating mental health outcome in 1993 and since then has continued this programme on an ongoing basis. In this chapter we start by describing the reasons for the introduction of the programme. We then consider a number of approaches for evaluating mental health outcome including the one chosen by the Centre. We discuss the implementation of the programme and finally report on various outcomes.

REASONS FOR EVALUATING MENTAL HEALTH OUTCOME

It is difficult to pin down precisely when demands for public services to be accountable permeated child and adolescent mental health services. However, by 1993 stakeholders in our psychotherapy service, such as the local authority, the health authority and charitable trusts and foundations, were beginning to want evidence for the effectiveness of psychotherapy. They were also demanding that we have the means to document the effectiveness of our work on an ongoing basis. Indeed, having in place the means for evaluation became a condition for receiving funding. Without this, the Brandon Centre's funding was, and would continue to be, particularly vulnerable.

The local context for adolescent mental health services and developments in the provision of adolescent mental health services also contributed to the impetus in implementing evaluation methodology. The presence of the Adolescent Department of the prestigious Tavistock Clinic as a geographical neighbour of the Centre obviously has an effect on funders' perception of the need for the Centre's psychotherapy service. The stimulus for the Centre to develop innovative psychotherapy services and a programme of evaluation is partly to do with creating a clinic whose identity is distinctive and is distinguishable from its illustrious neighbour. The proliferation of different types of counselling services for young people influenced the introduction of outcome evaluation at the Centre. Charitable trust administrators were being inundated with requests from youth counselling projects for financial support. They had no way of judging which services provided good quality care and met genuine need and hence deserved support. Because there was much greater competition for limited resources, the Brandon Centre needed to demonstrate empirically the quality of its work. Otherwise, from the perspective of funders, there might be little to distinguish the work of the Centre from youth counselling. The doctrinal debates that occur amongst professionals offering 'talking' treatments about what distinguishes different psychotherapies and counselling may be of great significance to us. To the average administrator of a charitable trust or a health authority commissioner such debates are meaningless. We passionately believe that we offer psychotherapy, not counselling, but referrers, clients and funders usually refer to our work as counselling. Moreover, the extravagant claims by some counselling organisations about the effectiveness of their work are not convincing to most administrators or commissioners and can bring all practitioners into disrepute.

Aside from these external pressures, there were a number of other reasons why we wanted to conduct a study of the effectiveness of our work. These reasons that perhaps were not properly articulated at the time are clearer now. Weiss' formulations of the reasons why a clinic might conduct a study of mental health outcome can be usefully applied to the Brandon Centre (Weiss, 1998). They are:

- To determine the effectiveness of open-ended, psychoanalytically oriented psychotherapy with young people. Psychoanalysis has been particularly influential in recognising the psychological needs of young people arising out of adolescent development. Pioneering psychoanalysts have been responsible for setting up clinics intended to be accessible and acceptable to this population (Laufer and Laufer, 1987). However, the very nature of adolescence, which includes separating from the primary objects and a tendency towards impulsive behaviour rather than being reflective, means that the length of treatment is unpredictable, a factor which militates against systematic evaluation such as periodic follow-ups during and after treatment. Yet there is a genuine need to know what impact treatment makes on the young person's adaptation.
- To demonstrate the effectiveness of a clinic as an institution. Stakeholders including users, funders and referrers may not be interested in whether a particular treatment is effective but want to know whether a clinic offers effective treatment.
- To identify, if possible, the groups of young people attending the clinic that benefit from the intervention being offered in terms of characteristics such as age, problem presented and family characteristics. For instance, it is important to know how much younger adolescents, who are less cognitively mature, benefit from psychotherapy compared to older adolescents and young adults. There is also the issue of whether the presenting problem matters in terms of

outcome. The outcome literature shows that young people who present with behavioural problems are less likely to benefit from an insight type of therapy than young people who predominantly present with emotional problems such as mood and anxiety disorders. Finally, a clinic might wish to establish whether young people who come from intact backgrounds and who are therefore likely to have a higher starting level of adaptation make better use of treatment than young people who come from disrupted backgrounds. Luborsky *et al.* (1993) concluded that the greatest change in psychotherapy was by individuals with a higher starting level of adaptation.

- To establish whether factors such as length of treatment, therapeutic technique, for instance interpretative versus supportive forms of psychotherapy, make a difference to outcome. Recent research by Piper *et al.* (1998; 1999) shows a complex interaction between these forms of therapeutic technique and client personality variables. Their study found that at post-therapy both techniques demonstrated significant improvement but there was a significantly higher drop-out rate for dynamically oriented interpretative therapy (23 per cent) than for dynamically oriented supportive therapy (6 per cent). In addition, quality of object relations was directly related to improvement in interpretative therapy and virtually unrelated to improvement in supportive therapy. Psychological-mindedness was related to improvement in both types of therapy.

OPTIONS FOR EVALUATING CHANGE

In the course of designing a programme for evaluating change the Centre considered a number of options. One option, that to some extent was already in existence, was to establish, as a group of experienced practitioners, what we considered to be effective practice in the treatment of troubled young people. Professionals build up a stock of clinical knowledge about the effectiveness of psychotherapy on the basis of their practice. This knowledge may not be clearly formulated, for instance in the form of a manual, but is communicated via training seminars or the supervision of candidates. At the Brandon Centre, like most psychotherapy organisations, psychotherapists are supervised and attend clinical meetings. It is assumed that through supervision and clinical meetings good practice is imparted and maintained. This system of evaluation can also be supported by a periodic review of clinic practice by peers whose expertise in the field is widely acknowledged. This already happens in connection with the work of training institutions. However, whilst comprehensive clinical supervision and management by experienced therapists are necessary and essential ingredients in maintaining rigorous standards for the quality of practice, it cannot be assumed that this is sufficient for determining treatment effectiveness. According to Roth and Fonagy (1996) the relationship between therapeutic outcome, training, experience and technique is complex and from their review of the relevant

literature it is clear that additional procedures for evaluating outcome are necessary. The Trustees of the Brandon Centre certainly considered the idea of peer
review of the work of the Centre but conceded that 'a label of approval' would not
be convincing to those funding the Centre's work.

Having recognised the need for a programme evaluating mental health outcome,
we considered designing our own assessment questionnaires. This option was
very tempting because we felt we knew our client group well and therefore
could design appropriate instruments for measuring change. However, we rejected
this approach for several reasons. First, without evaluating the reliability and
validity of the instrument its value is limited. This process of evaluation is time-
consuming and requires resources such as dedicated researchers who are experts in
the field. Such resources are beyond a community-based clinic like the Brandon
Centre. Second, the findings from proven instruments might have a wider
relevance than the narrow one of the local situation. It would be possible to
compare rates of change with other published studies using similar instruments
and so arrive at a judgement about whether the clinic was operating as effectively
as might be expected. A further aspect of the design of an outcome study that we
needed to consider was whether it would be possible to allocate young people
between a treatment group and either a randomised or non-randomised control
group. This is the preferred way of establishing treatment outcome. However, for
ethical reasons we could not do this since funding is given to the Centre in order to
provide a psychotherapy service. Also, we could not form a control group from
young people on our waiting list. Unlike some clinics that run lengthy waiting lists
where a patient can wait for up to 12 months before starting treatment, young
people referred to the Brandon Centre on average wait 5 to 6 weeks. This period of
time is too short to make a meaningful comparison between the outcome of treatment and no treatment. We needed to find a well-established way of measuring
adaptation which took account of a number of facets of adolescent and young adult
development so that the lack of a control group would not make outcome findings
redundant.

In the outcome literature there is widespread agreement amongst those working
on the evaluation of change of children and young people in psychotherapy on
the need to use consistent and accurate measures that take into account the full
symptomatic presentation with age. As development proceeds, this presentation
often changes predictably without the impact of treatment. Moreover, in adolescence behavioural norms change within a short space of time thus making the
assessment of psychopathology extremely hazardous. For instance, misuse of
alcohol in a 13-year-old might be more likely to be taken as a sign of maladaptive
behaviour than in a 15- or 16-year-old. Hence the need for measures which are
sensitive to the impact of development on child and adolescent experience and
behaviour.

We also needed instruments which would enable us to assess change in young
people from multiple vantage points. This is because change in the way the young
person functions can vary across different contexts and only a multiple perspective

assessment can capture all aspects of functioning. Achenbach and McConaughy (1987) note that the differences which may arise when using reports from different informants about a child or adolescent 'are as instructive as agreements, because they can highlight variations in judgements of the child's functioning across situations and interaction partners' (p. 228). A second reason for cross-informant assessment is the possibility of bias affecting the individual's rating. Lambert *et al.* (1986) note that therapists' ratings of a particular construct tend to show a larger degree of change than self-ratings of the same construct. Relatives' views may be biased negatively or positively by their emotional involvement with the young person. A third reason for cross-informant assessment is that informants differ in their ability to assess particular symptoms. For instance, a parent or a teacher is not necessarily as aware as the young person is of how anxious or depressed they feel. Obviously these states are important to identify in their own right. They may also underlie externalising problems such as self-harming behaviour, school refusal, substance abuse, conduct disorder and other problematic behaviours that put adolescent mental and physical well-being at risk (see Kolko and Kazdin, 1993; Capaldi and Stoolmiller, 1999; Miller-Johnson *et al.*, 1999). The effect of bias on the picture of the young person it is hoped can be controlled when there is more than one source of evaluation.

In designing a study we also needed to consider the frequency of follow-up, whether to use repeated measures of outcome during the course of treatment as well as measures at the beginning and end of treatment and a follow-up evaluation. Because there is a high rate of drop out amongst adolescents participating in long-term, open-ended psychotherapy, a valuable opportunity to assess the impact of treatment may be lost if evaluation is limited to the beginning and end of treatment. Repeated measures may also assist in assessing the relationship between the length of treatment in terms of the number of sessions and the benefit to the young person depending on the symptomatic presentation (Howard *et al.*, 1986; Howard *et al.*, 1993; Kordy *et al.*, 1988). This is critical in the treatment of young people because so many drop out prematurely (Baruch *et al.*, 1998). Researchers also stress the need to follow up adolescents after treatment has terminated since a number of studies have shown that they may continue to improve many months after the end of treatment (Levitt, 1957; Kolvin *et al.*, 1988). However, we have found that this requirement is especially difficult to fulfil with adolescents and young adults because many of them move address during their late teenage years and in early adulthood.

In devising our programme, we sought advice from experts in outcome methodology in child and adolescent mental health who were also aware of implementation issues in a psychotherapy clinic like the Brandon Centre.[1] Their advice was to

1   The Brandon Centre is indebted to Dr Mary Target, Professor Peter Fonagy and Andrew Gerber, Psychoanalysis Unit, University College London, for their invaluable advice and support in designing our study of mental health outcome.

use the Youth Self Report Form (YSR) (Achenbach, 1991a) and the Teacher's Report Form (TRF) (Achenbach, 1991b) which are modified versions of the Child Behaviour Checklist (CBCL) developed by Achenbach and Edelbrock (1986; 1987). We called the Teacher's Report Form (TRF) the Significant Other Form (SOF) because the young person was allowed to give the form to any significant other of their choice for completion. The SOF is essentially similar to the YSR. The patient's therapist (see Baruch, 1995) also completes the SOF. We decided to introduce the therapist's perspective 9 months after the study was under way because we noticed that approximately 25 per cent of young people were not obtaining a respondent for the SOF. In many instances this was due either to being socially isolated or the wish to keep their attendance at the Brandon Centre confidential.

These forms are designed for adolescents between 11 and 18 years old. We have modified them slightly to make them easier to fill in for young people and significant others who are not used to 'American' English. The YSR presents the adolescent with 118 statements which are rated according to whether the statement is not true, sometimes true, or very true/often true. The YSR is easy to administer and if the young person cannot read the statements they can be read to them by their therapist and rated in this way. The SOF is in all essential respects similar to the YSR

In 1997 we were one of the first clinics in this country to use the young adult versions of the CBCL, the Young Adult Self Report Form (YASR) and the Young Adult Behaviour Checklist (YABCL) designed for young adults aged 18 to 27 years (Achenbach, 1997). Until the availability of these forms young adults in psychotherapy at the Centre had completed the YSR version. This was unsatisfactory because the form was designed for young people up to the age of 18 years and so the norms established for the form were not applicable to an older age group. We were also hindered from properly tracing the progress of the young person by the discontinuity between instruments being available to assess adolescents and not being available to assess young adults.

The great strength of the YSR, TRF, YASR and YABCL is the way they allow a wide range of adolescent disorders to be assessed. In the YSR/TRF versions eight syndrome scales have been empirically identified, each of which is associated with a cluster of items on the questionnaire and reflects a common theme including: Withdrawn, Somatic Complaints, Anxious/Depressed, Social Problems, Thought Problems, Attention Problems, Delinquent Behaviour and Aggressive Behaviour. Norms for each syndrome scale, which take account of age and gender, have been calculated by Achenbach and Edelbrock from a carefully chosen sample designed to reflect a cross-section of the American population. Using these norms, it is possible to assign a T-score to the raw scores of each scale, which indicates whether the young person is within the normal or clinical range on a given syndrome scale. For the scales, a T-score of 67 (the ninety-fifth percentile) is normally considered to mark the cut-off point between the normal and the clinical ranges.

The syndromes have also been banded together so that scores exist for Internalising Problems (including Withdrawn, Somatic Complaints and Anxious/ Depressed), Externalising Problems (including Aggressive Behaviour and Delinquent Behaviour), and Total Problems. Norms have been calculated for these scales and the cut-off between the non-clinical and clinical populations is 60.

The young adult versions of the forms, although different in certain respects so that they are appropriate for an older age range, are essentially similar in terms of syndromes assessed and norms to the YSR and TRF.

One-week test–retest reliabilities have been calculated for the YSR, TRF, YASR and YABCL syndromes and their totals. The correlations are as follows:

Internalising/Externalising/Total

		Mean r	
YSR	0.91	0.91	0.91
TRF	0.91	0.92	0.95
YASR/YABCL	0.90	0.91	0.92

The CBCL, YSR, TRF, YASR and YABCL have been widely praised in the literature as a highly reliable and valid means for assessing child and adolescent psychopathology and are relatively easy to administer. As we noted earlier, many researchers stress the difficulties, particularly in adolescent disorders, of assessing behaviours that are deviant only when seen in combination and when compared in severity with norms for their age and gender (King and Noshpitz, 1991). The 'Achenbach' forms solve this problem by basing their entire set of results on comparisons with appropriately matched norms. The forms are the only questionnaires for young people, which look at a broad and meaningful range of disturbing behaviours and feelings and organise them into relevant disorders.

A potential limitation of the forms is whether they are applicable to young people from diverse cultures since their norms are based on a North American sample. However, a recent study has gone some way to show that results from populations from different cultures are meaningful. Crijnen et al. (1997) analysed CBCLs for 13,697 children and adolescents, aged 6 through to 17 years, from general population samples in Australia, Belgium, China, Germany, Greece, Israel, Jamaica, Holland, Puerto Rico, Sweden, Thailand and the USA. They concluded that the CBCL provides a robust methodology for assessing and comparing problems reported for children and adolescents from diverse cultures. Age and gender variations are cross-culturally consistent.

At the Brandon Centre the young person's therapist administers the forms. They are administered to all new young people at the beginning of treatment (no later than the second appointment) with follow-ups at 3 months, 6 months, 1 year and thereafter annually. If the young person has finished or dropped out of treatment then the forms are sent for completion. The percentage of forms completed drops a great deal between intake and the 12-month follow-up. Thus for the YSR and YASR, at 3 months follow-up, 50 per cent of forms are completed compared to intake, by 6 months the percentage is down to 35 per cent and by 12 months the percentage is 25 per cent. The completion rate for therapists' forms is similar to the YSR whereas for SOFs the completion rate is less. Dropping out of treatment, completion of treatment and personal factors to do with the young person, for instance leaving school and so not having access to a teacher who filled in the SOF form at intake, all contribute to the drop in the completion of forms between intake and 12 months. This means that our long-term outcome findings are based on a limited sample. However, as part of the programme of evaluating mental health outcome we also use a number of diagnostic assessments including ICD 10 diagnosis, Global Assessment of Functioning, Severity of Psychosocial Stressors for Children and Adolescents and a checklist of the young person's current problems at intake[2] and note the young person's relevant demographic details. These data enable us to compare the characteristics of the subjects of the outcome group with the characteristics of young people not included, and hence assess the generalisability of the results.

We have used three ways of measuring outcome. Outcome has been assessed by examining the change in mean Internalising, Externalising, and Total Problems scores. The advantage of this method of assessing outcome is that it is sensitive to relative change; for instance, the young person who has a very high clinical score at intake and improves substantially but does not improve enough to get into the non-clinical population.

Outcome has also been assessed by examining the change in numbers from the clinical to the non-clinical range or vice versa. The advantage of this method is that a clinically reliable and valid distinction established by Achenbach and Edelbrock and many others is used. The disadvantage of this method is its insensitivity to relative change. For instance a young person may be assessed at intake ten points above the cut-off between the clinical and non-clinical range and makes substantial change during treatment, for instance their score dropping by eight points

---

2 The Global Assessment of Functioning Scale (GAF) is a condensed version of the Global Assessment Scale (GAS) and Children's Assessment Scale included in DSM-IIIR and DSM-IV as axis V (American Psychiatric Association, 1994). The therapist rates the adolescent's level of functioning according to guidelines on a scale of 1 to 100 of decreasing severity. The young person is also rated for the severity of psychosocial and environmental stresses on a scale of increasing severity from 1 to 6 using the Severity of Psychosocial Stressors Scale for Children and Adolescents (SPS). The scale is taken from Axis IV of the DSM-IIIR. The therapist assigns a diagnosis using a slightly modified version of ICD-10 (World Health Organization, 1990) following two clinical interviews. There are nine commonly used diagnostic groupings describing psychological problems, all of which are rated by the therapist on a scale of 0 (None) to 3 (Severe). The therapist assigns a principal diagnosis. The therapist also fills out our own Presentation of Problems Form comprising a checklist of 39 items which describes the adolescent's current problems. The reliabilities for all these scales were reported in an earlier paper (Baruch, 1995).

at follow-up. Yet this change would not show up if the criterion for outcome were solely whether the young person moves into the non-clinical range.

Finally outcome has been assessed by categorising cases according to the presence of statistically reliable change in adaptation level using the method proposed by Jacobson, Follette and Revenstorf (1984) and modified by Christensen and Mendoza (1986). This uses the standard deviation for each scale, together with the interjudge reliability of the measure, to indicate the size of change necessary to identify cases where change could not be due to measurement error and chance. The index of reliable change in YSR ratings is given by the formula:

$$\text{Reliable change} = 1.96 \times \sqrt{2} \times s \times \sqrt{(1 - rxx)}$$

Where rxx is the best estimate of interrater reliability. In our data this gives the following reliable change index:

	YSR/YASR	SOF/YABCL	Therapist
		Points	
Internalising problems	8	7	8
Externalising problems	7	6	7
Total problems	7	6	7

IMPLEMENTATION

In the next chapter Zora Radonic describes the implementation of the Achenbach forms from a *clinical* perspective. In this chapter we shall discuss the issues that arise in *managing* the implementation of our programme. Proper management of the outcome programme is vital. There are two issues that need to be considered. First there is the introduction of the programme into the clinical sphere of the work of forms and its effect on the clinical process. Obviously the psychotherapists and I were anxious about whether the forms would deter young people from coming to the centre, and how much they would interfere with the therapeutic process. Second, there is the maintenance of the programme once it has become established. This requires the constant attention of a senior member of staff who is committed to outcome research. However, it is essential that the clinicians have a stake in the programme and that it is not the preserve of members of staff who are also researchers.

There were three factors that helped in managing the introduction of the programme. First, because the Centre is in the voluntary sector and therefore dependent for its survival on voluntary financial contributions, the staff have a stake in any activity which contributes to the Centre's future. Second, over a period of 6 months I ran a pilot study administering the forms to all my new clients. This was helpful in giving the staff confidence that the forms could be introduced without damaging the therapeutic relationship. The pilot study enabled us to learn about the problems of administration and so develop a procedure based on this experience. Third, the psychotherapists have been permitted a certain flexibility as to how to administer the forms. For instance, some young people are asked to fill the form in at home and return it at the next session, whereas others fill the form in during the session. The psychotherapist can exclude young people who are unwilling to participate or who are unable to fill in the form because they are severely disturbed and in crisis. Since the programme began only a handful of young people have been excluded on these grounds. Several young people with learning difficulties have been helped by their psychotherapist reading the questions.

The introduction of the forms had to be ratified by the centre's Council of Management, which is composed of lay people and mental health professionals. Strikingly some of the latter proved most resistant to and sceptical about their introduction. A sub-committee was formed in order to examine the problems their introduction posed and agreed to let the programme go ahead on the basis that it would be periodically reviewed. After 12 months they were convinced of its value.

The continuing management of the programme is essential. There needs to be at least one senior member of staff who keeps track of the assessments at intake, who knows when follow-ups take place and lets the therapists know which of their clients require forms. At the time of writing, over 550 young people have completed forms at intake. This means, apart from new clients who are assessed at intake, there are on average over thirty follow-ups every month. The senior member of staff responsible for the programme needs to ensure that the forms are analysed and that the analysed form is available to the therapist within 7 days, that is by the time the therapist next sees the young person. This is important because data from the questionnaires inform the therapist's clinical assessment of the young person. In this sense the outcome programme differs from outcome research where data may not usually be made routinely available to participants. Instead data are allowed to accumulate before being analysed.

The outcome programme affects recruitment of staff in so far as it is a condition of the employment of a psychotherapist that they agree to participate in the programme. The senior member of staff running the programme ensures that a procedure, including a manual, for training new recruits is in place. They need to be trained to administer the forms and other diagnostic assessments and to understand the meaning of the analysed Achenbach forms. During the existence of the programme at the Centre there have been several psychotherapy appointments of individuals from different types of training, including child and adolescent psychotherapy and adult psychotherapy, none of whom have had any experience of empirical assessment of psychopathology. It has been interesting to observe how they have successfully incorporated this into their work.

Another ingredient in implementing the programme is a link with a relevant university department. This is necessary if the clinic wishes to carry out an assessment of therapeutic change of its clinic population, rather than just on an individual basis, and to identify predictors of change. Such an analysis requires a level of expertise that is usually beyond the scope of a community-based psychotherapy clinic. The Brandon Centre is fortunate in having strong links with the Sub-Department of Clinical Health Psychology, University College, London. Both authors are attached to the Sub-Department, one of us (GB) is a part-time senior lecturer and the other (PF) is a full-time lecturer whose expertise is in the application of statistical analysis in psychology research. The value of such expertise for our programme cannot be underestimated. In summary the implementation and maintenance of a programme of outcome evaluation raises complex and demanding organisational issues. If these issues are to be resolved then psychotherapy staff need to feel they have a stake in the programme so that it is not the preserve of a small number of senior staff who share an interest in research. There also needs to be effective and continuing leadership of the project. Any let up in this respect, for instance failing to inform psychotherapists of follow-ups, 'chasing' therapists to ensure follow-up evaluations are completed as much as is practically possible, and the project is likely to collapse.

OUTCOMES

Clinical dimension

The data we collect inform the way we think about and discuss the problems presented by young people at weekly clinical meetings, especially the information obtained from the Achenbach forms. Many young people who use the Centre's psychotherapy service are unused to thinking and talking about themselves. We often find that they are able to use the YSR/YASR forms to communicate matters that they have been unable to talk about at their initial meetings with their therapist. For instance, at intake young people's responses to questions on the form about suicidal behaviour and intent and alcohol and drug abuse are particularly useful in assessing suicidal risk. Data from the SOF/YABCL forms are valuable at intake because they provide insights, especially when completed by an adult who knows the young person well, into their behavioural problems. These problems tend to be denied by the young person. Findings from the forms are also valuable in assessing the severity of the young person's clinical condition because they can be compared to well-established norms. Finally the therapists have welcomed being able to check the progress of their cases from the follow-up findings.

Outcome

We usually carry out a comprehensive analysis of all the data we collect once a year. Out of a total sample of 508 young people who had completed a YSR form at intake by 1 April 1999 there were 118 who had completed a form at 1 year. Out of the 508, 86 young people were ineligible for completing a form at 12 months because they had started therapy less than 12 months ago. We therefore have YSR follow-up data for 28 per cent of subjects who qualify for being followed up at 1 year. They differ from the unanalysed group in being older (mean 19.7 years [SD = 3.3] for the analysed group vs. mean 18.2 years [SD = 3.3] for the un-analysed group) and attending many more sessions (mean 46.1 [SD = 37.3] for the analysed group versus 8.9 [SD = 9.5] for the unanalysed group). The analysed group were less likely to receive a diagnosis of personality disorder, dis-order of gender identity or sexual orientation, habit/impulse disorder. We also have follow-up data at 1 year using the Therapists' and SOF forms for 71 and 49 young people respectively. The self-report findings for 1-year follow-up have remained consistent over the last 3 years despite the increase in the size of the sample.

- Mean change in YSR scores between intake and 1 year show a significant fall: for internalising problems from 68.1 (SD = 9.1) to 59.8 (SD = 10.2) ($t(117)$ = 9.9, $P \leq 0.001$), for externalising problems from 57.0 (SD = 8.6) to 52.6 (SD = 9.7) ($t(117)$ = 5.7, $P \leq 0.001$), for total problems from 64.1 (SD = 8.1) to 55.9 (SD = 9.9), ($t(117)$ = 10.5, $P \leq 0.001$).
- Mean change in SOF scores between intake and 1 year also show a significant fall: for internalising problems from 69.4 (SD = 10.1) to 61.5 (SD = 9.1) ($t(48)$ = 4.9, $P \leq 0.001$), for externalising problems 59.3 (SD = 8.4) to 55.6 ($t(48)$ = 3.5, $P \leq 0.001$), for total problems from 64.4 (SD = 8.6) to 58.1 (SD = 8.2), ($t(48)$ = 5.3, $P < 0.001$).
- Mean change in therapist scores between intake and 1 year show a significant fall: 72.8 (SD = 10.6) to 66.4 (SD = 8.1), ($t(70)$ = 5.6, $P < 0.001$), for extern-alising problems from 59.6 (SD = 8.3) to 56.2 (SD = 8.32), ($t(70)$ = 4.6, $P \leq 0.001$), for total problems from 66.0 (SD = 7.8) to 60.2, ($t(70)$ = 7.3, $P \leq 0.001$).
- Mean scores for YSR internalising problems and total problems and SOF total problems start in the clinical range but by 1 year are in the non-clinical range.
- YSR mean scores show the greatest change occurring between intake and 3 months, and 3 months and 6 months for all three domains, SOF mean scores follow a similar pattern except for externalising problems for which only the change between intake and 3 months shows significance. According to therapists' ratings most change in internalising problems occurs in the first 3 months of treatment and between 6 months and 12 months, there is a similar pattern for externalising problems and total problems.
- At intake 85.6 per cent of young people rate themselves in the clinical range for internalising problems, by 1 year the percentage has dropped to 52.5 per cent, for externalising problems the percentages are 50.7 per cent at intake and 20.3 per cent, and for total problems the percentages are 77 per cent to 35 per cent – all these reductions are statistically significant.
- At intake 85.7 per cent of young people are rated by significant others in the

clinical range for internalising problems, 12 months later 55.1 per cent are rated in the clinical range, for externalising problems the change is from 55.1 per cent to 34.7 per cent, for total problems the change is from 77.6 per cent to 38.8 per cent, all these changes are highly significant.

- At intake 90.1 per cent of young people are rated by therapists in the clinical range for internalising problems, 12 months later 78.9 per cent are rated in the clinical range, for externalising problems the change is from 54.9 per cent to 39.4 per cent, for total problems the change is from 81.7 per cent to 60.6 per cent, all these changes are highly significant.
- According to YSR scores, 50.8 per cent reliably change for internalising problems, 48.4 per cent stay the same and 0.8 per cent deteriorate, for externalising problems the percentages are 34.7 per cent, 58.5 per cent and 6.8 per cent respectively, and for total problems they are 55.9 per cent, 40.7 per cent and 3.4 per cent.
- According to SOF scores, 61.2 per cent reliably change for internalising problems, 26.5 per cent stay the same and 12.2 per cent deteriorate, for externalising problems the percentages are 36.7 per cent, 59.2 per cent and 4.1 per cent respectively, and for total problems they are 51.0 per cent, 40.8 per cent and 8.2 per cent.
- According to therapist scores 36.6 per cent reliably change for internalising problems, 54.9 per cent stay the same and 8.5 per cent deteriorate, for externalising problems the percentages are 36.6 per cent, 56.3 per cent and 7.0 per cent respectively, and for total problems they are 47.9 per cent, 49.3 per cent and 2.8 per cent.
- Predictors of change include fewer sessions in treatment, that is it appears that young people who attend for 33 sessions are more likely to improve than young people in treatment for 55 sessions.

Outcome research in child and adolescent psychotherapy tends to be conducted in a narrow way (Kazdin and Weisz, 1998), for instance using young people who are especially recruited for studies rather than being from a referred population. Treatments tested tend to be brief and group oriented and fail to test therapeutic techniques commonly used in clinical practice, including psychoanalytic psychotherapy and eclectic approaches involving a mixture of individual, parent and family-oriented techniques. The shortage of studies of psychoanalytic psychotherapy with children and young people is well documented (see Roth and Fonagy, 1996) and therefore makes comparison of our findings extremely difficult until other similar centres using a similar therapeutic approach with the same age range of young people carry out outcome studies.

Findings from our outcome work and study of patterns of attendance allow us to draw a number of conclusions which have affected the direction of clinic strategy. First, the greatest effect according to YSR and SOF scores appears to be on internalising problems and on older adolescents in terms of outcome and attendance. There is less impact on externalising problems and the problems of younger adolescents who tend to be referred for behavioural problems. Second, the follow-up findings at 1 year are largely confined to young people who remain in treatment. We do not know whether young people who engage in treatment (that is stay for longer than five sessions but end treatment prematurely [before 21 sessions] or before 12 months with the agreement of their therapist) show similar changes to the young people assessed at 1 year. Third, for the assessed group according to YSR and SOF scores it appears that the greatest change occurs within the first 6 months of treatment. This finding differs from a recent study of the dose-effect relationship in children's psychotherapy, which could find no general dose-effect relationship (Salzer *et al.*, 1999). However, in our study the number of sessions attended is a predictor of change. The finding that shorter length of treatment, *even though long-term*, predicts improvement suggests that young people who are in treatment for longer may have more intractable *underlying* problems (see Fonagy and Target, 1994). Certainly this fits with our clinical assessment of the young people who are part of this group. Finally, whereas there appears to be some consistency between the ratings of change made by young people and their significant others, there is considerable variance with therapist ratings who are more conservative in the amount of change they assess. This conservatism is unusual since according to Lambert *et al.* (1986) therapists' ratings of a particular construct are likely to show greater change than self-ratings of the same constuct.

A major weakness of our study of outcome is the lack of a control group allo-cated in a randomised way. A recent randomised controlled trial that compared child psychotherapy to teacher support for a school-based population with similar characteristics to a clinic-referred population concluded pessimistically that child psychotherapy did not reduce psychopathology compared to academic tutoring (Weiss *et al.*, 1999). In this study, the practitioners were allowed to use their usual therapeutic approach. This included cognitive and psychodynamic-humanistic approaches and behavioural approaches. The latter were less favoured by the clinicians participating in the study. There was a limit of up to 2 years for treat-ment. Children allocated to the control group received academic tutoring, sessions were up to 45 minutes in length and were also available for up to a period of 2 years. Together with other studies, the findings suggest that for treatments most commonly practised in clinical settings, evidence supporting their effectiveness is sparse (Kazdin, 1999). There is an urgent need to subject clinic-based treatments to randomised controlled trial evaluation.

Funding

We noted earlier that grant-awarding organisations in the public and charitable sectors make the demonstration of outcomes a condition of funding. Although it is difficult to assess accurately how much our programme for the evaluation of mental health outcome has contributed to the increase in grants obtained by the Centre there is no doubt that the expansion of the Centre's activities would not have occurred without the programme. We have found that many administrators and managers of grant-awarding organisations are relieved that there is a commitment to service assessment and evaluation because they frequently have to present our work to trustees and others who play a role in awarding grants who either know little about psychotherapy or are sceptical about its value. They are not looking for a picture of absolute effectiveness, rather findings that demonstrate their grant is being used to meet the needs of young people who really require help. They also hope that the findings are used reflectively to plan and think about service direction. Many of these people are extremely committed to making available psychotherapy to young people but find 'selling' our work to their colleagues difficult if all they have to go on are our *ex cathedra* statements about the success of our work with troubled young people (as a population) without empirical evidence to support these claims.

Finally, the evaluation of outcome has had a major impact on the direction of the Centre's work. Our project evaluating treatments for young people who present with severe antisocial behaviour and several school-based projects described in this book have developed from our outcome work as we seek to overcome barriers to effective treatment

References

Achenbach, T. M. (1991a). *Manual for the Youth Self-Report and 1991 Profile*. Burlington, VT: University of Vermont Department of Psychiatry.

—— (1991b). *Manual for the Teacher's Report Form and 1991 Profile*. Burlington, VT: University of Vermont Department of Psychiatry.

—— (1997). *Manual for the Young Adult Self-Report and Young Adult Behaviour Checklist*. Burlington, VT: University of Vermont Department of Psychiatry.

—— and Edelbrock, C. (1986). *Manual for the Teacher's Report Form and Teacher Version of the Child Behaviour Profile*. Burlington, VT: University of Vermont Department of Psychiatry.

—— and Edelbrock, C. (1987). *Manual for the Youth Self-Report and Profile*. Burlington, VT: University of Vermont Department of Psychiatry.

—— and McConaughy, S. H. (1987). *Empirically Based Assessment of Child and Adolescent Psychopathology: Practical Applications*. Newbury Park, CA: Sage Publications.

American Psychiatric Association (1994). *Diagnostic and Statistical Manual of Mental Disorders* (Fourth Edition). Washington DC: American Psychiatric Association.

Baruch, G. (1995). 'Evaluating the outcome of a community-based psychoanalytic psychotherapy service for young people between 12 and 25 years old: work in progress'. *Psychoanalytic Psychotherapy* 9: 243–67.

—— Gerber, A. and Fearon, P. (1998). 'Evaluating the outcome of a community-based psychoanalytic psychotherapy service for young people: One-year repeated follow-up'. In Davenhill, R. and Patrick, M. (eds), *Rethinking Clinical Audit: The Case of Psychotherapy Services in the NHS*. London: Routledge.

Capaldi, D. M. and Stoolmiller, M. (1999). 'Co-occurrence of conduct problems and depressive symptoms in early adolesecent boys: III. Prediction to young-adult adjustment'. *Development and Psychopathology* 11(1): 59–84.

Christensen, L. and Mendoza, J. L. (1986). 'A method of assessing change in a single subject: an alteration in the RC index'. *Behaviour Therapy* 17: 305–8.

Crijnen, A. A., Achenbach, T. M., and Verhulst, F. C. (1997). 'Comparisons of problems reported by parents of children in 12 cultures: Total problems, externalizing and internalizing'. *Journal of the American Academy of Child and Adolescent Psychiatry* 36(9): 1269–77.

Fonagy, P. and Target, M. (1994). 'The efficacy of psychoanalysis for children with disruptive disorders'. *Journal of the American Academy of Child and Adolescent Psychiatry* 33(1): 45–55.

Howard, K. I., Kopta, S. M., Krause, M. S. and Orlinsky, D. E. (1986). 'The dose effect relationship in psychotherapy'. *American Psychologist* 41: 159–64.

——Lueger, R. J., Maling, M. S. and Martinovich, Z. (1993). 'A phase model of psychotherapy outcome: Causal mediation of change'. *Journal of Consulting and Clinical Psychology* 61: 678–85.

Jacobson, N. S., Follette, W. C. and Revenstorf, D. (1984). 'Psychotherapy outcome research: methods of reporting variability and evaluating clinical significance'. *Behaviour Therapy* 15: 336–52.

Kazdin, A. (1999). Commentary on 'Weiss, B., Catron, T., Harris, V. and Phung, T. M. (1999). "Traditional child psychotherapy did not reduce psychopathology compared with academic tutoring". *Journal of Consulting and Clinical Psychology* 67(1): 82–94'. In *Evidence-Based Mental Health* 2(3): 86.

——and Weisz, J. R. (1998). 'Identifying and developing empirically supported child and adolescent treatements'. *Journal of Consulting and Clinical Psychology* 66(1): 19–36.

King, R. A. and Noshpitz, J. D. (1991). *Pathways to Growth: Essentials of Child Psychiatry*, vol. 2: Psychopathology. New York: Wiley.

Kolko, D. J. and Kazdin, A. E. (1993). 'Emotional/Behavioural problems in clinic and non-clinic children: correspondence among child, parent and teacher reports'. *Journal of Child Psychology and Psychiatry* 34: 991–1006.

Kolvin, I., Nicol, A. E. and Wrate, R. M. (1988). 'Psychotherapy is effective'. *Journal of the Royal Society of Medicine* 81: 261–6.

Kordy, H., von Rad, M. and Senf, W. (1988). *Psychotherapy Psychosomatics* 49: 212–22.

Lambert, M. J., Hatch, D. R., Kingston, M. D. and Edwards, B. C. (1986). 'Zung, Beck, and Hamilton Rating Scales as measures of treatment outcome: a meta-analytic comparison'. *Journal of Consulting and Clinical Psychology* 54: 54–9.

Laufer, M. and Laufer, M. E. (1987). *Adolescence and Developmental Breakdown: A Psychoanalytic View*. New Haven and London: Yale University Press.

Levitt, E. E.(1957). 'The results of psychotherapy with children: an evaluation'. *Journal of Consulting Psychology* 21: 186–9.

Luborsky, L., Diguer, L., Luborsky, E., McLellan, A. T., Woody, G. and Alexander, L. (1993). 'Psychological Health-Sickness (PHS) as a predictor of outcomes in dynamic and other psychotherapies'. *Journal of Consulting and Clinical Psychology* 61: 542–9.

Miller-Johnson, S., Winn, D-M., Coie, J., Maumary-Gremaud, A., Hyman, C., Terry, R. and Lochman, J. (1999). 'Motherhood during the teen years: A developmental perspective on risk factors for childbearing'. *Development and Psychopathology* 11(1): 85–100.

Piper, W. E., Joyce, S., McCallum, M. and Azim, H. F. (1998). 'Interpretive and supportive forms of psychotherapy and patient personality variables'. *Journal of Consulting and Clinical Psychology* 66(3): 558–67.

——and Ogrodniczuk, J. S. (1999). 'Follow-up findings for interpretive and supportive forms of psychotherapy and patient personality variables'. *Journal of Consulting and Clinical Psychology* 67(2): 267–73.

Roth, A. and Fonagy, P. (1996). *What Works for Whom? A Critical Review of Psychotherapy Research*. New York, London: The Guilford Press.

Salzer, M. S., Bickman, L. and Lambert, E. W. (1999). 'Dose-effect relationship in children's psychotherapy services'. *Journal of Consulting and Clinical Psychology* 67(2): 228–38.

Target, M. and Fonagy, P. (1994). 'The efficacy of psychoanalysis for children: prediction of outcome in a developmental context'. *Journal of the American Academy of Child and Adolescent Psychiatry* 33: 1134–44.

Weiss, B. (1998). 'Annotation: Routine monitoring of the effectiveness of child psychotherapy'. *Journal of Child Psychology and Psychiatry* 39(7): 943–50.

——Catron, T., Harris, V. and Phung, T. M. (1999). 'Traditional child psychotherapy did not reduce psychopathology compared with academic tutoring'. *Journal of Consulting and Clinical Psychology* 67(1): 82–94.

World Health Organization (1990). ICD-10, 1990 Draft of Chapter V, 'Mental and Behavioural Disorders (including disorders of psychological development)'. Geneva: World Health Organization.

Chapter 12

The clinician's experience of implementing audit

Impact on the clinical process in the treatment of troubled young people

Zora Radonic

In this chapter I shall describe my experience of implementing the questionnaires (that is the Youth Self Report Form, the Significant Other Form, the Young Adult Self Report Form and the Young Adult Behaviour Checklist) described in the previous chapter.

When I was first introduced to audit methodology at the Brandon Centre I was immediately anxious about administering questionnaires in my ordinary clinical practice. I was worried that they would interfere with the engagement phase of the therapeutic process and later on with the development of the transference and counter-transference.

Young people come to the Brandon Centre for different reasons: they usually say that they are depressed, they feel hopeless and desperate, they have problems with their parents, siblings or something is wrong in their boyfriend/girlfriend relationship. Younger adolescents usually report that their problems are external to themselves whereas older adolescents are more aware of the internal difficulties. However differently they see their problems, when they come to the Centre they are overwhelmed by the intensity of their feelings as well as by the anxiety that they cannot deal with them. Most adolescents are reluctant about seeking help and I have found that even if they say that they would like some help, they are often mistrustful of the adult who is there to help them.

Given the young person's ambivalence about asking for help, the first contact with a therapist is of great importance. With younger adolescents and with very reluctant adolescents the first meeting is crucial as to whether they will continue to come. The aim of this first meeting is to provide a space for listening as the young person in one way or another always brings their story and wants to be heard. A further aim is to supply the young person with understanding by putting them in contact with their immediate anxiety, for instance about being out of control, or feeling hopeless and helpless. In summary, the first meeting also gives the therapist an opportunity to establish a partnership with the young person, which promotes a desire to meet again to find out more about themselves.

I was worried that in giving the young person a questionnaire in the first meeting the delicate and sensitive task of establishing this partnership would be undermined. The questionnaire is quite long and takes time to introduce and to complete, so I decided to administer the questionnaire in the second session. Of course with some adolescents there isn't a second session!

To begin with I introduced the questionnaire in an uncertain manner as if its purpose was for the Centre's research therefore putting the Centre in the position of a third object of the Oedipal situation, such as a demanding parent, and keeping myself available for a different kind of relationship. This is to some extent helpful since the young person then has an opportunity for different links – with the therapist, as well as with the Centre. For young people the transference to the Centre operates from the very beginning. The Centre has a very important role in their minds. It provides them with, so to speak, a home – with a certain stability and security and a point of reference during the holidays when, for instance, the therapist is away.

I would briefly like to illustrate the usefulness of the form in facilitating contact by describing my work with Carl. Carl was16 years old when he was referred by his school. On more than one occasion he had had a fight with another young pupil. Carl's behaviour was disruptive and he was threatened with expulsion if he didn't go for counselling. Carl phoned the Centre to make an appointment and he arrived for the first session about 4 hours early. When we met he said that he was expecting the Centre to be a very big place, something like a school or a youth club with many young people around. I immediately wondered if he was disappointed by the size of the Centre. Carl was very anxious and suspicious about me being 'big' and finding things out about him. It was very difficult to make contact so I decided to introduce the form. He wasn't willing to fill it in at first but when I asked him about his reluctance we began to talk. It was soon clear to me that he was worried that I would use the form to let his school know about Carl. The link between the school and myself, as the link between two 'big' parents in Carl's mind, seemed potentially dangerous. However, it was now possible to begin to talk about it. After working in this area for a while, Carl relaxed and with my help he filled in the form. He continued coming to his sessions and after a while he kept asking me when we were going to do the forms again. He said that the questions were good and just right for him.

Carl was a young, unpsychologically minded adolescent boy who had difficulty in thinking about himself just like many young people who are referred to the Centre. However, I felt that the form was helpful in engaging him and that it opened up the possibility of links and relationships in his mind. He came for about 6 months. He became more trustful of me and managed to tell me in the last session before he stopped attending (the ending wasn't planned) that his father was seriously ill, he went to a hospital and subsequently he died there in tragic circumstances. The fact that Carl was able to tell me about his father's complex illness, which was disturbing him very much, was a very significant moment for him. And indeed his 6-monthly self-report showed a significant improvement in his symptoms.

The way I use the questionnaires in my clinical practice and the way I view them has changed over time. I began to be more curious about whether they might be clinically useful. I became more confident in the way I introduced them. I introduce them as a way to open up a potential link between a young person and me and between the young person and the Centre. I then found that the young people also started filling in the questionnaire with more interest. No young person has refused to complete the form. Young people are very used to being asked to fill in different kinds of forms and are usually not anxious about them.

The manner in which each young person relates to the questionnaires can tell us much about them. A 22-year-old student, Martha, came to the Centre in a panic that she wasn't going to be able to pass her exams. Martha was repeating the second year of college and she was desperate to find help. She appeared to be manic. She was unable to sit still in the first few sessions. I introduced the questionnaire; she started completing it but somehow couldn't settle with it. When she finished she smiled, looking anxious and uncertain but also pleased. She then asked me if I had created this questionnaire for her. In asking this question I thought that she needed to believe that I was the creator of the questionnaire for her as she perceived me as an unreal, ideal and grandiose person. I think she believed these were the characteristics that could help her.

I have found the questionnaires helpful with silent, younger adolescents who come to the Centre reluctantly and who are difficult to reach with words. They often relate to the questionnaire in an 'intimate' way. They reply honestly and they reveal their difficulties, including suicidal and self-harming behaviour. Younger adolescents, aged between 13 and 16 years, are usually referred by their parents, teachers and sometimes their GP. They often feel pushed to come for help. Often they don't recognise themselves as having problems. If they do, they look for concrete solutions to resolve them. If they are in a very angry state they can be tempted to attack the therapeutic setting. Their projections are intense and they can leave the therapist feeling anxious and rejected. In these situations the questionnaires are useful for the picture they provide of the young person. Often their score is high on the aggressive and delinquent behaviour scales. If the questionnaire is sensitively introduced to a young person who presents these problems and the questions and the answers are discussed the form can be very containing. It helps such young people feel that they are in control and that their views and opinions are important and respected.

When the therapeutic process is established and the development and the movements in the transference and counter-transference can be observed and interpreted, I find that the follow-up questionnaire after 3 months and after 6 months has a very strong impact on the therapeutic relationship. The time intervals are short and somehow interfere with the early stages of therapy. I feel uncomfortable asking for the questionnaire to be completed again so soon as if I am expecting a different result. It is, however, possible to interpret the young person's responses in and out of the transference.

I will now present two cases which illustrate the use of the forms in longer-term work.

DINA

Dina was aged 17 years in the last year of her A levels. She was doing badly at school and felt depressed, tired and unmotivated. She came to the Centre because she was worried that she wasn't going to be able to do enough work to pass her exams. She was also uncertain what to do after her A levels. I asked her to fill out the questionnaire and she seemed interested in doing this. Figure 12.1 shows the analysis at intake – she is in the clinical range, high on two syndromes; anxiety/depression and attention problems.

Dina's home situation was very difficult. She was an only child. She lived with her mother who was recovering from alcoholism. She drank a lot when Dina was growing up. Dina was very close to her and protective of her. Her father also drank heavily. It seemed that he had battled with his wife to stop drinking but after many years he lost the battle. Dina moved out of the family home and some time later Dina's father re-married. Dina's mother carried on drinking and her situation worsened. Dina went to live with her father when she was about 15 years but she behaved badly and the stepmother sent her away. Dina described a good relationship with her father but saw him as weak in relation to his 'powerful', drunken mother. During the 12 months before Dina came to the Centre she found her relationship with her mother impossible. She argued with her a lot and felt pushed out by her. She went to live with a friend twice but she returned home.

Dina was unsure about her sexual identity. She had a boyfriend but not 'a proper relationship'. She found herself being obsessed with very beautiful boys and girls as well, 'ideal' young people, the very opposite of the picture she had of her mother and her father. Dina was keen to start therapy. However, the beginning of therapy was difficult. In her sessions Dina appeared to be depressed; she was always very tired and sleepy. She didn't know what to talk about and sometimes she missed her appointments. I felt that it was very important to work on these absences as I could see the danger of her disappearing rather than engaging. I also thought that she couldn't really begin to speak about how she felt about herself but that she was very occupied with herself, especially with her looks. Her 3 months' self-report form shows that she is very high on social problems.

This high score is common for adolescents who are narcissistically preoccupied with themselves. Looking at the graph more closely we can see how Dina feels about herself: she sees herself as clumsy, she acts too young for her age, she is teased a lot, she feels not liked by others. When we began to speak about these problems in her sessions, Dina was also able to tell me more about her family. She started attending her sessions more regularly. She seemed more engaged and sometimes she was even keen to come to her sessions. She also appeared to be less depressed. The issues about her mother, their relationship and the coming separation between the two of them became the focus of our work. She was very ambivalent. She was keen to leave her mother but was worried about her too. She was less aware of her worry, which was split off and was causing some of her depression. In the transference she was unsure if I wanted her to leave or stay,

Figure 12.1 Dina: Youth Self Report Form/Young Adult Self Report Form

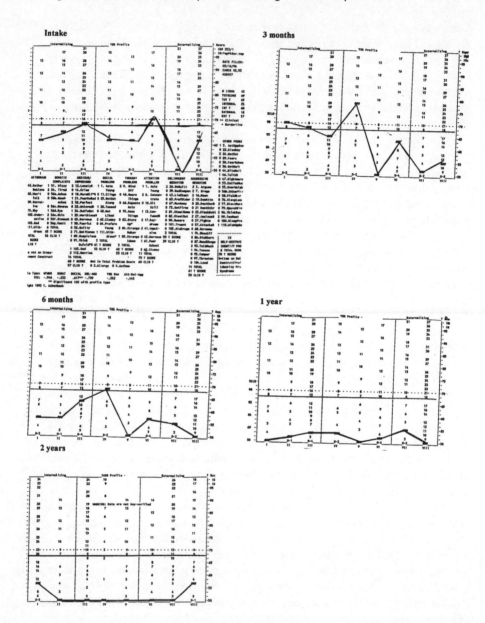

especially as she was beginning to feel better. Working through these anxieties helped Dina to feel less depressed and enabled her to become more involved with her work at school and her exams. The outcome of her self-report form after 1 year confirmed the progress of her therapy.

In Dina's case the forms suggest that the therapy was effective: Dina appears less depressed and anxious. I can also conclude that there were improvements in other areas of Dina's life, for instance at school, with her family and in other social relationships. A further follow-up was needed to find out how Dina managed the separation with her mother and how she coped at university. A year later I sent Dina a questionnaire which she returned completed. This doesn't always happen but when it does happen it is informative and rewarding to see that the contact has been maintained (see 2 years in Figure 12.1).

I am a bit concerned that the flat line is too good to be true. It could be that Dina settled but I suspect that she is not revealing the negative side of her experience. Closer observation of the findings shows some old difficulties, for instance drinking and problems with the opposite sex, with her family, especially with her mother, and a preoccupation with her looks.

LUCIAN

Lucian was 22 years old when he came to the Centre in a desperate state. He felt helpless as if he was losing control over his mind and overwhelmed by feelings of guilt. Lucian requested to see a female therapist and when we met he was very anxious.

Figures 12.2, 12.3 and 12.4 show Lucian's state from the forms completed at intake by Lucian, his girlfriend and by the therapist. I think that the high clinical ranges depicted in these charts are common for very needy, desperate young people who are screaming 'help me'.

Lucian was born in a Latin American country. He moved to London after finishing his degree in the country of his origin. He was involved in a 'difficult' relationship with a few girlfriends. At times he felt very anxious in the presence of girls and women, especially women who were in a position of authority. He felt driven to run away from the situations in which he felt unable to be in control of his feelings. He was aware that at times he behaved inappropriately. But he wasn't aware why he felt so anxious and he also felt very guilty about his behaviour. The arguments and fights with his girlfriends as well as the storms inside his mind interfered with his final exams. He struggled a lot, he was on the border of giving up, but in the end he managed to pull himself together enough to finish his degree. He 'escaped' hoping to start a new life in England. Some of his relations lived in London and they offered to help him to settle down.

Lucian's parents divorced when he was a young child. He lived with his mother and his older brother and saw his father regularly. Lucian was jealous of his older brother and he saw him as a rival for his mother's love. In addition to this Lucian

Figure 12.2 Lucian: Youth Self Report Form/Young Adult Self Report Form

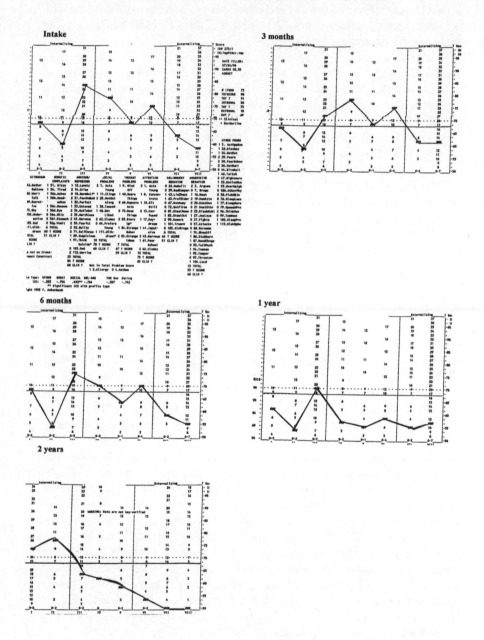

Figure 12.3 Lucian: girlfriend's version (significant other version of the Teacher's Report Form/Young Adult Behaviour Checklist)

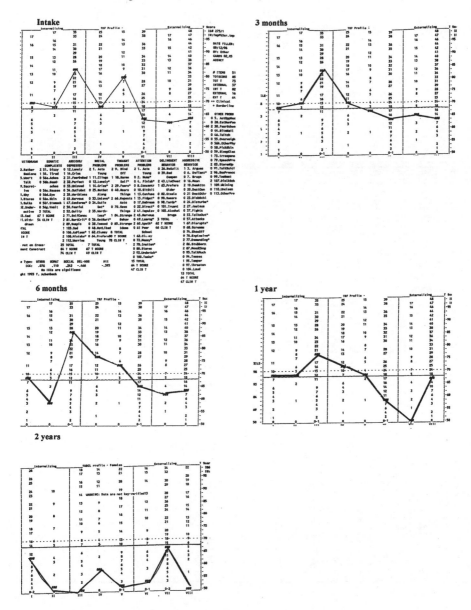

Figure 12.4 Lucian: therapist's version (significant other version of the Teacher's Report Form/Young Adult Behaviour Checklist)

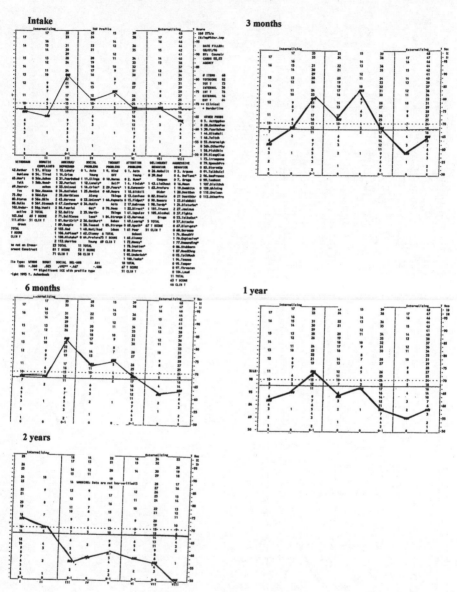

was very insecure about his mother's attention. Lucian's mother had a series of unsuccessful relationships that made her depressed and unhappy. Lucian disliked his mother for having relationships, for being needy and feeling sad. When he arrived in London, Lucian was offered an interesting job. He behaved irresponsibly at work in the way he related to his colleagues, especially women. He could not bear to be asked to improve his behaviour and promptly resigned.

Lucian was depressed, withdrawn and very anxious. He had no friends, no job and he didn't want to know anyone. He met a woman and started a relationship with her. It looked as though this relationship was a 'retreat' for Lucian. He was expecting a great deal from her, mainly to look after him and to save him from anxieties and feelings of being out of control. His girlfriend was working as a lawyer, constantly in contact with people, especially men, which made Lucian feel jealous and left out. He became clingy and demanding and she suggested that he seek therapy.

Therapy started but Lucian seemed very stuck. In some ways his state became worse as he seemed to be trying to rely on his girlfriend even more. Although he came to his sessions regularly he seemed mistrustful of me, ambivalent and uncertain that I could help. At times, in the first 6 months, I felt stuck too and worried that his therapy would not progress. However, there were some changes after 3 months and some improvements after 6 months of therapy.

These charts show that Lucian was still very anxious, needing a lot of attention, and feeling depressed and withdrawn. Just looking at the outcome of the graphs they show that at this stage the therapy was not very effective, especially as the therapist saw little improvement in the symptoms too. This is a difficult although not uncommon situation for any therapist when treatment seems to be stuck. The treatment can break down at this point. The young person might feel even more depressed and hopeless and the therapist might feel frustrated and depressed too.

Lucian's therapy carried on. I persisted and after a while some internal dynamics were beginning to unfold. In the transference I was often seen as a mother Lucian didn't want to be with, whilst the girlfriend was like a desirable mother. He hoped that she was going to sort everything out for him. I think that working through these hopes and engaging Lucian to think about his relationship with me so that he could find out about his feelings towards his mother brought some significant changes that were confirmed in the follow-up outcomes after 1 year of therapy.

It is interesting to see the different ways Lucian, his girlfriend and the therapist saw change (see Figures 12.2, 12.3 and 12.4). In Lucian's view there was an improvement in all areas in a gradual way between intake and 1 year. In the girlfriend's and the therapist's view change occurred after a year.

After a longer period of depression Lucian's mood began to improve. He started a new job. Although he was still very anxious, especially about slipping back into old ways of relating to other people, there were signs that he was managing. He seemed more in contact with his feelings and was less likely to act them out. In his sessions with me he also changed. He seemed able to be closer to me. He was much more open in talking about himself and being able to listen to my interpretations. He became interested in what was going on in his mind and his relationships outside as well as inside the therapy. These changes were very important. However, I do not think that they can be captured or measured by the questionnaires. Indeed, I was worried that giving him the questionnaire after 2 years of therapy would interfere with this different, more in-depth work. It was interesting that he didn't bring back his girlfriend's questionnaire for a long time, which was unusual for Lucian. I think that he was worried that I would see how much better he was doing in his outside life (see 2 years in Figures 12.2, 12.3 and 12.4).

In his sessions Lucian seemed aware that he was in a very different situation now compared to when he started but he still felt anxious and vulnerable and wished to carry on with his therapy.

CONCLUSION

In my opinion it is possible to accommodate therapy and the implementation of a questionnaire in ordinary clinical work with troubled adolescents. The questionnaires are not as intrusive as I initially feared them to be. In the present climate of measuring and evaluating the effectiveness of our work and demonstrating that we make a difference to the lives of young people, I have found the questionnaires appropriate for an adolescent population. Young people are usually less anxious about them than the therapist. The questionnaires are standardised, widely used and they are fair. They are there to measure the identified syndromes, which they do well. The findings are informative and helpful. The questionnaires are useful in engaging some younger adolescents at intake. They are also helpful with other young people in enabling them to think about their difficulties when therapy is ongoing or is coming to an end. The questionnaires can and sometimes do interfere with the ongoing therapeutic process but they have not distracted me from what remains central in my clinical work: namely, thinking about the young person's inner world, that is the dynamics, movements and changes in their internal object relationships.

Part IV

Conclusion

Chapter 13

Conclusion

What is the future for community-based psychotherapy for young people?

Geoffrey Baruch

The idea of a community-based contraceptive and psychotherapy service for troubled young people was the inspiration of a far-sighted pioneer. The recent recognition by professionals and policy-makers that troubled adolescents and young adults are a group with distinctive needs who require services that are separate from services for children and adults was anticipated by the Brandon Centre by 30 years.

During this period there have been enormous advances in the understanding of child and adolescent mental health problems and the way they are treated (Rutter, 1998; 1999). Undoubtedly there will be further advances that will have a considerable impact on community-based psychotherapy. In this chapter I would like to consider the future prospects for community-based psychotherapy for young people.

THE SETTING AND THE CONTRIBUTION OF USERS' VIEWS

The great strength of the Brandon Centre model of community-based psychotherapy is the acceptability of the setting to young people. The non-medical and non-institutional character of the setting fits in with the aspiration of young people to have access to a setting that has a separate identity from institutions for children and adults. However, it is only recently that we have begun to consult users for their detailed views of our service and facilities.

We were persuaded to introduce a survey mainly because, in recent years under the Labour Government, providers in all areas of the public services have been expected to be accountable to the people they serve. The incorporation of users' views into the development of any service, including psychotherapy and contraception, is now commonplace and is expected by funders. At the Brandon Centre we have approached this requirement in the spirit that users' views can make a real contribution to the way we provide help rather than simply going through the motions of eliciting views of users for the sake of appearances. We have learned about aspects of our service that are highly regarded. They include the warm contact made by reception staff with clients over the telephone and when they arrive for their appointment, especially for the first time, and the appreciation of the genuine understanding provided by the doctors and psychotherapists. We have also learned about aspects of the setting that could be improved, for instance the provision of a water cooler for drinking water, the size of our waiting room and more flexible opening hours. The data from questionnaires are fed back to all members of staff and the Centre's Council of Management and then considered at staff meetings and meetings of the Council of Management.

Our survey, which is an ongoing survey of user views, is in its infancy but already we can appreciate its value. It certainly makes us think about how young people feel when they contact the Centre and how we can best respond to their fears.

However, we are concerned that the ethos of user consultation can turn into making users' views sovereign in how a service is provided. Users' views relate to the acceptability of the way the service is delivered and not to its effectiveness. Indeed, acceptability can be in conflict with what is needed to deliver and maintain an effective service. On the other hand a service that is effective but is not acceptable to users is of little value. The challenge in planning psychotherapy especially, and contraception and sexual health services, is to find the balance between service acceptability and treatment effectiveness. To give an example from the Centre's experience: it is generally felt by providers of health services for young people that allowing them to bring friends to their appointment can be very useful in enabling the client to overcome their anxieties. It can also facilitate friends accessing help they might otherwise feel too fearful about using on their own. Certainly our contraceptive service is much more accessible to young women, especially younger adolescents who are too anxious to attend on their own, because they come with a small group of friends. However, we have seen from Charles Wells's chapter that young offenders who attend their sessions with a group of friends hanging around outside the Centre or in the waiting room are undermining the therapeutic work by turning their attendance into a social gathering.

In conclusion, a combination of measures for user consultation and for the evaluation of treatment effectiveness (that also includes the user's perspective) provides a means for demystifying psychotherapy and medical practice whilst at the same time adhering to those aspects of practice that contribute to good outcomes.

RESEARCH

As I noted, there have been considerable advances in research in child and adolescent mental health. Rutter (1998) has reviewed the impact of this research on the field, how it has affected clinical practice and how it may do so in the future. A clear implication of his thesis is that the relationship between research and clinical practice will continue to grow. The challenge for the Brandon Centre and other providers of adolescent mental health services will be twofold. First there will be the challenge of keeping abreast of research findings in child and adolescent mental health, identifying those findings that are relevant to community-based practice and determining ways of integrating them into treatment strategies. To some extent the Centre is already doing this, for instance in the treatment of young people who present with severe conduct problems. It seems likely that practitioners will increasingly be expected to note evidence from evaluation studies that support a treatment strategy and use that strategy (Kazdin, 1999).

The second challenge is to strengthen the link between research and clinical practice within one's own setting. A genuine community service, like the Brandon Centre, offers fertile ground for research initiatives. We started a programme of evaluation in 1993 long before treatment evaluation, outcome and evidence-based practice became fashionable in child and adolescent mental health in the UK. We have published many of our observations and have used them to review the direction of our work. The randomised controlled trial evaluating treatments for severe antisocial behaviour, described by Charles Wells, and our school-based services are a result of findings from this programme of evaluation. Currently we are also investigating the association between emotional and behavioural problems of young women and contraceptive use, using the Achenbach forms. Recent research shows a link between conduct problems and unwanted pregnancy in teenagers. We wish to see whether this link is relevant to the population that uses our contraceptive service (Miller-Johnson *et al.*, 1999; Woodward and Fergusson, 1999). The possibility of being able to predict which young people are at risk of pregnancy would allow us to develop preventive strategies.

In promoting research, there is a danger that the perception of the Centre among young people, referrers and other stakeholders as a confidential setting where they can talk about their problems will be affected and accessibility will be undermined. Certainly the impact of research on accessibility has to be monitored. There is also a danger of this research interfering with therapeutic practice, although Zora Radonic's chapter shows how the two can be sensitively combined. None the less, as noted earlier, accessibility in itself is of limited value unless it is harnessed to delivering effective treatment strategies and, as we have shown, on-site research contributes to the latter. We believe we have been able to demonstrate that research can be integrated with clinical practice whilst maintaining the accessibility of the setting.

As well as the impact of research on clinical practice, our understanding of adolescent mental health has been enhanced by a growing body of research in all aspects of adolescent development. The Brandon Centre's psychotherapy service was inspired by psychoanalytic ideas about adolescence. These ideas also influenced the counselling approach of the contraceptive service. Psychoanalytic ideas about adolescent mental health are now augmented by findings from developmental psychology, for instance the factors that threaten development such as at-risk behaviour engaged in by young people, including delinquent behaviour, substance abuse and unprotected sexual activity. There is also the effect on development and mental health of conditions to which adolescents are exposed that are beyond their control, for instance parental disharmony, mental illness in a parent, parental divorce and remarriage, single parenthood, homelessness, physical and sexual abuse, and poverty. Consciously or unconsciously practitioners are and will continue to be influenced by findings from many empirical studies that have examined in great detail the impact these conditions and at-risk behaviours have on adolescent mental health.

PSYCHOTHERAPY

The basic model of intervention as exemplified in several chapters remains with the young person meeting with a therapist for a period of 50 minutes. The therapist administers psychoanalytic or psychodynamic therapy using a mixture of interpretative and supportive interventions. However, this book shows that far more is involved in the treatment of some young people than psychotherapy. For instance drug therapies often play a role in treatment. Indeed, young people suffering from depression who are referred to the Centre by their GP frequently have been prescribed a course of antidepressant medication. We also noted in Olivia Amiel's chapter the important role anti-psychotic medication played in the treatment of her patients and how this helped her to sustain psychotherapeutic work.

Psychotherapeutic adaptations suitable for different groups of troubled young people include George Mak-Pearce's description of a six-session intervention that seems to meet the initial needs of many young people seeking help who may be put off and frightened by the prospect of open-ended, long-term therapy. The book has shown how, in our mission to ensure that we engage young people who are difficult to reach, have serious mental health problems and are therefore in great need of help, we have had to adapt traditional psychoanalytic methodology. We have also *combined* other treatment modalities with the Centre's psychoanalytic approach, principally cognitive-behavioural approaches for the treatment of severely antisocial youth. We have also applied adapted versions of psychoanalytic methodology in settings outside the Centre in order to engage difficult-to-reach young people in treatment, such as the school-based projects described by Caroline Essenhigh and David Trevatt.

At present, because psychotherapy training is driven by what Rutter (1999) has called a mono-theory and mono-treatment, psychotherapists can find that the adaptations that they have to make, in order to engage effectively with young people, are a great challenge to their skill base and their professional self-perception. Psychotherapists face similar problems to those of researchers who find that a treatment that is tested and is efficacious in a randomised controlled trial translates poorly into routine clinical practice. Similarly psychotherapists find that the skills they learned in psychotherapy training may translate poorly into routine clinical work with young people unless they are adapted to specific aspects of the population being treated and the setting where services are being delivered.

An enormous challenge for psychotherapy is the adaptation of therapeutic approach for young people from minority ethnic backgrounds, especially since many of the conditions that contribute to mental health problems, such as socio-economic disadvantage, poor living conditions and disrupted family structures, are in some cases associated with these backgrounds. At present psychotherapy is only beginning to take account of cultural, ethnic and racial differences. As Rajinder Bains's chapter shows, these differences significantly affect how problems are presented, attitudes to treatment, patterns of seeking help and the usage of treatment. The challenge of developing interventions that are culturally appropriate, sensitive and acceptable to young people is even greater because of the diversity of backgrounds that young people come from in the particular area in which the Brandon Centre is situated. As Kazdin (1993) argues, it is impossible to formulate a limitless number of models of therapy that accommodate each group. However, it should be possible to develop principles of practice that are culturally flexible by assessing the ways in which therapeutic interventions are used by young people from diverse backgrounds and by developing a greater understanding of how their background relates to mental health problems when they occur.

CONCLUDING REMARKS

The excellent reputation of the voluntary sector in the UK is based on the way it responds rapidly and creatively to the needs and problems of disadvantaged populations without being hamstrung by bureaucratic practice that tends to permeate state-funded services. The Centre was created in response to a vacuum within the NHS in the provision of contraceptive services specifically geared for the needs of teenagers. The downside of the approach of the voluntary sector is that services can become isolated, fragmented and duplicated. Certainly there is a case for partnerships to be created whereby therapy organisations for young people and contraceptive services in the voluntary sector and the NHS share their expertise and services so that there is greater equality of access for users. The Brandon Centre would like to build on the relationships we have already developed with local providers and referrers. We believe that by creating a wide range of partnerships we shall be able to offer users the benefits of therapeutic and contraceptive services they would otherwise not have access to. We are very much at the early stages of this proposal. However, we can already see that a different attitude is necessary for partnerships to work. We are used to considering our plans and projects in terms of what is best for the Brandon Centre and the population we serve, whereas working in partnership with other organisations necessarily means considering their interests as well as our own. Obviously this creates tensions which we believe are well worth struggling with since partnership and joined-up thinking are the way health and social services are evolving at the start of the new millennium. We believe that the Brandon Centre with its track record for innovation and flexibility is uniquely positioned to put the new ethos into practice.

References

Kazdin, A. (1993). 'Adolescent mental health: Prevention and treatment programs'. *American Psychologist* 48(2): 127–41.

——(1999). Commentary on 'Weiss, B., Catron, T., Harris, V. and Phung, T. M. (1999). "Traditional child psychotherapy did not reduce psychopathology compared with academic tutoring". *Journal of Consulting and Clinical Psychology* 67(1): 82–94'. In *Evidence-Based Mental Health* 2(3): 86.

Miller-Johnson, S., Winn, D-M., Coie, J., Maumary-Gremaud, A., Hyman, C., Terry, R. and Lochman, J. (1999). 'Motherhood during the teen years: a developmental perspective on risk factors for childbearing'. *Development and Psychopathology* 11(1): 85–100.

Rutter, M. (1998). 'Practitioner review: routes from research to clinical practice in child psychiatry: retrospect and prospect'. *Journal of Child Psychology and Psychiatry* 39(6): 805–16.

——(1999). 'Services for children with mental health problems: How should they be developed?' Presentation at conference 'Developing Effective Child and Adolescent Mental Health Services: Current Initiatives and Innovations', Royal College of Psychiatrists, 2 February 2000.

Woodward, L. J. and Fergusson, D. M.(1999). 'Early conduct problems and later risk of teenage pregnancy in girls'. *Development and Psychopathology* 11(1): 127–42.

Index